SIXTH EDITION

INTERACTIONS

Listening/Speaking

2

Judith Tanka

Lida R. Baker

McGraw Hill

Interactions 2 Listening/Speaking, Sixth Edition

Published by McGraw-Hill ESL/ELT, a business unit of The McGraw-Hill Companies, Inc.
1221 Avenue of the Americas, New York, NY 10020. Copyright © 2014 by The McGraw-Hill
Companies, Inc. All rights reserved. Printed in the United States of America. Previous editions
© 2007, 2001, and 1995. No part of this publication may be reproduced or distributed in any
form or by any means, or stored in a database or retrieval system, without the prior written
consent of The McGraw-Hill Companies, Inc., including, but not limited to, in any network or
other electronic storage or transmission, or broadcast for distance learning.

Some ancillaries, including electronic and print components, may not be available to customers
outside the United States.

This book is printed on acid-free paper.

7 8 9 0 DOW/DOW 1 0 9 8 7 6 5

ISBN: 978-0-07-759519-7
MHID: 0-07-759519-X

Senior Vice President, Products & Markets: Kurt L. Strand
Vice President, General Manager, Products & Markets: Michael J. Ryan
Vice President, Content Production & Technology Services: Kimberly Meriwether David
Director of Development: Valerie Kelemen
Marketing Manager: Cambridge University Press
Lead Project Manager: Rick Hecker
Senior Buyer: Michael R. McCormick
Designer: Page2, LLC
Cover/Interior Designer: Page2, LLC
Senior Content Licensing Specialist: Keri Johnson
Manager, Digital Production: Janean A. Utley
Compositor: Page2, LLC
Printer: RR Donnelley

Cover photo: Anna Omelchenko/Shutterstock.com

All credits appearing on page iv or at the end of the book are considered to be an extension of
the copyright page.

The Internet addresses listed in the text were accurate at the time of publication. The inclusion
of a website does not indicate an endorsement by the authors or McGraw-Hill, and McGraw-
Hill does not guarantee the accuracy of the information presented at these sites.

www.mhhe.com

www.elt.mcgraw-hill.com

A Special Thank You

The Interactions/Mosaic 6th edition team wishes to thank our extended team: teachers, students, administrators, and teacher trainers, all of whom contributed invaluably to the making of this edition.

Maiko Berger, **Ritsumeikan Asia Pacific University**, Oita, Japan • Aaron Martinson, **Sejong Cyber University**, Seoul, Korea • Aisha Osman, Egypt • Amy Stotts, **Chubu University**, Aichi, Japan • Charles Copeland, **Dankook University**, Yongin City, Korea • Christen Savage, **University of Houston**, Texas, USA • Daniel Fitzgerald, **Metropolitan Community College**, Kansas, USA • Deborah Bollinger, **Aoyama Gakuin University**, Tokyo, Japan • Duane Fitzhugh, **Northern Virginia Community College**, Virginia, USA • Gregory Strong, **Aoyama Gakuin University**, Tokyo, Japan • James Blackwell, **Ritsumeikan Asia Pacific University**, Oita, Japan • Janet Harclerode, **Santa Monica College**, California, USA • Jinyoung Hong, **Sogang University**, Seoul, Korea • Lakkana Chaisaklert, **Rajamangala University of Technology Krung Thep**, Bangkok, Thailand • Lee Wonhee, **Sogang University**, Seoul, Korea • Matthew Gross, **Konkuk University**, Seoul, Korea • Matthew Stivener, **Santa Monica College**, California, USA • Pawadee Srisang, **Burapha University**, Chantaburi, Thailand • Steven M. Rashba, **University of Bridgeport**, Connecticut, USA • Sudatip Prapunta, **Prince of Songkla University**, Trang, Thailand • Tony Carnerie, **University of California San Diego**, California, USA

Photo Credits

Text Credits

Table of Contents

A 21st-Century Course for the Modern Student

Interactions/Mosaic prepares students for university classes by fully integrating every aspect of student life. Based on 28 years of classroom-tested best practices, the new and revised content, fresh modern look, and new online component make this the perfect series for contemporary classrooms.

Proven Instruction that Ensures Academic Success

Modern Content:
From social networking to gender issues and from academic honesty to discussions of Skype, *Interactions/Mosaic* keeps students connected to learning by selecting topics that are interesting and relevant to modern students.

Digital Component:
The fully integrated online course offers a rich environment that expands students' learning and supports teachers' teaching with automatically graded practice, assessment, classroom presentation tools, online community, and more.

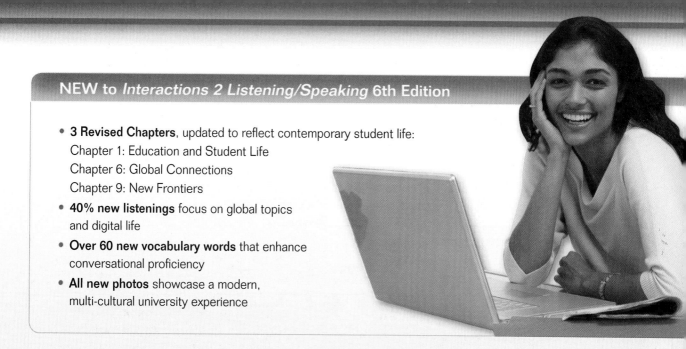

NEW to *Interactions 2 Listening/Speaking* 6th Edition

- **3 Revised Chapters**, updated to reflect contemporary student life:
  Chapter 1: Education and Student Life
  Chapter 6: Global Connections
  Chapter 9: New Frontiers
- **40% new listenings** focus on global topics and digital life
- **Over 60 new vocabulary words** that enhance conversational proficiency
- **All new photos** showcase a modern, multi-cultural university experience

Emphasis on Vocabulary:

Each chapter teaches vocabulary intensively and comprehensively. This focus on learning new words is informed by more than 28 years of classroom testing and provides students with the exact language they need to communicate confidently and fluently.

Practical Critical Thinking:

Students develop their ability to synthesize, analyze, and apply information from different sources in a variety of contexts: from comparing academic articles to negotiating informal conversations.

Highlights of *Interactions 2 Listening/Speaking* 6th Edition

Part 1: Conversation Each chapter begins with short conversations related to academic life. The activities that follow help students develop important listening skills.

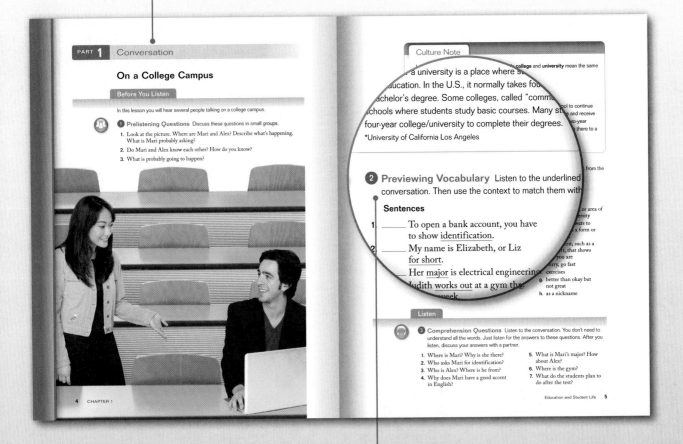

PART 1 Conversation

On a College Campus

Before You Listen

In this lesson you will hear several people talking on a college campus.

1 Prelistening Questions Discuss these questions in small groups.

1. Look at the picture. Where are Mari and Alex? Describe what's happening. What is Mari probably asking?
2. Do Mari and Alex know each other? How do you know?
3. What is probably going to happen?

4   CHAPTER 1

Culture Note

college and university mean the same
a university is a place where s...
...ucation. In the U.S., it normally takes fo...
...achelor's degree. Some colleges, called "comm...
...chools where students study basic courses. Many st...   ...ool to continue
four-year college/university to complete their degrees.   ...e and receive
*University of California Los Angeles   ...there to a

...from the

2 Previewing Vocabulary Listen to the underlined...
conversation. Then use the context to match them with...

Sentences

1. _____ To open a bank account, you have   ...or area of
to show identification.   ...rsity
2. _____ My name is Elizabeth, or Liz   ...vers to
for short.   ...a form or
_____ Her major is electrical engineerin...   ...nt, such as a
_____ Judith works out at a gym th...   ...t, that shows
...week   ...you are
...rry, go fast
...exercises
g. better than okay but
not great
h. as a nickname

Listen

3 Comprehension Questions Listen to the conversation. You don't need to understand all the words. Just listen for the answers to these questions. After you listen, discuss your answers with a partner.

1. Where is Mari? Why is she there?
2. Who asks Mari for identification?
3. Who is Alex? Where is he from?
4. Why does Mari have a good accent in English?
5. What is Mari's major? How about Alex?
6. Where is the gym?
7. What do the students plan to do after the test?

Education and Student Life   **5**

Emphasis on Vocabulary Each chapter presents, practices, and carefully recycles vocabulary-learning strategies and vocabulary words essential to the modern student.

B Asking for Clarification Work in small groups. Take turns telling your classmates about a holiday, custom, or tradition from your family or culture. When it is your turn to listen, use expressions from the box if you need the speaker to explain, repeat, or define something.

Example

A: In my city, it's customary to have a parade every year on New Year's Day.

B: What do you mean… a parade?

A: It's a public celebration that includes people, musical groups, and sometimes horses walking or riding down the main street of a town or city. For example, have you ever heard of the Rose Parade?

B: What?

A: The Rose Parade. It's in Pasadena, California every year on January 1. You can watch it on television.

PART 2 Lecture

Academic Honesty

Before You Listen

On Mari's first day in a writing class, the professor explains the course syllabus and gives some important information about academic honesty.

◄ What is the young woman doing?
What is the young man doing?

10   CHAPTER 1

Part 2: Lecture Students prepare for academic courses by listening to extended lectures. Key note-taking skills are taught.

Listen

Strategy

Using the Introduction to Predict Lecture Content
Like an essay, a lecture usually has three main parts: the introduction, the body, and the conclusion. You should listen very carefully to the introduction because it will usually have two important pieces of information:

1. the topic of the lecture
2. a brief summary or list of the main ideas the speaker will talk about

*Note: Lecturers often start their lectures with announcements, a review of the last lecture, or a story. It is usually not necessary to take notes on these things.

3 Taking Notes on the Introduction Listen to the lecture introduction and fill in the blanks.

General topic of the lecture: _____

Main ideas that the speaker will talk about: _____
_____
_____
_____

12   CHAPTER 1

Practical Critical Thinking Each chapter focuses on a few key strategies for academic and social communication, which support language learning and encourage independence in student thinking.

PART 3 Strategies for Better Listening and Speaking

Getting Meaning from Context

FOCUS

When you listen to people talking in English, it is probably hard to understand all the words. However, you can usually get a general idea of what they are saying. How? By using *clues* that help you to *guess*. These clues include:

- words
- synonyms and paraphrases
- transitions
- stressed words
- intonation
- a speaker's tone of voice
- your knowledge of the culture, speakers, or situation

Many tests such as the TOEFL® iBT measure your academic listening and speaking abilities. This activity, and others in the book, will develop your social and academic conversation skills, and provide a foundation for success on a variety of standardized tests.

Using Context Clues

The following conversations take place on a college campus.

1. Listen to the beginning of each conversation.
2. Listen to the question for each conversation. Stop the recording and choose the best answer to each question.
3. In the **Clues** column, write the words that helped you choose your answer. Discuss them with your teacher and classmates.
4. Listen to the last part of each conversation to hear the correct answer.

Answers	Clues
1. Ⓐ going to the post office Ⓑ their grades in a course Ⓒ parents coming to visit Ⓓ going to the beach	*posted, coming out, C*
2. Ⓐ He doesn't like his major. Ⓑ He isn't going to graduate on time. Ⓒ His parents are disappointed. Ⓓ He's only in his third year.	

TOEFL® iBT is a registered trademark of Educational Testing Service (ETS). This product is not endorsed or approved by ETS.

Education and Student Life **17**

Answers	Clues
3. Ⓐ a physician Ⓑ a professor Ⓒ a student advisor Ⓓ a teaching assistant	
4. Ⓐ The student wrote an excellent essay. Ⓑ The student plagiarized a large part of her essay. Ⓒ The student is a very original writer. Ⓓ The student used too many words.	

Focused Listening

FOCUS

Getting Meaning from Intonation

Meaning comes not only from words but also from the way English speakers use their voices. The *tone* (feeling) and rising or falling *intonation* of a speaker's voice can be important clues. Listen to a short conversation. It will be repeated three times. Circle the second speaker's feeling in each case.

1. sad   happy   neutral
2. sad   happy   neutral
3. sad   happy   neutral

1 Listening for Intonation Cues In the items that follow, you will hear two conversations. Each of them is spoken in two ways. Use the differences in intonation and tone to decide what the speakers are feeling.

1a. Ⓐ happy   1b. Ⓐ happy
    Ⓑ disappointed   Ⓑ disappointed
    Ⓒ neutral   Ⓒ neutral

2a. Ⓐ annoyed   2b. Ⓐ annoyed
    Ⓑ calm   Ⓑ calm
    Ⓒ disappointed   Ⓐ disappointed

18 CHAPTER 1

Part 3: Strategies for Better Listening and Speaking
Impactful listening exercises help students practice getting meaning from context.

Communication for the Modern Student
A focus on real-life and academic communication prepares students for success in school and in life.

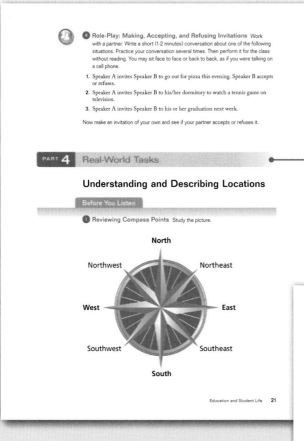

④ Role-Play: Making, Accepting, and Refusing Invitations Work with a partner. Write a short (1-2 minutes) conversation about one of the following situations. Practice your conversation several times. Then perform it for the class without reading. You may sit face to face or back to back, as if you were talking on a cell phone.

1. Speaker A invites Speaker B to go out for pizza this evening. Speaker B accepts or refuses.

2. Speaker A invites Speaker B to his/her dormitory to watch a tennis game on television.

3. Speaker A invites Speaker B to his or her graduation next week.

Now make an invitation of your own and see if your partner accepts or refuses it.

PART 4 Real-World Tasks

Understanding and Describing Locations

Before You Listen

① Reviewing Compass Points Study the picture.

North

Northwest   **Northeast**

West   **East**

Southwest   **Southeast**

South

Part 4: Real-World Tasks Students learn to apply their listening and speaking skills to a variety of practical interactions such as understanding and describing locations.

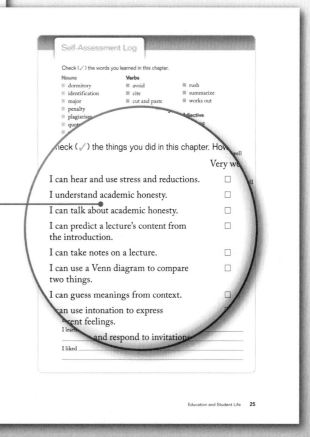

Self-Assessment Log

Check (✓) the words you learned in this chapter.

Nouns	Verbs	
dormitory	avoid	rush
identification	cite	summarize
major	cut and paste	works out
penalty		
plagiarism		**Adjective**
quot		

heck (✓) the things you did in this chapter. How well

Very we

I can hear and use stress and reductions.	☐
I understand academic honesty.	☐
I can talk about academic honesty.	☐
I can predict a lecture's content from the introduction.	☐
I can take notes on a lecture.	☐
I can use a Venn diagram to compare two things.	☐
I can guess meanings from context.	☐
can use intonation to express ·ent feelings.	

I lear   and respond to invitation

I liked _____

Results for Students A carefully structured program presents and practices academic skills and strategies purposefully, leading to strong student results and more independent learners.

Scope and Sequence

Chapter	Listening	Speaking
1 Education and Student Life p2 	Listening for main ideas and details Getting meaning from intonation Recognizing compass directions Understanding expressions and statements of location Using the prepositions *in*, *on*, and *at* in addresses and locations	Asking for clarification Discussing personal views on academic honesty and cheating in the U.S. Talking about academic honesty in different countries' education systems Using expressions of location Describing map locations
2 City Life p26 	Listening for main ideas and details Making inferences Listening for clues to relationships between people Following directions	Using the phrase *by the way* Opening and closing phone conversations Talking about crime Expressing frustration Learning names of professions Requesting and giving directions Saying you don't understand
3 Business and Money p50 	Listening for main ideas and details Making inferences Distinguishing between *can* and *can't* Distinguishing between teens and tens Recognizing expressions of advice	Talking about managing money Talking about entrepreneurs Talking about abilities Using the words *borrow* and *lend* Asking for, giving, and refusing advice
4 Jobs and Professions p74 	Listening for main ideas and details Making inferences Recognizing the intonation of tag questions Recognizing a sequence of events Taking notes on causes and effects Creating abbreviations Taking notes on statistics	Talking about jobs and careers Apologizing and reconciling Role-playing a job interview Learning idioms related to housework Talking about "men's" and "women's" jobs Interviewing a person about his or her job Giving a short oral report

Critical-Thinking Skills	Vocabulary Building	Pronunciation	Language Skills
Interpreting a photo Using a lecture introduction to predict content Taking effective lecture notes using indentation, keywords, and abbreviations and symbols Using a Venn diagram to compare and contrast Getting meaning from context	Terms for academic life Terms for writing papers and academic honesty Expressions for making, accepting, and refusing invitations Compass directions Expressions of location *In*, *on*, and *at* in addresses and locations	Identifying and practicing stressed words Identifying and practicing reduced pronunciation	Using context clues to guess information from conversations Using intonation to express feelings
Predicting questions speakers will ask Getting meaning from context Speculating about hypothetical situations Taking notes on statistics Using transitions as cues for note-taking Taking notes on an informal talk	Expressions for opening and closing conversations Terms for expressing frustration Expressions for requesting and giving directions Names of professions Terms for expressing lack of understanding Using the phrase *by the way*	Identifying and practicing stressed words Identifying and practicing reduced pronunciation	Using context clues to identify a speaker
Outlining a lecture Getting meaning from context Taking notes on a process	Terms for talking about money *Borrow* vs. *lend* Expressions for asking for, giving, accepting, and rejecting advice Terms for talking about entrepreneurs and the entrepreneurial process Terms related to banking	Identifying and practicing stressed words Identifying and practicing reduced pronunciation Pronouncing *can* and *can't* Pronouncing teens and tens	Using context clues to identify banking services
Interpreting information in a table Getting meaning from context Speculating about hypothetical situations Taking notes on a lecture Predicting the order of a set of pictures Using a matrix diagram to organize ideas	Terms related to jobs and careers Expressions for apologizing and reconciling Idioms related to housework Terms signaling cause and effect	Identifying and practicing stressed words Identifying and practicing reduced pronunciation Asking and answering negative tag questions	Using context clues to guess people's jobs

Scope and Sequence

Chapter	Listening	Speaking
5 **Lifestyles Around the World** p100 	Listening for main ideas and details Making inferences Recognizing stress in two- and three-word verbs	Talking about single parents Talking about changes in the American family Asking for help and favors Talking about numbers and percentages Comparing lifestyles in different countries
6 **Global Connections** p124 	Listening for main ideas and details Taking notes on similarities and differences Identifying blended consonants Listening to a phone survey	Talking about taking courses online Asking for help and permission, and information questions Interrupting politely Talking about body language customs in different cultures Discussing pros and cons in different situations Talking about different ways to travel Conducting a phone survey
7 **Language and Communication** p148 	Listening for main ideas and details Making inferences Understanding statements with rising intonation Identifying correct spellings in a spelling bee	Discussing the meaning of friendship Comparing American and British English Contradicting politely Talking about stereotypes Using interjections Using expressions for guessing
8 **Tastes and Preferences** p172 	Listening for main ideas and details Making inferences Understanding reduced questions Distinguishing between present and past yes/no questions Understanding comparisons of people Recognizing paraphrases	Talking about likes and dislikes Giving an impromptu speech Comparing the characteristics of generations Talking about fads Expressing approval and disapproval Describing your ideal partner

Critical-Thinking Skills	Vocabulary Building	Pronunciation	Language Skills
Interpreting information in a line graph Taking notes on a lecture Getting meaning from context	Two- and three-word verbs used in a conversation between neighbors Expressions used to ask for help or a favor Terms used to talk about changes in the American family Expressions used to signal examples Terms used for discussing lifestyles	Identifying and practicing stressed words Identifying and practicing the dropped *h* in unstressed words Pronouncing linked phrases	Using context clues to guess people's lifestyles
Interpreting body language in photos Taking effective notes on a lecture to put into an outline Getting meaning from context Using a chart to conduct a phone survey with your classmates	Expressions for interrupting Expressions signaling similarity and difference Expressions used in phone surveys	Identifying and practicing stressed words Identifying intonation patterns Pronouncing names and sentences with blended consonants	Using context clues to guess about ways to travel
Getting meaning from context Taking notes on classifications	Terms used to talk about friendship vs. friendliness Terms used for talking about languages and dialects Examples of vocabulary differences between American and British English Interjections Expressions for guessing Slang expressions	Identifying and practicing stressed words	Using context clues to guess about language and communication
Getting meaning from context Speculating about hypothetical situations Evaluating people's positive and negative qualities Interpreting the language of personal ads Taking notes in columns Predicting note organization	Expressions for likes and dislikes Expressions of approval and disapproval Terms signaling paraphrases Ways to say that something is popular	Identifying and practicing stressed words	Using context clues to identify people's tastes and preferences Using intonation to identify feelings

Scope and Sequence

Critical-Thinking Skills	Vocabulary Building	Pronunciation	Language Skills
Getting meaning from context Taking notes and outlining based on a lecture Recognizing signposts in a speech or lecture	Terms for talking about home efficiency Terms for technological advancements Expressions for persuasive language Terms for talking about voyages and discoveries Expressions that signal surprise	Identifying and practicing stressed words Pronouncing the *th* sound Pronouncing *–ed* endings	Recognizing signal words to guess the correct answer
Getting meaning from context Recognizing digressions in a lecture Comparing celebrations across cultures	Expressions to offer, accept, or decline help Terms to express congratulations and sympathy Expressions signaling digressions in a lecture Terms related to ceremonies	Identifying and practicing stressed words Using correct stress in compound phrases	Using context clues to identify ceremonies

Introducing the Interactions 2 Listening/Speaking Characters

Name: Ali
Nationality: American

Name: Mari
Nationality: Japanese

Name: Jeff
Nationality: American

Name: Dan
Nationality: American

Name: Nancy
Nationality: American

Name: Lee
Nationality: Korean

Name: Alex
Nationality: Mexican

Name: Yolanda
Nationality: American

Name: Alicia
Nationality: Mexican

Name: Andrew
Nationality: American

1 Education and Student Life

> "Education is not the filling of a bucket but the lighting of a fire."

William Butler Yeats
Irish poet and dramatist

In this
CHAPTER

Conversation On a College Campus

Lecture Academic Honesty

Getting Meaning from Context Using Context Clues

Real-World Task Describing Locations

Connecting to the Topic

1. What are these students celebrating?

2. Tell about one happy event during your high school or university years.

3. What are the steps to getting a bachelor's degree (B.A.) in your country? What about a master's degree (M.A.) or a Ph.D.?

On a College Campus

Before You Listen

In this lesson you will hear several people talking on a college campus.

1 **Prelistening Questions** Discuss these questions in small groups.

1. Look at the picture. Where are Mari and Alex? Describe what's happening. What is Mari probably asking?

2. Do Mari and Alex know each other? How do you know?

3. What is probably going to happen?

Culture Note

In conversational American English, the words **college** and **university** mean the same thing. Example:

A: Hey, Bob, where did you go to college?
B: Boston University. And you?
A: UCLA*.

A college or a university is a place where students go after high school to continue their education. In the U.S., it normally takes four years to finish college and receive a bachelor's degree. Some colleges, called "community colleges," are two-year schools where students study basic courses. Many students transfer from there to a four-year college/university to complete their degrees.

*University of California Los Angeles

2 Previewing Vocabulary Listen to the underlined words and phrases from the conversation. Then use the context to match them with their definitions.

Sentences

1. _d_ To open a bank account, you have to show <u>identification</u>.
2. _h_ My name is Elizabeth, or Liz <u>for short</u>.
3. _b_ Her <u>major</u> is electrical engineering.
4. _f_ Judith <u>works out</u> at a gym three times a week.
5. _a_ My <u>dormitory</u> is about five minutes from the Student Center.
6. _c_ The secretary asked me to <u>fill out</u> some forms.
7. _e_ There's no need to <u>rush</u>. We have plenty of time.
8. _g_ **A:** What did you think of the movie?
   B: It was <u>pretty good</u>.

Definitions

a. building where students live

b. a student's field or area of study at a university

c. write the answers to questions on a form or application

d. a document, such as a passport, that shows who you are

e. hurry, go fast

f. exercises

g. better than okay but not great

h. as a nickname

Listen

3 Comprehension Questions Listen to the conversation. You don't need to understand all the words. Just listen for the answers to these questions. After you listen, discuss your answers with a partner.   _Alex from mexico_

Marika

English test

japan, my grandmather is american

1. Where is Mari? Why is she there?
2. Who asks Mari for identification?
3. Who is Alex? Where is he from?
4. Why does Mari have a good accent in English?

5. What is Mari's major? How about Alex? _bissnes administrien_
6. Where is the gym? _next to the student Senter_
7. What do the students plan to do after the test?

Education and Student Life **5**

this sit is takken

Stress

FOCUS

In spoken English, important words that carry information, such as nouns, verbs, and adjectives are usually stressed. This means they are

- higher   • louder   • spoken more clearly

than other (unstressed) words. Stress is an important part of correct pronunciation. Listen to this example:

Could you **tell** me how to **get** to the **gym**?

In this example, the words *tell*, *get*, and *gym* are stressed.

---

4 **Listening for Stressed Words** Listen to part of the conversation again. Some of the stressed words are missing. During each pause, repeat the phrase or sentence. Then fill in the missing stressed words.

Mari: _Excuse_ me, is _this_ seat taken?

Alex: Pardon?

Mari: Is anyone _sitting_ here?

Alex: Ah, no.

Mari: Thanks. I'm _glad_ the test hasn't _started_ yet. I _thought_ I was going to be _late_.

Alex: Me too. I had to _rush_ here to be on _time_. I'm Alex, by the way.

Mari: Oh, _nice_ to _met_ you. _My_ name is Mariko. Or just Mari, for _short_.

Alex: Nice to meet you, Mari.

Mari: _Where_ are _you_ from?

Alex: Mexico. And ~~Japan~~ _you_?

Mari: Japan.

Alex: Really? Your English _accent_ is really good.

Mari: Oh, _that is_ because my _grandmother_ is American. We _always_ spoke English when I was _____little_____, so I can ___speak___ pretty well, but my ___reading___ and writing are really ___weak___.

Alex: I see. So, um, are you planning to go to ___college___ here?

Mari: Yes, ___exactly___.

Alex: What's your ___major___?

Mari: ___Business___ administration. How about ___you___?

Alex: The ___same___!

Mari: Cool! How long have you been ___study___ here?

Alex: You mean in the ___English___ program?

Mari: Yeah.

Alex: This is my ___second___ semester.

Mari: Oh, so you know the ___campus is___ pretty well!

Alex: Oh, yeah.

Mari: Could you ___tell___ me how to ___get___ to the ___gym___? I want to go work ___out___ after the ___test___.

Alex: The ___gym___? Yeah, it's next to the ___student___ Center, ___across___ from the grad dorms.

Mari: Sorry… the ___what___?

Alex: The grad dorms. Um, the ___dormitoris___ for graduate students. Here, I can show you on the campus map…

Mari: That's OK, I ___know___.

Alex: I'm actually planning to go there, ___too___. Want to go ___together___?

Mari: Sounds ___great___!

Check your answers using the listening script on page 263. Then read the conversation with a partner. Pronounce stressed words louder, higher, and more clearly than unstressed words.

Reductions

FOCUS

Reductions

In spoken English, words that are not stressed are often shortened, or reduced. For example, we write: "Could you tell me how to get to the gym?" But we say, "Cudja tell me howda get ta the gym?" Listen to the difference:

Unreduced Pronunciation	Reduced Pronunciation
could you	cudja
how to	howda

Reduced forms are a natural part of spoken English. They are not slang. However, reduced forms are not acceptable spellings in written English.

5 **Comparing Unreduced and Reduced Pronunciation** The following sentences are from the conversation. Listen for the difference between unreduced and reduced pronunciation. Repeat both forms after the speaker.

Unreduced Pronunciation	Reduced Pronunciation*
1. I thought I was going to be late.	I thought I was gonna be late.
2. I had to rush here to be on time.	I hadta rush here to be on time.
3. Nice to meet you.	Nice ta meetcha.
4. What's your major?	Whatcher major?
5. How about you?	How boutchu?
6. You mean in the English program?	Y'mean in the English program?
7. Could you tell me how to get to the gym?	Couldja tell me how to get ta the gym?
8. I want to go work out after the test.	I wanna go work out after the test.

6 **Listening for Reductions** Listen to the following conversations. You'll hear the reduced pronunciation of some words. Write the unreduced forms of the missing words in the blanks.

1. **Student:** Hi. I'm here _____get_____ take the English placement test.

   Teacher: OK. ___what___ ___is___ ___your___ name?

   Student: Phailin Montri.

   Teacher: ___could___ ___you___ spell that for me, please?

*The reduced forms are not acceptable spellings in written English.

2. **Paul:** I _____want_____ _____to_____ leave early tomorrow. This

morning I _____had_____ _____to_____ rush to catch the

bus and I was almost late _____ work.

Marine: What time are you _____gonna_____ _____to_____ leave?

Paul: Around 7:30.

3. **Lara:** Ann, this is my friend Richard.

Richard: Nice _____to_____ _____meet_____ _____you_____.

Where are you from?

Ann: Toronto.

Richard: Oh, _____you_____ _____mean_____ you're Canadian?

Ann: Right.

After You Listen

7 Reviewing Vocabulary Discuss your answers to the following questions with a partner. Use the underlined vocabulary in your answers.

1. If you are a college student, what is your major? If you are not a college student, what would you like to study?

2. What is your full name? Do you have a nickname that people call you for short?

3. Have you ever lived in a dormitory? If not, would you like to? Why or why not?

4. Do you work out at a gym? How often? What exercises do you do?

5. What kind of identification do you have to show before you can get on an airplane?

6. How many forms did you have to fill out when you registered for your English course?

7. Is there a sport or a musical instrument that you play pretty well?

8. Describe a time when you had to rush. What happened?

Using Language Functions

FOCUS

Asking for Clarification

If someone uses words you don't understand, you can signal that you don't understand by using one of the following expressions.

Excuse me?	What did you say?	You mean...?
Pardon?	What do you mean?	What? (informal)
Sorry?	What was that?	Huh? (informal)

8 **Asking for Clarification** Work in small groups. Take turns telling your classmates about a holiday, custom, or tradition from your family or culture. When it is your turn to listen, use expressions from the box if you need the speaker to explain, repeat, or define something.

Example

A: In my city, it's customary to have a parade every year on New Year's Day.

B: What do you mean... a parade?

A: It's a public celebration that includes people, musical groups, and sometimes horses walking or riding down the main street of a town or city. For example, have you ever heard of the Rose Parade?

B: What?

A: The Rose Parade. It's in Pasadena, California every year on January 1. You can watch it on television.

PART **2**   Lecture

Academic Honesty

Before You Listen

On Mari's first day in a writing class, the professor explains the course syllabus and gives some important information about academic honesty.

◄ What is the young woman doing?
What is the young man doing?

Honor Code

University students in the U.S. and Canada must promise to follow a set of rules about honest behavior. These rules are called the "Academic Honor Code." Some universities ask students to read the honor code. Others require students to sign it. Here are some examples of honor codes from well-known universities:

- "I pledge my honor that I have not violated the honor code during this examination." — Princeton University
- "On my honor I have neither given nor received any unauthorized aid on this (exam, test, paper)." — Rice University
- "On my honor as a University of Colorado student, I have neither given nor received unauthorized assistance." — University of Colorado
- I am aware of what constitutes academic misconduct and the disciplinary actions that may be taken against it, and agree not to cheat. — University of British Columbia

1 **Prelistening Discussion** Read the following situations. If you think these actions are okay to do, write "+". If you think these actions are wrong, write "–". Then discuss your responses with your classmates.

1. _____ Your classmate is looking at your paper during an exam. You let him see your answers because you believe it's important for students to help each other. You also think that if the teacher catches him, your classmate will be in trouble, not you.

2. _____ You find some interesting information on the Internet. You decide to copy this information and include it in your essay.

3. _____ Your English vocabulary and grammar are weak. To be sure that your homework is correct, you ask your American neighbor to check and correct your work.

2 **Previewing Vocabulary** You will hear the following words and phrases in the lecture. Check (✓) the words you don't know. Discuss their meanings with a partner.

Nouns	Verbs		Adjective
penalty	avoid	paraphrase	unique
plagiarism	cite	quote	
quotation marks	cut and paste	summarize	
source	expect		
syllabus	get caught		
term paper	give credit		

Strategy

Using the Introduction to Predict Lecture Content

Like an essay, a lecture usually has three main parts: the introduction, the body, and the conclusion. You should listen very carefully to the introduction because it will usually have two important pieces of information:

1. the topic of the lecture
2. a brief summary or list of the main ideas the speaker will talk about

*Note: Lecturers often start their lectures with announcements, a review of the last lecture, or a story. It is usually not necessary to take notes on these things.

3 Taking Notes on the Introduction Listen to the lecture introduction and fill in the blanks.

General topic of the lecture: _about academic honesty._

Main ideas that the speaker will talk about: _academic honesty is very important and speaker talk about citting._

Strategy

Three Keys to Writing Effective Lecture Notes

Indentation Indent means "move your text to the right." Indent to show the relationship between main ideas and specific details. Write main ideas next to the left margin. Indent about 1.5 cm as information becomes more specific:

Main idea
    Detail
        More Specific Detail

Key Words When you take notes, do not write every word, and do not write complete sentences. Instead, write only the most important or "key" words. Key words are usually nouns, verb, adjectives, and adverbs.

Abbreviations and Symbols You can save time if you abbreviate (shorten) words and use symbols as much as possible. For example, write ≠ instead of "different from" or "not the same." Write "info" instead of "information." You can create your own symbols and abbreviations or use those listed on page 262.

4 Taking Effective Lecture Notes (Part 1) Listen to the first part of the lecture. Take notes here. Remember to write key words, indent and abbreviate.

> Main idea is plagiasm
> Detail
>   1. copy text of onther student,
>   2. copy homwork from classelmates.
>   3. texting by phone, using notes.
>   4. When you plagiaze (_____)
>   other pepole
>   5. septensis
>   6. unic ideas
> More Specific detail.
>   1. cutting and pastin from website
>   2. _____ book, magazin
>   3. buying essy on online
>   4. some paragraf

5 Identifying the Three Keys to Taking Effective Lecture Notes Look at the notes on page 14. They were written by two different students. Which notes are better? Why? Which notes resemble yours more closely?

STUDENT A	STUDENT B
I. Intro	Syllabus: lot of writing: will be four essays,
A. Syllabus: lot of writing: 4 essays, 1 term paper	one term paper
B. Academic Honesty	Academic honesty
1. Types of cheating	Types of cheating
2. How to avoid	How to avoid cheating?
3. If caught ?	What can happen if you get caught?
II. Types of cheating	Types of cheating
A. copying test answ.	copying test answers
B. using notes	using notes
C. copying hw	copying homework from classmates
D. texting answ.	texting answers
E. plagiarism = borrow sentences, parag., ideas from others, w/o quotation or source	plagiarism means to borrow sentences, paragraphs, ideas from others, without quotation or mentioning the source
Ex: — cut & paste from web	cut and paste from the web
— copy from bk., newspaper, etc.	copy from book, newspaper, etc.
— buy essay online	buy essay online
— ask friend to write paper	ask friend or cousin to write your essay, including just sentences or paragraphs
Cultural differences: Asia, Middle East ≠ western cult.: give credit to source	Asia and Middle East have different ideas about cheating
	western culture: you must give credit to source

(handwritten margin notes: "delete", "Mor specific / ditto")

 6 Taking Effective Lecture Notes (Part 2) Listen to the second part of the lecture. Take notes on page 15. Remember to indent, abbreviate, and write key words.

I. How to avoid *plagiazm* (handwritten)

A. Show _2 thing_

1. _cout them, cout means speaks exacs words_
2. _don't cheange the paragraf mainnig idea_

B. _You have to give (handwritten)._

1. This means (handwritten)
2. (handwritten)
3. (handwritten)

C. Remember to _site soures_ (handwritten)

1. _____
2. _source - (handwritten)_

   a. website _____
   b. article _____

(left margin handwritten notes in Armenian script)

After You Listen

7 **Reviewing Vocabulary** Work in small groups. Look back at the vocabulary list in Activity 2 on page 11. Quiz each other on the terms and their meanings.

Example

Student A: What does "source" mean?

Student B: A person or place that your information came from.

Student C: That's correct.

Strategy

Graphic Organizer: Venn Diagram

A Venn diagram can help you compare two topics. With a Venn diagram, you can see how the topics are different and how they are similar.

Must cite sources   **Use sources in our writing**   **No need to cite sources**

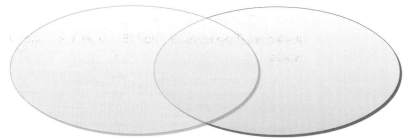

Example In my country, like in the U.S., we're expected to use information from famous people in our writing. The difference is that in the U.S., you have to cite the source of the information you use. But in my country, we don't have to cite sources because our teachers already know the source of the famous quotations.

8 Discussing the Lecture Compare your country's rules and customs related to academic honesty with the rules you learned from the lecture. Topics to discuss:

- common types of cheating
- high school or university rules about cheating
- the meaning of *plagiarism*
- penalties for cheating
- what teachers do to prevent cheating
- reasons why students cheat

On the Spot!*

9 What Would You Do?

Situation

Last year you took a Business Writing class. One of the course requirements was a ten-page term paper. You worked hard on your paper and received an A.

This year, a close friend of yours is taking the same class. Your friend is a good student, but recently her mother has been sick, and she has been busy taking care of her younger brother and sister.

Your friend asks to copy and turn in your paper from last year. There is a new professor for the class, so your friend is sure the teacher will not recognize the paper.

1. Would you allow your friend to use your paper? Why or why not?
2. Do you think your friend could get caught?
3. If you are sure your friend will not be caught, will it change your decision?
4. Have you ever witnessed cheating? Describe.
5. Have you ever asked a friend to copy a report or homework? Why or why not?
6. If a person cheats in school, will this person also be dishonest in other areas of life?

*When you're "put on the spot", you are asked to make a difficult decision or answer an uncomfortable question without much time to think about it. In the On the Spot! activities in this book, you work with your classmates to solve difficult problems or discuss difficult situations.

Getting Meaning from Context

FOCUS ON TESTING

TOEFL® iBT

When you listen to people talking in English, it is probably hard to understand all the words. However, you can usually get a general idea of what they are saying. How? By using *clues* that help you to *guess*. These clues include:

- words
- synonyms and paraphrases
- transitions
- stressed words
- intonation
- a speaker's tone of voice
- your knowledge of the culture, speakers, or situation

Many tests such as the TOEFL® iBT measure your academic listening and speaking abilities. This activity, and others in the book, will develop your social and academic conversation skills, and provide a foundation for success on a variety of standardized tests.

Using Context Clues

The following conversations take place on a college campus.

1. Listen to the beginning of each conversation.

2. Listen to the question for each conversation. Stop the recording and choose the best answer to each question.

3. In the **Clues** column, write the words that helped you choose your answer. Discuss them with your teacher and classmates.

4. Listen to the last part of each conversation to hear the correct answer.

Answers	Clues

1. (A) going to the post office
  (B) their grades in a course
  (C) parents coming to visit
  (D) going to the beach
	posted, coming out, C

2. (A) He doesn't like his major.
  (B) He isn't going to graduate on time.
  (C) His parents are disappointed.
  (D) He's only in his third year.	

TOEFL® is a registered trademark of Educational Testing Service (ETS). This product is not endorsed or approved by ETS.

Answers	Clues
3. (A) a physician (B) a professor (C) a student advisor (D) a teaching assistant	
4. (A) The student wrote an excellent essay. (B) The student plagiarized a large part of her essay. (C) The student is a very original writer. (D) The student used too many words.	

Focused Listening

FOCUS

Getting Meaning from Intonation

Meaning comes not only from words but also from the way English speakers use their voices. The *tone* (feeling) and rising or falling *intonation* of a speaker's voice can be important clues. Listen to a short conversation. It will be repeated three times. Circle the second speaker's feeling in each case.

1. sad   happy   neutral
2. sad   happy   neutral
3. sad   happy   neutral

1 **Listening for Intonation Cues** In the items that follow, you will hear two conversations. Each of them is spoken in two ways. Use the differences in intonation and tone to decide what the speakers are feeling.

1a. (A) happy
(B) disappointed
(C) neutral

1b. (A) happy
(B) disappointed
(C) neutral

2a. (A) annoyed
(B) calm
(C) disappointed

2b. (A) annoyed
(B) calm
(A) disappointed

2 **Using Intonation To Express Feelings** Work with a partner. Choose one of the sentences below.

1. I got 80% on my chemistry test.
2. We're having chicken for dinner again.

Read your sentences to your partner in three different ways. Your partner will say which feeling you are trying to express each time.

| upset | surprised | neutral |

Now write your own sentence. Say it to your partner with different emotions. Your partner will guess which feeling you are expressing.

Using Language Functions

F⊙CUS

Making, Accepting, and Refusing Invitations

Read Sarah and Mark's conversation. How does Mark invite Sarah to go out with him? What does Sarah say to accept or refuse the invitation?

Sarah: Hello?

Mark: Hi Sarah. How's it going?

Sarah: Pretty good, thanks. How are you?

Mark: Good. Listen, I finished work early and I was wondering if you'd like to go to a movie with me.

Sarah: When—tonight?

Mark: Yeah.

Sarah: Oh Mark, thanks for asking, but I can't. I have to take care of some things here at my apartment....

OR

Sarah: Sure! That sounds like fun!

3 **Making, Accepting, and Refusing Invitations** Work with a partner. Complete this chart with expressions from the conversation. Add other expressions that you know.

Language Tip

To refuse the invitation, Sarah does not just say, "No, thank you." Instead, she gives a reason for refusing. This kind of reason (which may or may not be true) is called an **excuse**, and refusing an invitation this way is called **making (or giving) an excuse**.

Inviting	Accepting	Refusing
I was wondering if you'd like to...	Sure! That sound like fun!	Thanks for asking, but (+ excuse)

4 **Role-Play: Making, Accepting, and Refusing Invitations** Work with a partner. Write a short (1-2 minutes) conversation about one of the following situations. Practice your conversation several times. Then perform it for the class without reading. You may sit face to face or back to back, as if you were talking on a cell phone.

1. Speaker A invites Speaker B to go out for pizza this evening. Speaker B accepts or refuses.

2. Speaker A invites Speaker B to his/her dormitory to watch a tennis game on television.

3. Speaker A invites Speaker B to his or her graduation next week.

Now make an invitation of your own and see if your partner accepts or refuses it.

PART 4 Real-World Tasks

Understanding and Describing Locations

Before You Listen

1 **Reviewing Compass Points** Study the picture.

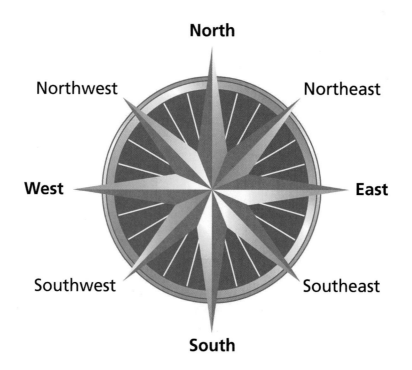

2 Expressions of Location Listen and repeat each expression after the speaker. Then write the numbers from the map next to the matching expressions from the list.

8 a. _____ on the northwest corner of Harris Avenue and Madison Street
2 b. _____ at the intersection of Harris and Madison
4 c. _____ beside / next to (the electronics store)
1 d. _____ across the street from the shoe store / opposite the shoe store
5 e. _____ on both sides of the street
6 f. _____ in the middle of the block
7 g. _____ in the middle of the street
3 h. _____ between the coffee shop and the Indian restaurant
9 i. _____ around the corner from the office supply store

Write the numbers from the map next to the matching expressions on the list above.

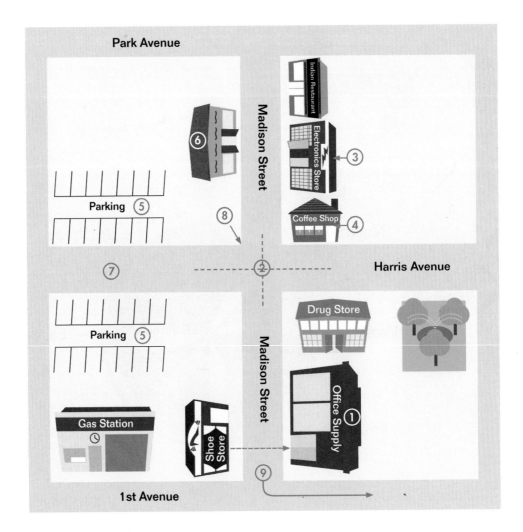

Language Tip

The prepositions *in*, *on*, and *at* can be confusing. Look at these examples.

Examples

I live <u>on</u> Lakeside Drive.

The school is <u>at</u> 4909 Michigan Avenue.

Washington University is <u>in</u> St. Louis.

It is <u>in</u> Missouri.

It is <u>in</u> the United States.

Hints

on + street

at + address

in + city, state, country

3 Expressions of Location in Context Study the map of a college campus. Read the names of the buildings and streets. Then listen to statements about the map. Write *T* if a statement is true and *F* if it is false, based on the map. You will hear each statement twice.

1. T
2. F
3. F
4. T

5. T
6. F
7. F
8. F

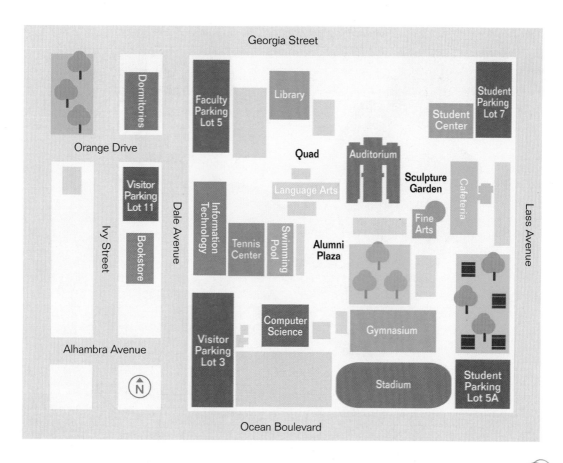

4 **Using Expressions of Location** Write five true or false statements about the map on page 23. Use a different expression from Activity 2 on page 22 in each statement. Then read your statements to one or more classmate. Your classmates will say if your statements are *true* or *false*.

1. _____

_____

2. _____

_____

3. _____

_____

4. _____

_____

5. _____

_____

5 **Describing Map Locations** Work in pairs to ask and answer questions about locations. Student A should look at the map on page 244. Student B should look at the map on page 252.

◄ How do you find your way? Do you use a print map, a GPS, or both?

◄ A map

Self-Assessment Log

Check (✓) the words you learned in this chapter.

Nouns
- dormitory
- identification
- major
- penalty
- plagiarism
- quotation marks
- source
- syllabus
- term paper

Verbs
- avoid
- cite
- cut and paste
- expect
- fill out
- get caught
- give credit
- paraphrase
- quote
- rush
- summarize
- works out

Adjective
- unique

Expressions
- for short
- pretty good/pretty well

Check (✓) the things you did in this chapter. How well can you do each one?

	Very well	Fairly well	Not very well
I can hear and use stress and reductions.	☐	☐	☐
I understand academic honesty.	☐	☐	☐
I can talk about academic honesty.	☐	☐	☐
I can predict a lecture's content from the introduction.	☐	☐	☐
I can take notes on a lecture.	☐	☐	☐
I can use a Venn diagram to compare two things.	☐	☐	☐
I can guess meanings from context.	☐	☐	☐
I can use intonation to express different feelings.	☐	☐	☐
I can make and respond to invitations.	☐	☐	☐
I can read a map and describe locations.	☐	☐	☐

Write what you learned and what you liked in this chapter.

In this chapter,

I learned _____

_____

I liked _____

_____

2 City Life

"I love cities. I love
neighborhoods and the ways
in which they interact with
each other... I love the long
gradual shifts in culture they
contain. I love the fact that
they work at all."

Jason Sutter
U.S. blogger

In this
CHAPTER

Conversation Finding a Place to Live

Lecture Neighborhood Watch Meeting

Getting Meaning from Context
Conversations in an Apartment Building

Real-World Task Following Directions

 Connecting to the Topic

1 What do you see in the photo? Where are the people?
   What are they doing?

2 How is your neighborhood different from this neighborhood?

3 What are some different kinds of places to live? Name seven.

Finding a Place to Live

Before You Listen

The following telephone conversation is about an advertisement ("ad") for a roommate to share a house.

> Roommate wanted to share 5–bdr. house near campus w/3 working people. Furnished room, private bath, kitchen priv., backyard. $800/month + util. Call Nancy at 555–5949.

Culture Note

Student Housing Offices

In North America, most universities have housing offices. Students looking for places to live and people who are looking for **roommates** can advertise in these offices. It is quite common for students to move into a **dormitory**, house, or apartment with people they have not met before.

1 **Prelistening Questions** Discuss these questions in small groups.

1. Look at the picture. What is Mari doing? Where is she?

2. If Mari calls about the ad, what questions will she probably ask? What questions will the owner of the house probably ask her?

3. Where are you living now? Do you have roommates? How did you find each other?

2 **Previewing Vocabulary** Listen to the underlined words and phrases from the conversation. Then use the context to match them with their definitions.

Sentences

1. _b_ My roommate Sarah is a real slob.

2. _e_ Sarah never lifts a finger to clean up after herself.

3. _d_ It really bugs me that I have to do all the housework myself.

4. _f_ **A:** Are you going to Nadia's party tonight?
   B: No, I can't make it. I have to study.

5. _a_ **A:** Do you want to go out to dinner?
   B: Thanks, but I can't leave the house because my sister is going to come by around six o'clock.

6. _c_ **A:** Where is the language lab?
   B: Go upstairs. It's the first door on your right. You can't miss it.

Definitions

a. to stop somewhere for a short visit

b. a messy person (*slang*)

c. to be able to see (something) easily

d. to irritate, annoy, bother (*slang*)

e. to help with work

f. to come or go (to a particular event)

Listen

3 **Comprehension Questions** Listen to the conversation. You don't need to understand all the words. Just listen for the answers to these questions. After you listen, discuss your answers with a partner.

1. Who are the speakers?

2. What is the student calling about?

3. Where does the student live now? What is the problem there?

4. Who lives in the house that the student is asking about?

5. How is the neighborhood?

6. At the end of the conversation, what do the speakers agree to do?

Stress

4. Listening for Stressed Words Listen to the conversation again. Some of the stressed words are missing. During each pause, repeat the phrase or sentence. Then fill in the missing stressed words.

Nancy: Hello?

Mari: May I speak to Nancy, please?

Nancy: _Speaking_.

Mari: Uh hi, uh, my name is Mari, and I'm calling about the _room_ for rent. I saw your _ad_ at the campus _housing_ office.

Nancy: Oh, right. OK, uh, are you a _student_?

Mari: Well, right now I'm just studying _English_, but I'm planning to start _college_ full-time in _March_.

Nancy: I see. _Where_ are you living _now_?

Mari: I've been living in a _house_ with some other students, but I _don't_ _like_ it there.

Nancy: Why? What's the _problem_?

Mari: Well, _first_ of all, it's really _noisy_, and it's not very clean. The other people in the house are real _slobs_. I mean they never lift a _finger_ to clean _up_ after themselves. It really _bugs_ me! I need a place that's cleaner and more _pravét_.

Nancy: Well, it's really _quite_ here. We're not _home_ very much.

Mari: What do you _do_?

Nancy: I teach _English_ at the college.

Mari: _Waite_ a minute! Didn't we meet yesterday at the _plasment_ exam?

Nancy: Oh... _you are_ the girl from _Japan_! What was your name again?

Mari: Mari.

Nancy: Right. What a _slow_ _word_!

Mari: It really is. By the way, who _as_ lives in the house? The ad said there are _3_ people.

Nancy: Well, besides me there's my _hasbund_, Andrew, and my _cousen_, Jeff. He's a musician and a part-time _studen_. Uh, are you OK with having _mail-yroudayrs_ roommates?

Mari: Sure, as long as they're clean and not too _noisy_.

Nancy: _Don't_ worry. They're both _esily_ to live with.

Mari: OK. Um, is the _neborhud_ safe?

Nancy: Oh sure. We haven't had _any_ problems, and you can _smoke_ to school from here.

Mari: Well, it sounds really _nice_. When can I come by and _see_ it?

Nancy: Can you make it this _evining_ around _five_? Then you can meet the _pays_ too.

Mari: Yeah, five o'clock is _good_. What's the _adress_?

Nancy: It's 3475 Hayworth Avenue. Do you know where _that_ is?

Mari: No, I don't.

Nancy: OK. From University Village you go seven blocks _is_ on Olympic Avenue. At the intersection of Olympic and Alfred, there's a _staplite_. Turn _left_ and go _up_ one and a half blocks. Our house is in the _middle_ of the block on the _left_.

Mari: That sounds _essy_.

Nancy: Yeah, you _can't_ _miss_ it. Listen, I've got to go. Someone's at the door. See you this _evening_.

Mari: OK, see you _later_. Bye.

Nancy: Bye-bye.

Check your answers in the listening script on pages 267–268. Then read the conversation with a partner. Pronounce stressed words louder, higher, and more clearly than unstressed words.

Many students of English have difficulty with the phrase *by the way.* Speakers use this phrase to introduce a new topic in a discussion or conversation.

For example, in the conversation you heard:

Nancy: Oh… you're the girl from Japan! What was your name again?
Mari: Mari.
Nancy: Right. What a small world!
Mari: It really is. **By the way**, who else lives in the house? The ad said there are three people.

At first, Mari and Nancy are speaking about their meeting at the placement test the day before. Mari says "by the way" because she wants to interrupt this topic to introduce another topic.

Andrew: I love this dog!
Nancy: Me too. **By the way**, we need to buy some dog food and treats!

Reductions

5 **Comparing Unreduced and Reduced Pronunciation** The following sentences are from the conversation. Listen for the difference between unreduced and reduced pronunciation. Repeat both forms after the speaker.

Unreduced Pronunciation	Reduced Pronunciation
1. Where are you living now?	Where're ya living now?
2. What do you do?	Whaddaya do?
3. You can walk to school from here.	Ya kin walk ta school from here.
4. When can I come by and see it?	When kin I come by 'n see it?
5. Can you make it this evening around five?	Kinya make it this evening around five?
6. Do you know where that is?	D'ya know where that is?
7. I've got to go.[1]	I've gotta go.

[1]*I've got to* means "I must" or "I have to."

hamwork

6 **Listening for Reductions** Listen to the following conversations. You'll hear the reduced pronunciation of some words. Write the unreduced forms of the missing words in the blanks.

Conversation 1

Mari: Hey Jeff, _____ _____ _____ going?

Jeff: I _____ _____ get a present for Nancy. It's her birthday, _____ know.

Mari: Yeah, I know. _____ _____ _____ think I should get her?

Jeff: Well, she likes music. _____ _____ a CD?

Conversation 2

Nancy: _____ _____ _____ like my new haircut, Mari?

Mari: It's great! Who's your hairstylist?

Nancy: His name's José.

Mari: _____ _____ give me his phone number?

Nancy: Sure, but he's always very busy. _____ _____ try calling him, but he might not be able _____ see _____ until next month.

Conversation 3

Andrew: _____ _____ _____ _____ _____ do tonight, Nancy?

Nancy: Nothing special. I've _____ _____ stay home _____ correct my students' compositions.

Check your answers in the listening script on pages 268–269. Then read the conversation with a partner. Try to use reduced forms.

7 **Reviewing Vocabulary** With a partner, read the beginning of the following phone conversation. Then complete the conversation. Try to use all the words and phrases in the box. Perform your conversation in front of the class.

Noun	Verbs	Expressions	
slob	bug	can't miss	never lifts a finger
	come by	make it	

Speaker 1: Hello?

Speaker 2: Hi _____. This is _____.
                 [name of partner]   [your name]

Speaker 1: Oh hi! How are you?

Speaker 2: Well, I got a new roommate last week.

Speaker 1: Really? How is [he or she]?

Speaker 2: Terrible!...

Using Language Functions

FOCUS

Starting a Phone Conversation

Reread the beginning of the phone conversation between Mari and Nancy in Activity 4 on page 30. Phone conversations between strangers often begin similarly. Typically, they contain these functions and expressions:

Function	Expressions
• A caller asks to speak to a person.	Can/Could/May I please speak to _____? Is _____ there? I'd like to speak to _____.
• The person that the caller asked for identifies himself or herself.	Speaking. This is he/she. This is _____.
• The caller identifies himself or herself.	My name is _____. [used by strangers talking for the first time] This is _____. [used when people know each other]
• The caller gives a reason for calling.	I'm calling about... I'm calling because... Let me tell you why I called.

Ending a Phone Conversation

Reread the end of the phone conversation between Mari and Nancy in Activity 4 on page 31. It has these typical elements:

Functions	Expressions
• One speaker signals that the conversation is finished.	I've got to go.
• The other speaker uses a closing expression.	See you later. Bye.
• The first speaker uses a closing expression.	Bye.

Other Expressions to Signal the End of a Conversation

Well, thanks for the information.
It was nice talking to you.
Thanks for calling.
I'll be in touch (with you).

8 Role-Play Work with a partner. Role-play phone conversations. Be sure to use the expressions for opening and closing a phone conversation. Student A should look at page 245. Student B should look at page 253.

9 Telephone Game For this activity your teacher will divide you into groups of five or six. Each person in the group will receive a number from 1 to 5 (or 6).

1. Exchange phone numbers with the people in your group.

2. Your teacher will give a "secret" message to each person who got number 1.

3. This evening, person 1 will call person 2 in your group and give him or her the message. Person 2 will call person 3, and so on until everyone is called.

4. The next day, person 5 (or 6) from each group will repeat the message in class. See if the message changed as it passed from person to person.

Remember: When you call your classmate:

- ask for your classmate by name
- identify yourself
- say why you are calling
- give the message
- use the expressions you learned for ending the conversation

Neighborhood Watch Meeting

Before You Listen

Culture Note

In many American cities, neighbors join together to form a **Neighborhood Watch**. They agree to work together to stop crimes in their area. They watch out for unusual activity in their neighborhood. If they see anything suspicious, they call the police.

At the first Neighborhood Watch meeting, a police officer usually comes to speak about crime prevention.

Last week there was a burglary in Nancy's neighborhood. The people on her street decided to form a Neighborhood Watch. This is their first meeting. A police officer is speaking about ways to prevent crime.

▲ Neighborhood Watch signs ▲

1 **Prelistening Discussion** Discuss these questions in small groups.

1. Look up the meaning of the following word pairs: neighbor/neighborhood; burglar/burglary; robber/robbery; thief/theft.

2. Is there much crime in the area where you live? What kind? Do you feel safe in your area?

3. Does your area have something like a Neighborhood Watch? Do you think it would be a good idea? Why or why not?

4. What are some things you can do to protect yourself and your home against crime?

2 Previewing Vocabulary Listen to these words and phrases from the lecture. Check (✓) the words you don't know. Discuss their meanings with a partner.

Nouns
- alarm
- break-in
- deadbolt
- decal
- device
- front/back (of)
- license
- right
- slob
- (car) theft
- timer
- valuables

Verbs
- break into
- prevent

Adjective
- violent

Expression
- get into the habit

▲ A deadbolt lock: one way to secure your home

Culture Note

How do people in the United States protect their homes from theft? People use a variety of approaches and products, including security systems, dogs that bark, and lights to discourage thieves from trying to break into their homes. Some homeowners even keep a gun in their home to defend themselves against criminals.

Strategy

Taking Notes on Statistics

Statistics are numbers that give facts about a situation. Often, statistics are expressed as a percentage or fraction; for example, "Thirty percent of the students in our class are men" or "People spend about one-fourth of their salaries on rent." Statistics are very common in lectures. When people talk about statistics, the following terms appear frequently:

Nouns

_____ % _____ percent

_____ number

_____ half

_____ third

_____ quarter

Verbs

_____ increase, go up, rise

_____ decrease, decline, go down

_____ double

Other phrases

_____ less than

_____ more than

_____ equal to or the same as

About 66 percent (%) of the people ▶ in this photo are women.

3 **Abbreviating Statistics** Write abbreviations or symbols next to the items in the chart above. If you don't know the abbreviation or symbol for an item, create one.

4 **Taking Notes on Statistics** Listen to sentences from the lecture. Use abbreviations and symbols from above to take notes. You will hear each sentence twice.

1. _____

2. _____

3. _____

Exchange notes with a partner. Try to repeat the sentences you heard by using your partner's notes.

Strategy

Transitions (Connecting Words)

Transitions are words and phrases that connect the parts of a speech or composition. There are usually transitions *between* the major sections of a talk. In addition, we also use transitions to connect details *within* each main section. If you listen for transitions, you can tell when a new idea or topic is starting.

Example

"Tonight I'd like to give you some simple suggestions to make your homes and cars safer. OK? So <u>first of all</u>, let's talk about lights."

"<u>Next</u>, let's talk about lights inside the house."

5 Listening for Transitions Following is a list of transitions from the lecture. Listen to the lecture. When you hear each transition, write the topic or suggestion that follows it.

PART 1

First of all, *you need* _____

Next, _____

All right then. The next topic I want to discuss is _____

    First of all, _____

    Also, _____

PART 2

OK, now let's move on and talk about _____

    First, _____

    The most important thing is _____

Now my last point is _____

    The main thing is _____

    Also, _____

    And one more thing: _____

Answer these questions with your classmates.

1. How many main ideas did the speaker discuss? Which transitions introduced them?

2. Why are some of the transitions indented in the outline on page 39?

3. When you take notes, should you write transitions in your notes? Why or why not?

 6 **Taking Notes** Following are sample notes on the police officer's suggestions. Notice that they do not contain transitions; instead, the relationship among main ideas and details is shown by underlining, indenting, and listing.

Use your notes from Activities 4 and 5 to fill in the missing information. Remember to use abbreviations and symbols. If necessary, listen to the lecture again.

Date: _____

Ways to Prevent Crime

PART 1

<u>Intro:</u>

Very little violent crime in neigh'hood. But:

Burglaries ↑:

    Last yr: _____

    This yr: _____

Car theft ↑: _____

<u>How to keep home & auto safe:</u>

1. House lights

    need lights in front and _____

    turn on at _____

2. _____

    bright lights in garage, hallway, apt. door

    fix broken lights

    house or apt: use automatic _____

3. _____

—_____ not safe

—every door needs _____

—get special locks for _____

    —50% _____

PART 2

4. _____

    —use _____

    —put _____

    —alarms don't _____

    —better to have _____

5. _____

    —Go on vacation, _____

    —See someth. unusual, _____

    —Put _____

◀ Is this home safe from burglars?
Why or why not?

7 **Discussing the Lecture** Discuss the following questions about the lecture and your own experience. Refer to your notes as necessary.

Part 1

1. Has anyone ever broken into your home or your car? If yes, what did the burglars steal?

2. What advice did the police officer give about lights? Do you do these things in your house or apartment?

3. How does an automatic timer work? Do you use timers in your home?

4. What types of locks did the officer recommend? Do you use locks like that?

Part 2

5. According to the officer, how can you prevent car theft? Do you follow these suggestions?

6. What is the officer's opinion about car alarms? What do you think?

7. What is a decal? Where do people often put them? Do you have any?

8. How do people in a Neighborhood Watch help each other? Do you help your neighbors this way?

8 **Reviewing Vocabulary** Work in small groups. Look back at the vocabulary list in Activity 2 on page 37. Quiz each other on the terms and their meanings.

On the Spot!

9 **What Would You Do?** Read the situation and discuss the following questions.

> **Situation**
>
> You have come to the United States to study at a university. You have rented a room in the home of a very nice American family. The neighborhood is quiet and pretty, and the house is near your school. You are comfortable and happy in your new home.
>
> One day, while preparing food in the kitchen, you discover a gun inside a cabinet.

Discuss the following questions in small groups.

1. Imagine that you have just discovered the gun. How do you feel?

2. What will you do next? Will you speak to the homeowners about the gun? What will you say?

3. Will you look for another place to live?

4. Imagine that the family with the gun lives next door to you. You have a young child, and this family also has a young child. The two children want to play together. Would you allow your child to play at this house?

5. Do you believe that people have the right to own guns, or should guns be illegal?

6. If a person illegally owns a gun, what should the punishment be?

▲ According to a Police Foundation report, over 35% of American households contain at least one firearm (gun). Do you think this home contains any firearms?

Getting Meaning from Context

FOCUS ON TESTING

TOEFL® iBT

Using Context Clues

Many tests such as the TOEFL® iBT measure your academic listening and speaking abilities. This activity, and others in the book, will develop your social and academic conversation skills, and provide a foundation for success on a variety of standardized tests. The following conversations take place in an apartment building.

1. Listen to the beginning of each conversation.
2. Listen to the question for each conversation. Stop the recording and choose the best answer.
3. In the **Clues** column, write the words that helped you choose your answer. Discuss them with your teacher and classmates.
4. Listen to the last part of each conversation to hear the correct answer.

Answers	Clues
Questions 1 through 3 are based on a conversation between a man and a woman.	
1. Ⓐ a neighbor Ⓑ the apartment manager Ⓒ Donna's father Ⓓ a repairman	
2. Ⓐ a repairperson Ⓑ a painter Ⓒ an exterminator[1] Ⓓ a plumber[2]	
3. Ⓐ It's on the third floor. Ⓑ It's in bad condition. Ⓒ It's in a good neighborhood. Ⓓ It's cheap.	

[1]An exterminator is a professional who uses poison to kill insects.
[2]A plumber is a person who installs and repairs water pipes, sinks, toilets, and so on.

Answers	Clues
Questions 4 and 5 are based on a conversation between two neighbors.	
4. (A) He thinks it's very funny. (B) He's surprised to see Donna. (C) He's a little angry. (D) He is happy to help Donna.	
5. (A) He is happy to help Donna. (B) He's surprised to see Donna. (C) He's annoyed with Donna. (D) He's very worried.	

Focused Listening

FOCUS

Guessing Relationships Between People

The way people address each other in North America can give clues about their relationships. For example:

- In very formal situations, it is polite to use the titles "Sir" or "Ma'am" when you are talking to an older person or someone important. With adults you do not know well, it is correct to use a title with the person's last name. For example, "Ms. Adams" or "Dr. Snow."
- On the other hand, two people who are equal in age or equal in position, or who are meeting in a casual situation, usually use each other's first names.
- People in close personal relationships often use nicknames to address each other.

For example:

- Married people, people in romantic relationships, or relatives speaking to children: *honey, dear, sweetheart, darling*
- Children to parents: *Mom, Mommy, Mama, Dad, Daddy, Papa*
- Children to grandparents: *Grandma, Granny, Grammy, Grandpa*
- Friends: *pal, buddy, brother, sister, girl*

 1 Listening for Clues to Relationships Between People

1. Work in groups of four, divided into two pairs. Pair A, turn to page 245. Pair B, turn to page 253. Look only at your list and follow the instructions. Study the information in your list for a few minutes before you begin.

Using Language Functions

FOCUS

Expressing Frustration

Frustration is what people feel when they cannot get what they want, even after many tries. For example, imagine that your neighbor's dog wakes you up every night. You complain to your neighbor many times, but the situation does not improve.

In this situation you would feel *frustrated*.

The underlined idioms in the following sentences mean that a speaker is frustrated. Notice the grammar in each sentence.

- My roommate is a total slob! She never cleans up after herself! <u>I am fed up with</u> her mess!
- **Mother (to fighting children):** <u>I've had it with</u> your fighting! Go outside right now. I want some quiet in here!
- **Student:** I've been working on this physics problem for three hours. <u>I'm sick of it!</u>

---

2 Role-Play Work in pairs to role-play situations in an apartment building. Student A should look at page 246. Student B should look at page 254.

3 Follow-up Discussion Discuss the following questions with your classmates.

1. Do you live in an apartment? If yes, does your building have a manager? What responsibilities does he or she have?

2. In Activity 1, you learned that a person who kills insects is called an exterminator. Below is a list of other professionals who work in houses and apartments. Use a dictionary to find out what each person does. Then tell your group if you have ever called this kind of person to fix a problem in your home. Describe the problem.

architect	electrician	phone technician
cable/Internet installer	gardener	plumber
carpenter	painter	roofer
carpet cleaner		

3. Tell your classmates about any other problems you have had in your home or with your neighbors. Also, explain what you did to solve the problem(s).

Following Directions

1 **Prelistening Questions** Look at the map. Imagine that two people are standing at the spot marked with a red X. Speaker A wants to go to the Chinese restaurant.

1. What expressions can Speaker A use to ask for directions?
2. Imagine that you are Speaker B. How would you answer Speaker A?

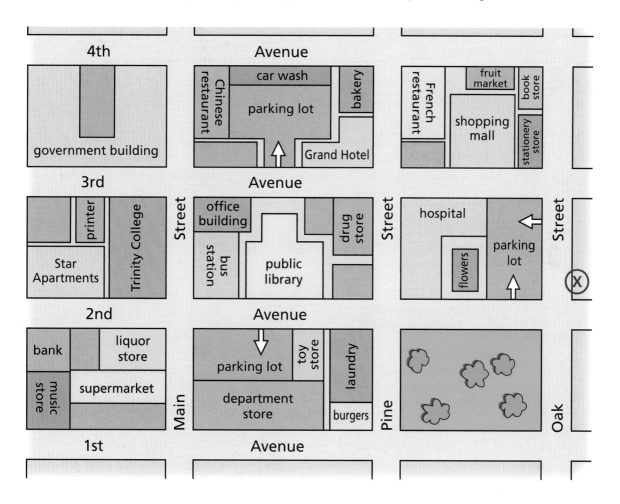

Requesting and Giving Directions

Function	Expressions
Use these expressions to *request* directions.	Excuse me, where is _____? Can/could you tell me where _____ is? How do I get to _____? Do you know where _____ is?

Use these expressions to *give* directions.	**Verbs:** go, walk, drive, turn
	 Directions: up/down the street;
	            north, south, east, west;
	            right, left; straight
	 Distance: half a block, one mile, two kilometers
	 Prepositions: on the left/right; on _____ Street;

2 **Following Directions** You will hear directions based on the map on page 47. Follow the directions on the map. At the end of each item you will hear a question. Write the answer to the question in the space. You will hear each item twice.

1. _____

2. _____

3. _____

4. _____

After You Listen

Saying You Don't Understand

If you don't understand the directions that someone gives you, use one of these expressions.

I don't understand.	I'm lost.	I didn't catch that.
I'm confused.	I'm in the dark.	I'm not following you.
I don't get it.		

3 **Requesting and Giving Directions** Work in pairs to request and give directions using maps. Student A should look at page 246. Student B should look at page 254. Follow the instructions on those pages.

Self-Assessment Log

Check (✓) the words you learned in this chapter.

Nouns
- alarm
- break-in
- deadbolt
- decal
- device
- front/back (of)
- license
- right
- slob

- (car) theft
- timer
- valuables

Verbs
- break into
- bug
- come by
- prevent

Adjective
- violent

Expressions
- can't miss
- get into the habit
- (can/can't) make it
- never lift a finger

Check (✓) the things you did in this chapter. How well can you do each one?

	Very well	Fairly well	Not very well
I can hear and use stress and reductions.	☐	☐	☐
I can make telephone calls.	☐	☐	☐
I can talk about crime and crime prevention.	☐	☐	☐
I can take notes on statistics and transitions.	☐	☐	☐
I can guess meanings from context.	☐	☐	☐
I can use phrases to express frustration.	☐	☐	☐
I can ask for and give directions.	☐	☐	☐

Write what you learned and what you liked in this chapter.

In this chapter,

I learned _____

_____

I liked _____

_____

CHAPTER 3

Business and Money

"If you work just for money,
you'll never make it, but if you
love what you're doing and you
always put the customer first,
success will be yours."

Ray Kroc
U.S. businessman,
founder of McDonald's Corp.

In this CHAPTER

Conversation Borrowing Money

Lecture Entrepreneurs

Getting Meaning from Context Banking Services

Real-World Task Balancing a Checkbook

Connecting to the Topic

1. What kind of products and services do you think this man's business offers?

2. Name and describe three small business you know.

3. Imagine you were to start a small business. What kind of business would you start? Describe it.

Borrowing Money

Before You Listen

In the following conversation, Jeff talks with his father about borrowing money.

Jeff's father ▶

◀ Jeff

1 **Prelistening Questions** Discuss these questions in small groups.

1. Look at the photos. Jeff is asking his father for money. Do you think his father will give it to him? Why or why not?

2. In your community, who usually pays for a person's education after high school?

3. Is it easy or difficult for you to manage your money?

4. What do you do when you need more money?

5. Do you know anyone who works and goes to school at the same time?

2 **Previewing Vocabulary** Listen to the underlined words and phrases from the conversation. Then use the context to match them with their definitions.

Sentences

1. __a__ It's hard to live alone in the United States because everything costs an arm and a leg.

2. __d__ Serena can't make ends meet because she doesn't earn enough money.

3. __e__ We didn't go away on vacation last summer because we were broke.

4. __b__ I can't buy everything I want, because I am living on a budget.

5. __f__ With his two jobs, Tom has an income of $3,200 a month.

6. __e__ You don't earn much money as a server at a fast-food restaurant.

Definitions

a. a lot of money

b. a plan for how to spend one's money each month

c. without any money

d. to pay all one's bills

e. to receive money for work

f. all the money you receive for work or any other reason

Listen

3 **Comprehension Questions** Listen to the conversation. You don't need to understand all the words. Just listen for the answers to these questions. After you listen, discuss your answers with a partner.

1. What is Jeff's problem?

2. What solutions does his father suggest?

3. Why can't Jeff work more hours?

4. How does Jeff feel at the end of the conversation?

Stress

4 **Listening for Stressed Words** Listen to the conversation again. Some of the stressed words are missing. During each pause, repeat the phrase or sentence. Then fill in the missing stressed words.

Dad: Hello?

Jeff: Hi, Dad.

Dad: Jeff! How ___are___ you?

Jeff: I'm fine, Dad. How's Mom? Did she get over her ___cold___?

Dad: Yes, she's ___fine___ now. She went back to ___work___ yesterday.

Jeff: That's good. Um, Dad, I need to ___ask___ you something.

Dad: Sure, son, what ___is___ it?

Jeff: Well, uh, the truth is, I'm ___broked___ again. Could you ___lend___ me $200 just till the end of the month?

Dad: Broke again? Jeff, when you moved ___in___ with Nancy and Andrew, you said you could ___make___ ends ___meet___. But this is the ___third___ time you've asked me for help!

Jeff: I know, I know, I'm sorry. But, see, my old guitar broke, and I had to buy a ___new___ one. I ___can't___ ___play___ on a broken guitar, right?

Dad: Look Jeff, if you want to play in a ___band___, that's OK with me. But you ___can't___ keep asking ___me___ to pay for it!

Jeff: OK, OK, you're right. But what do you think I ought to ___do___? Everything costs an ___arm___ and a ___leg___ around here.

Dad: Well, first of all, I think you'd better go on a ___budget___. Make a list of all your ___income___ and all your expenses. And then it's simple. Don't ___spend___ more than you ___earn___.

Jeff: But that's ___exactly___ the problem! My expenses are ___always___ larger than my income. That's why I need to borrow money from ___you___.

Dad: Then maybe you should work more hours at the ___computer___ store.

Jeff: Dad! I ___already___ work 15 hours a week! How can I ___study___ and ___work___ and find time to play with my band?

Dad: Come ___on___, Jeff, when ___I___ was your age…

Jeff: I know, I know. When ___you___ were my age you were already ___married___ and working and going to school.

Dad: That's right. And if I could do it, why can't ___you___?

Jeff: Because ___I'm___ not ___you___, Dad, that's why!

Dad: All right, Jeff, calm down. I don't ___expect___ you to be like me. But I ___can't___ ___lend___ you any more money. Your mother and I are on a budget ___too___, you know.

Jeff: Maybe I should just drop ___out___ of school, ___work___ full-time, and play in the band in the evenings. I can go back to school ___later___.

Dad: I wouldn't do that if I were you.

Jeff: Yeah, but you're ___not___ me, remember? It's my life!

Dad: All right, Jeff. Let's not ___argue___. Why don't you ___think___ about this very carefully and call me ___back___ in a few days. In the meantime, you'd ___better___ find a way to ___pay___ for that new guitar.

Jeff: Yes, Dad.

Dad: All right. Good-bye, son.

Jeff: Bye.

Check your answers in the listening script on pages 271–272. Then read the conversation with a partner. Remember that stressed words are louder, higher, and pronounced more clearly than unstressed words.

Language Tip

The words *borrow* and *lend* can be confusing. Look at this example:

Jeff wants to *borrow* money from his father, but his father doesn't want to *lend* money to him.

An easy way to remember the difference is like this:

borrow = take
lend = give

Also notice the grammar:

to borrow (something) **from** (someone)
to lend (something) **to** (someone)

Reductions

5 **Comparing Unreduced and Reduced Pronunciation** The following sentences are from the conversation. Listen for the difference between unreduced and reduced pronunciation. Repeat both forms after the speaker.

Unreduced Pronunciation	Reduced Pronunciation
1. I need to ask you something.	I need <u>ta</u> ask you something.
2. This is the third time you've asked me for help.	This is the third time you've <u>ast</u> me for help.
3. My old guitar broke, and I had to buy a new one.	My old guitar broke, 'n I <u>hadta</u> buy a new one.
4. What do you think I ought to do?	<u>Whaddaya</u> think I <u>oughta</u> do?
5. If I could do it, why can't you?	If I could do it, why <u>cantchu</u>?
6. Why don't you think about this very carefully and call me back in a few days?	Why <u>dontchu</u> think about this very carefully 'n call me back in a few days?

6 **Listening for Reductions** Listen to the following conversation between a bank teller and a customer. You'll hear reduced forms from Chapters 1, 2, and 3. Write the unreduced forms of the missing words in the blanks.

Customer: Hi, my name is Chang Lee.

Teller: How _____can_____ I help you?

Customer: I _____want_____ _____to_____ check my balance.

Teller: OK. _____can_____ I have your account number, please?

Customer: 381335.

Teller: Your balance is $201.

Customer: OK. _____and_____ I _____asked_____ my father _____to_____ wire me some money. I'd like _____to_____ know if it's arrived.

Teller: I'm sorry. Your account doesn't show any deposits.

Customer: Oh, no. I need _____to_____ pay my rent tomorrow. _____What_____ _____do_____ _____you_____ think I _____ought_____ _____to_____ do?

Teller: Well, we're having some computer problems today. So, why _____don't_____ _____you_____ call us later to check again? Or _____you_____ _____can_____ come back. We're open till 5:00.

Customer: OK, thanks.

Teller: You're welcome.

Check your answers in the listening script on page 272. Then read the conversation with a partner. Try to use reduced forms.

7 Using Vocabulary Write a question using each of these words. Then use your questions to interview a classmate.

1. borrow_____

2. lend _____

3. earn _____

4. income _____

5. budget _____

In pairs, practice the words and idioms from this section. Student A should look at page 247. Student B should look at page 255.

Pronunciation

In pairs, practice the words and idioms from this section. Student A should look at page 247. Student B should look at page 255.

FOCUS

Can Versus *Can't*

To hear the difference between *can* and *can't*, you must listen to the differences in vowel quality and stress.

Examples

1. You can **buy** a cheap house these days. (Pronounce: kin buy)
2. You **can't buy** a cheap house these days. (Pronounce: kant buy)

Remember: *Can't* is always stressed.
Can is normally reduced and the main verb is stressed.

8 Pronouncing *Can* and *Can't* Listen and repeat the following pairs of sentences. Place an accent mark over the stressed words *can't* and the main verb. The first one is done for you.

Affirmative	**Negative**
1. Jeff can play on a broken guitar.	**1.** Jeff can't play on a broken guitar.
2. Jeff's father can pay for his new guitar.	**2.** Jeff's father can't pay for his new guitar.
3. Jeff can work more hours at the computer store.	**3.** Jeff can't work more hours at the computer store.
4. I can lend you more money.	**4.** I can't lend you more money.
5. Jeff can go back to school later.	**5.** Jeff can't go back to school later.

9 **Distinguishing Between *Can* and *Can't*** Listen to the sentences. Decide if they are affirmative or negative. Circle *can* or *can't*.

1. (can)   can't   6. can   (can't)
2. can   (can't)   7. (can)   can't
3. can   (can't)   8. can   (can't)
4. (can)   can't   9. (can)   can't
5. can   (can't)   10. (can)   can't

10 **Talking About Abilities** Look at the following list of activities. Which ones can you do? With a partner, take turns making true sentences with *can* and *can't*. As you listen to your partner, put a check in the *Can* or *Can't* column.

Example

Student A says, "I can sew a button on a shirt."

	My Partner Can...	My Partner Can't...
a. sew a button on a shirt	✓	
b. bake a cake		
c. stand on his or her head		
d. do a handstand		
e. water-ski		
f. snowboard		
g. sing		
h. dance		
i. drive a stick-shift car		
j. pilot a plane		
k. understand our teacher		
l. understand TV news in English		
m. run a mile (1.6 kilometers)		
n. run a marathon		
o. speak Latin		
p. play a musical instrument		

▲ I can stand on my head.

Check with your partner to make sure you understood his or her sentences correctly. Ask your partner about additional skills or abilities that are not on the list. Tell the class three things your partner can and can't do.

Using Language Functions

11 **Recognizing Expressions of Advice** Reread the conversation from Activity 4 in the listening script on pages 271–272. Find one place where Jeff asks his father for advice. Find four places where his father gives him advice. Fill in the chart with the language they use.

Asking for Advice	Giving Advice
Jeff: _____ _____ _____ _____	Jeff's father: 1. _____ _____ 2. _____ _____ 3. _____ _____ 4. _____ _____

12 **Role-Play** With a partner, role-play one of the following situations. Use expressions from the chart below. Your teacher may ask you to perform your role-play in front of the class.

Useful Expressions of Advice			
Asking	**Giving**	**Accepting**	**Rejecting**
Can you give me any/some advice? What should I do? What do you suggest/recommend/advise? What do you think I should/ought to do?	You should + *verb*. I advise you to + *verb*. I suggest that you + *verb*. You can/could + *verb*. Why don't you + *verb*? Verb/Don't + *verb*.	Thanks for the advice. That sounds like a good idea. Thanks. I'll do that.	Thanks, but I don't think that's a good idea. Thanks. I'll think about it. Thanks, but I'm not so sure.

Situation 1

Person A is spending more money each month than he or she is earning.

Person B gives suggestions for managing money.

Situation 2

Person A bought a radio and paid cash for it. Unfortunately, he or she didn't keep the receipt. Two days later, the radio broke. Person A asks Person B for advice on how to get his or her money back.

Situation 3

Person A doesn't trust banks and keeps all his or her money in a box under the bed. Person B explains why this is a bad idea and gives Person A advice about safer places to keep his or her money.

Situation 4

Person A, a foreign student, is planning a vacation to Person B's home city. Person A asks Person B for advice on ways to have a good time without spending a lot of money. (Example: Person A asks about inexpensive places to stay and eat.)

PART 2 Lecture

Entrepreneurs

Before You Listen

The following lecture is about people who start new businesses or industries—they are called entrepreneurs—and about the process they follow in creating their businesses.

◀ Jeff Bezos, founder of Amazon.com

1 **Prelistening Discussion** Discuss these questions in small groups.

1. Have you ever seen or heard the word *entrepreneur*? Tell what you know about this word.

2. What makes a business leader successful? Knowledge? Skill? Personal characteristics? Make a list on the board. Write both the noun and adjective forms of the words.

Example

creativity/creative

3. Give examples of people you know about who have started their own businesses. Which of the characteristics listed on the board do they have?

4. Which of the characteristics listed on the board do *you* have? Do you think you would be a good entrepreneur? Why or why not?

2 **Previewing Vocabulary** Listen to these words and phrases from the lecture. Check (✓) the ones you don't know. Discuss the meanings of new words with a partner.

Nouns
- ▓ brilliant idea
- ▓ quality
- ▓ solution
- ▓ team
- ▓ vision

Verbs
- ▓ found
- ▓ have (something) in common
- ▓ hire
- ▓ identify

- ▓ raise capital
- ▓ solve
- ▓ surf the Internet
- ▓ take risks

Culture Note

Steve Jobs (1955–2011) was one of the most famous entrepreneurs in the revolution of the personal computer and mobile technology. We all know the name of the company he cofounded: Apple. Chances are you use one of the innovative technology products he designed: the iPod, iPhone, iPad, an iMac or a MacBook. Jobs brought Apple back from the edge of bankruptcy in the late 1990s. The company now has the honor of being the most profitable corporation in the United States. Some people wonder how the Apple team will continue Jobs' vision, and if they will be as successful without him. What do you think?

Listen

3 **Taking Notes** Listen to the first part of the lecture and take notes in the best way you can. Use your own paper. Listen specifically for the following information:

- What are entrepreneurs?
- What characteristics do they have?

Strategy

Outlining

In Chapters 1 and 2 you learned how to indent to show the relationship between main ideas and specific details. You can also show this relationship by using an outline. An outline looks like this:

I. First main topic

    A. First subtopic

        1. First detail about subtopic A

        2. Second detail

    B. Second subtopic

II. Second main topic

(Etc.)

You can see that outlines use indentation together with letters and numbers to organize information. Outlining is a very common way of taking notes in English.

▲ Frederick Smith, founder of FedEx

▲ Anita Roddick, founder of The Body Shop

◄ Jerry Yang, founder of Yahoo!

4 **Outlining the Lecture** Here is a sample outline of the first part of the lecture. Use your notes from Activity 3 to fill in as much information as you can. Remember to use abbreviations and symbols and write key words only. Listen again if necessary.

Date: _____

Topic: Entrepreneurs

I. Intro

  A. Example: _____

  B. Def. of entrep.: _____

II. Characteristics (similar)

  A. _____

    1. Ex.: _____

  B. _____

    1. Ex.: _____

III. Background (diff.)

  A. _____

    1. Ex.: _____

    2. Ex.: _____

  B. Rich and poor

    1. Ex.: _____

  C. Many ent. are

    1. Ex.: _____

  D. _____

  E. _____

    1. Ex.: _____

5 **Taking Notes on a Process** Listen to the second part of the lecture. Continue taking notes on your own paper. After listening, use your notes to fill in the missing information below.

IV. Entrepreneurial process

A. Identify a problem

B. _____

C. _____

D. _____

E. _____

F. _____

After You Listen

6 **Discussing the Lecture** Discuss the following questions about the lecture and your own experience. Refer to your notes as necessary.

1. Match each person with the company he or she founded. Have you ever used any of these companies' products?

   1. __e__ Jeff Bezos   **a.** Microsoft Corporation
   2. __a__ Bill Gates   **b.** FedEx
   3. __d__ Jerry Yang   **c.** The Body Shop
   4. __c__ Anita Roddick   **d.** Yahoo!
   5. __b__ Frederick Smith   **e.** Amazon

2. What qualities do all entrepreneurs have in common? Do you have these qualities?

3. In what ways can entrepreneurs be different from each other?

4. What are the six steps in the entrepreneurial process?

5. Why are entrepreneurs cultural heroes in the United States?

6. Would you like to be an entrepreneur? Why or why not?

7 **Reviewing Vocabulary** Work in small groups. Look back at the vocabulary list in Activity 2 on page 61. Quiz each other on the words and their meanings.

8 Become an Entrepreneur! Work in small groups. Pretend that you are an entrepreneurial team. Design a product or service together. Use the following questions to guide you. When you are finished, make a presentation to your classmates. Use pictures, posters, sliderocket.com, or PowerPoint to make your presentation more interesting.

1. Think of a problem, need, or opportunity on which you would like to focus.

2. Invent a solution to the problem. It can be a product or a service.

3. Design a business plan. Make decisions about the following items:

   a. Will you need any special equipment?

   b. Where will your business be located?

   c. Who will you need to hire in order to produce your product or provide your service?

   d. Where or how will you get the money to create and market your product or service?

   e. Where, when, and how will you test-market it?

   f. How will you raise capital to make and sell your product?

PART 3 Strategies for Better Listening and Speaking

Getting Meaning from Context

1 Prelistening Questions Discuss these questions with your classmates.

1. Most American banks offer many different services. Look at the lettered list of banking services in the Focus on Testing box on page 66. Define the unfamiliar items with the help of your teacher.

2. Which of these services are offered by your bank? Which ones have you used?

3. Have you ever tried banking by phone, by mail, or online?

Getting money from an ATM ▶

FOCUS ON TESTING

Using Context Clues

Many tests such as the TOEFL® iBT measure your academic listening and speaking abilities. This activity, and others in the book, will develop your social and academic conversation skills, and provide a foundation for success on a variety of standardized tests. You are going to hear some advertisements about banking services.

1. Listen to the beginning of each advertisement.
2. Listen to the question for each ad. Stop the recording and write the letter of the best answer on the line next to each question.
3. In the **Clues** column, write the words that helped you choose your answer.
4. Listen to the last part of each advertisement to hear the correct answer.

Banking Services		
a. a safe deposit box	**c.** a home improvement loan	**e.** a credit card
b. a savings account	**d.** an automated teller machine (ATM)	**f.** a car loan

Questions	Clues
1. _____ What is the speaker talking about?	_____
2. _____ What is the speaker talking about?	_____
3. _____ What is the speaker talking about?	_____
4. _____ What is the speaker talking about?	_____

Pronunciation

FOCUS

Teens and Tens

In American English, it is hard to hear the difference between the "teens," 13 to 19— and the "tens," every tenth number from 30 to 90. To hear the difference, pay attention to the following:

1. In the *teen* numbers, the *t* sounds like /t/.

   Example   seventeen

2. In the *ten* numbers, the *t* sounds similar to /d/.

   Example   seventy

3. Speakers usually stress the *ten* numbers on the first syllable and the *teen* numbers on the last.

   Example   thír̓ty   thirteéń

2 **Pronouncing Teens and Tens** Listen and then repeat the pairs of numbers after the speaker.

1. thirteen   thirty
2. fourteen   forty
3. fifteen   fifty
4. sixteen   sixty
5. seventeen   seventy
6. eighteen   eighty
7. nineteen   ninety

3 **Distinguishing Between Teens and Tens** Listen and then circle the numbers you hear.

1. $40.10 $14.10
2. $16.99 $60.99
3. 18%   80%
4. 90   19
5. 230   213
6. 216   260
7. 40.5   14.5
8. $2,250 $2,215
9. 7064   1764
10. 8090   1890

▲"They're eighteen."

4 **Pair Practice with Teens and Tens**
Work in pairs to practice teens and tens. Student A should look at page 247. Student B should look at page 255.

▼"They're eighty."

5 **What Would You Do?** Read the following situations. Decide what to do in each case. Choose the best answer to each question, or write your own answer in the space provided.

1. While walking down the street, you find a wallet. It contains $100 and an identification card with the owner's name, address, and phone number. What would you do?

   ✓ (A) Call the owner and return the wallet with the money.

   (B) Keep the money and mail the empty wallet to the owner.

   (C) Keep the money and throw away the wallet.

   USA (D) Take the wallet with the money to a police station.

   (E) Other: _____

2. It's the same situation as No. 1, but the wallet contains only $5. What would you do?

   ✓ (A) Call the owner and return the wallet with the money.

   (B) Keep the money and mail the empty wallet to the owner.

   (C) Keep the money and throw away the wallet.

   (D) Take the wallet with the money to a police station.

   (E) Other: _____

3. You went to the bank to take money out of your account. By mistake, the bank teller gave you more money than you requested. What would you do?

   ✓ (A) Return the extra money immediately. The amount doesn't matter.

   (B) Keep the extra money.

   (C) It depends on the amount.

   (D) Other: _____

4. You went to your favorite department store and bought four items. When you got home, you noticed that the clerk only charged you for three items. What would you do?

   (A) Keep the extra item and use it.

   (B) Give the extra item to a friend or to charity.

   ✓ (C) Return the extra item to the store.

   (D) Other: _____

6 **Discussing the Situations** Discuss the following questions in small groups.

1. What answers did you select for the situations? Explain your choices.

2. Have any of these situations ever happened to you? What did you do with the money or items?

3. Do you think you are an honest person?

Balancing a Checkbook

Most adults in the United States have a checking account. Once a month, they receive a *statement* from the bank, which lists all their *deposits* and *withdrawals* for the month. At that time they must *balance their checkbook*. This means they check to make sure that they, or the bank, did not make a mistake in adding or subtracting. Many people do online banking and balance their checking accounts online.

▶ Do you do your banking online?

Before You Listen

1 **Prelistening Questions** Answer these questions in a small group.

1. Do you have a checking account at a bank?
2. How often do you write checks?
3. How often do you balance your checkbook?
4. In Activity 3 on page 70 you can see a sample page from a couple's checkbook record. It has six columns. What kind of information is in each column?

2 **Previewing Vocabulary** Listen to these words and expressions from the conversation. Match them with their definitions.

Vocabulary

1. _____ balance (noun)
2. _____ balance a checkbook (verb)
3. _____ pay off (a credit card) (verb)
4. _____ interest (noun)
5. _____ enter (an amount) (verb)

Definitions

a. a monthly percentage that is paid on borrowed money

b. to write an amount on a check or in a checkbook record

c. the amount of money in an account

d. to pay all of a bill with one payment

e. to check all payments and deposits in a checking account

3 **Balancing a Checkbook** George and Martha Spendthrift have a joint checking account; that is, they share one checking account and both of them can write checks from it. Here is one page from their checkbook record. Listen as they try to balance their checkbook. Fill in the missing information.

———— CHECKBOOK RECORD ————

NAME: _George & Martha Spendthrift_

ACCOUNT: 132-98804

NO.	DATE	DESCRIPTION	PAYMENT	DEPOSIT	BALANCE
200	10/25		30.21		490.31
201	10/27	Electric Company	57.82		
202	10/27	Time magazine			
203	10/30		70.00		327.49
204	11/1	Compu-Tech	125.00		202.49
205		Dr. Painless	40.00		162.49
	11/1	Deposit		1234.69	
206	11/2				985.18
207	11/4	Visa Payment	155.00		830.18
208	11/8		305.00		525.18
209	11/10	Traffic ticket			

4 **Discussion** Discuss the following questions in small groups.

1. Look at the checkbook record. What could the couple do to spend less money?
2. Do you think a joint checking account is a good idea? Why or why not?
3. Who manages the money in your family?

5 Find Someone Who... Walk around the room and find one person who fits each of the descriptions in the chart below. Write that person's name in the blank space. Then move on and talk to a different person. Collect as many names as possible.

Example

You read: "Find someone who… has used an ATM this week."

You ask a classmate: "Excuse me, can I ask you something? Have you used an ATM this week?"

Language Tip

Question Openers

Before asking someone a question, especially a personal question, it is polite to use one of the following conversation openers:

- Excuse me, can/could/may I ask you a question?
- Can/could/may I ask you something?
- Do you mind if I ask you a (personal) question?

Find Someone Who...	Name
is not carrying any money today	
works or has worked in a bank	
has a checking account	
pays bills online	
has her or his own business	
has borrowed money to buy a car	
has a credit card	
has used an ATM this week	
knows how to read the stock market numbers online	
owns a house or an apartment	
bought something and returned it to the store the next day	
has shopped at a second-hand store	
wants to start a new business in the future	

Talk It Over

6 Interview Attitudes about money vary from culture to culture, family to family, and person to person. Interview someone outside your class about his or her attitude about money. Use the following questions. Take notes in the spaces provided. When you return to class, share what you've learned in small groups.

Name of the person you interviewed: _____

Questions	Answers
1. Would you normally ask a friend how much money he or she makes?	
2. Would you feel comfortable borrowing money from your relatives? In what situation? How much?	
3. If you borrowed a dollar from a classmate, how soon would you return the money?	
4. *Ask a man:* How would you feel if your wife earned more money than you? *Ask a woman:* How would you feel if your husband earned more money than you?	
5. When you want to buy an expensive item like a car, do you pay the listed price or do you bargain for a lower price?	
6. When you buy something expensive, do you pay for the whole thing at one time or do you prefer to make payments (pay a little each month)?	
7. Do you think children should receive money (an allowance) from their parents to spend as they like? At what age should they begin receiving it?	

Self-Assessment Log

Check (✓) the words you learned in this chapter.

Nouns
- balance
- brilliant idea
- budget
- income
- interest
- quality
- solution
- team
- vision

Verbs
- balance a checkbook
- earn
- enter
- found
- have (something) in common
- hire
- identify
- pay off
- raise capital
- solve
- surf the Internet
- take risks

Adjective
- broke

Expressions
- an arm and a leg
- make ends meet

Check (✓) the things you did in this chapter. How well can you do each one?

	Very well	Fairly well	Not very well
I can hear and use stress and reductions.	☐	☐	☐
I can distinguish between *can* and *can't*.	☐	☐	☐
I can talk about abilities.	☐	☐	☐
I can ask for and give advice.	☐	☐	☐
I can take notes on a process, using an outline.	☐	☐	☐
I can guess meanings from context.	☐	☐	☐
I can talk about starting a business.	☐	☐	☐
I can distinguish between tens and teens.	☐	☐	☐
I can talk about money and banking.	☐	☐	☐

Write about what you learned and liked in this chapter.

In this chapter,

I learned _____

_____

I liked _____

_____

CHAPTER 4

Jobs and Professions

"Work and play are words used to describe the same thing under differing conditions."

Mark Twain
U.S. author and humorist

Connecting to the Topic

1. Describe this woman's job. What does she do every day?

2. What is your ideal job? Why?

3. What do you need to do to get your ideal job?

Finding a Job

In the following conversation, Jeff, Mari, and Nancy talk about jobs.

JOB search | any job title | skills | in | state

| Senior Retail Sales Associate and/or Assistant Manager - **(New York)** sales |
| Co-Manager Opportunity, Premium Outlets - **(New York)** sales |
| Store Associate Dog Trainers - **(New York)** animals |
| Music Blogger - **(Anywhere)** writing/editing |
| Chocolate Shop Salesperson - **(New York)** sales/food |

▼ Jeff looks for a job online.

1 Prelistening Questions Discuss these questions with your classmates.

1. Nancy is a teacher; Jeff plays guitar in a rock band; Mari is an international student. What job-related problems might each of them have?

2. Look at the picture. How is Jeff looking for a job? Have you ever done an online job search?

3. How do people in your home country find jobs?

4. Have you ever had a job? What was your first job?

2 Previewing Vocabulary Listen to the underlined words and phrases from the conversation. Then use the context to match them with their definitions.

Sentences

1. ___d___ I'm not <u>in the mood</u> to go to a movie tonight.

2. ___c___ He has two jobs because he is <u>supporting</u> his mother.

3. ___e___ He <u>spends</u> a lot of <u>time</u> playing his guitar.

4. ___b___ **A:** How was your day today?
   B: It was <u>the worst</u>.

5. ___a___ The students <u>complained</u> about the bad food in the cafeteria.

Definitions

a. to say that you are unhappy or angry with someone or something

b. terrible (*slang*)

c. to pay for (someone's) expenses

d. (not) to want (to do or to have something)

e. to use time (doing something)

Listen

3 Comprehension Questions Listen to the conversation. You don't need to understand all the words. Just listen for the answers to these questions. After you listen, discuss your answers with a partner.

[handwritten: time]
[handwritten: computer part]

1. Why is Jeff looking at <u>classified ads</u> online?   *[handwritten: full time]*   *[handwritten: record store]*

2. What kind of job would Jeff prefer?   *[handwritten: involving music,]*

3. What was Jeff's first job?   *[handwritten: berger fleper past food]*   *[handwritten: fast food place]*

4. What was the problem with Jeff's first job?   *[handwritten: borring job.]*   *[handwritten: pretty ouf]*

5. Why is Nancy unhappy with her job?   *[handwritten: 4 different classes]*   *[handwritten: 12 years]*

6. Why can't Mari work in the United States?   *[handwritten: writter]*   *[handwritten: enternashenal student]*

7. What does Jeff suggest at the end of the conversation?   *[handwritten: go to up the dinner]*

Stress

4 **Listening for Stressed Words** Listen to the conversation again. Some of the stressed words are missing. During each pause, repeat the phrase or sentence. Then fill in the missing stressed words.

Mari: Hey, Jeff, what's going ___on___?

Jeff: Oh, I'm looking at the ___classified___ ads. It looks like I have to get a ___job___.

Mari: I thought you ___had___ a job, at a computer store or something.

Jeff: Yeah, but that's ___part___-time. I need something ___full___-time.

Mari: Really? But what about ___school___? What about your ___band___? How can you work full-time?

Jeff: Well, to tell you the ___truth___, I'm probably going to drop ___out___ of school for a while. I'm just not in the ___mood___ for ___studying___ these days. I'd rather spend my time ___playing___ with my band. But my father won't ___support___ me if I'm not in school.

Mari: I see... Well, what kind of job do you want to ___get___?

Jeff: Well ideally, something involving ___music___, like in a record store. But if ___that is___ not possible... I don't know. But whatever I do, it'll be better than my ___first___ job.

Mari: Oh yeah? What was ___that___?

Jeff: Believe it or not, the summer after I finished ___high___ school I worked at Burger Ranch.

Mari: You? In a ___fast___-food place? What did you ___do___ there?

Jeff: I was a ___burger___ flipper. You know, I made hamburgers all day long.

Mari: That sounds like a pretty ___boring___ job!

Jeff: It was the ___worst___. And I haven't gone inside a Burger Ranch since I ___quit___ that job.

Nancy: Hi, what's so _funny_?

Jeff: Do you remember my _job_ at the Burger Ranch?

Nancy: Oh yeah. That was pretty _awful_. But actually, it doesn't sound so bad to me right now.

Mari: Why, Nancy? What's _wrong_?

Nancy: Oh, I'm just really, really _tired_. I'm teaching four different _classes_ this term, and _two_ of them are really _large_. Sometimes I think I've been _teaching_ too long.

Mari: How long have you been _teaching_?

Nancy: Twelve years. Maybe it's time to try something _else_.

Mari: Like _what_?

Nancy: Well, I've always wanted to be a _writer_. I could work at home...

Jeff: Oh, _don't_ listen to her, Mari. She _always_ talks this way when she's had a bad day at school. At least you _have_ a good _job_, Nancy. Look at me: I'm _broke_, and Dad won't _lend_ me any more money...

Nancy: Oh, stop _complaining_. If you're so poor, why don't you go _back_ to the Burger Ranch?

Mari: Listen you two, stop _argu_. Look at me! I _can't_ work at _all_ because I'm an international student.

Jeff: OK, OK. I'm _sorry_, Nancy. Tell you what. Let's go out to _dinner_. _I'll_ pay.

Nancy: But you're _broke_!

Jeff: All right, _you_ pay!

Check your answers in the listening script on pages 275–276. Then read the conversation with two classmates. Remember that stressed words are louder, higher, and pronounced more clearly than unstressed words.

Reductions

5 Comparing Unreduced and Reduced Pronunciation The following sentences are from the conversation. Listen for the difference between unreduced and reduced pronunciation. Repeat both forms after the speaker.

Unreduced Pronunciation	Reduced Pronunciation
1. What's going on?	What's goin' on?
2. I'm probably going to drop out of school for a while.	I'm probably gonna drop outa school for a while.
3. What did you do there?	What didja do there?
4. What kind of job do you want to get?	What kinda job dya wanna get?
5. Oh, I don't know.	Oh, I dunno.
6. If you're so poor, why don't you go back to the Burger Ranch?	If you're so poor, why doncha go back ta the Burger Ranch?

6 Listening for Reductions Listen to the following conversation. It contains reduced forms. Write the unreduced forms of the missing words in the blanks.

Manager: I'm ___going___ ___to___ ask you some questions, OK? What ___kind___ ___of___ jobs have you had?

Applicant: Mostly factory jobs. The last five years I worked in a plastics factory.

Manager: ___did___ ___you___ ___do___ do there?

Applicant: I ___used___ ___to___ cut sheets of plastic.

Manager: ___What___ ___do___ ___you___ ___want___ ___to___ do here?

Applicant: I ___don't___ ___know___. I'll do anything. I'm good with my hands and I'm a hard worker.

Manager: Why ___don't___ ___you___ fill out an application in the office. It looks like we're ___going___ ___to___ have an opening next week. I'll call you.

Applicant: Thanks.

Check your answers in the listening script on page 276. Then read the conversation with a partner. Try to use the reduced forms.

> ### After You Listen

7 Reviewing Vocabulary Work in pairs to practice the new vocabulary. Student A should look at page 248. Student B should look at page 256.

Using Language Functions

FOCUS

Apologizing and Reconciling

At the end of the conversation, Jeff and Nancy have a short argument. It ends like this:

Mari: Listen you two, stop arguing. Look at me! I can't work at all because I'm an international student.

Jeff: OK, OK. I'm sorry, Nancy. Tell you what. Let's go out to dinner. I'll pay.

Notice that Jeff does two things. First he *apologizes* to Nancy. He says, "I'm sorry." Then he *reconciles* with her. This means that he offers to do something nice for her—to take her out to dinner—so that she will not be angry anymore. Here are some expressions you can use to apologize:

• I'm sorry.

• I apologize.

• (Please) Forgive me.

8 Role-Play Prepare short conversations with a partner for the following situations. Take turns apologizing and reconciling. Then role-play one of the situations for the class.

1. You forgot your boyfriend's/girlfriend's birthday.

2. You came to work late. As you came in, your boss was standing by the door waiting for you. Your boss is angry.

3. You had a loud party in your apartment, and your neighbor is very upset with you.

4. While arguing with your roommate, you called him or her "stupid" and slammed the door on your way out of the room.

9 Discussion Work in groups of three or four and discuss the following questions.

1. In the conversation, Mari complains that she can't work because she is an international student. This is the law in the United States.

   • Do you think this law is fair? What might be the reasons for this law?

   • If you were a student in the United States and needed money, what would you do?

2. After twelve years of teaching, Nancy is thinking about changing careers. This is not unusual in the United States and Canada.

   • Is it easy for people to change careers in other countries?

   • If, after working for several years, you discovered that you hated your career, what would you do?

3. In North America, it is very common for people to go to college and have jobs at the same time.

   • Do you think this is common in other countries?

   • Do you or any of your friends have jobs right now? What kind?

Changes in the U.S. Job Market

Before You Listen

In the following lecture, a job counselor is speaking to a group of students about changes in the U.S. job market and future job possibilities.

1 **Prelistening Discussion** Study the table and answer the questions that follow.

Fastest Growing Occupations, 2002–2012

Job	Percent Change	Salary Rank[1]	Training Needed Post-High School[2]
1. Medical assistants	59%	3	On the job
2. Network systems and data communications analysts	57%	1	B.A.
3. Physician's assistants	49%	1	B.A.
4. Home health aides	48%	4	On the job
5. Computer software engineers, applications	46%	1	B.A.
6. Computer software engineers, systems software	45%	1	B.A.
7. Fitness trainers and aerobics instructors	44%	3	Vocational
8. Database administrators	44%	1	B.A.
9. Veterinary technologists and technicians	44%	3	Associate degree
10. Hazardous materials removal workers	43%	2	On the job
11. Dental hygienists	43%	1	Associate degree
12. Personal and home care aides	40%	4	On the job

[1]Jobs are divided into four groups according to salary. Number 1 means a salary in the top 25 percent, and so on.
[2]*Associate degree* means a diploma from a two-year community college. *On the job* means no previous training or education is needed. *Vocational* refers to schools that offer training in nonacademic fields.

Job	Percent Change	Salary Rank[1]	Training Needed Post-High School[2]
13. Computer systems analysts	39%	1	B.A.
14. Environmental engineers	38%	1	B.A.
15. Postsecondary teachers	38%	1	M.A. or Ph.D.
16. Network and computer systems administrators	37%	1	B.A.
17. Preschool teachers, except special education	36%	4	Vocational
18. Computer and information systems managers	36%	1	B.A. or higher
19. Physical therapists	35%	1	M.A.
20. Occupational therapists	35%	1	B.A.

Source: "Fastest Growing Occupations, 2002–2012," U.S. Department of Labor

1. What information is given in this table?

2. What years are covered?

3. The table has four columns. What information is given in each one?

4. What job do you hope to have in the future? Is it on this list?

5. Which jobs require a college education?

6. Which jobs have the highest salaries?

 2 Previewing Vocabulary Listen to these words and phrases from the lecture. Check (✓) the ones you don't know. Discuss the meanings of new words with a partner.

Nouns

▓ automation
▓ bottom line
▓ category
▓ competition
▓ economy
▓ health care

▓ illness
▓ job market
▓ labor costs
▓ manufacturing
▓ rank
▓ salary

▓ service
▓ trend

Verb
▓ grow by X%

Strategy

Taking Notes on Causes and Effects

To understand the main points in a lecture, you need to recognize the relationship between *causes* (reasons) and *effects* (results). Study the examples below. Notice that sometimes the cause is mentioned first, and other times the effect is first. In some sentences the order can be switched.

Many people use arrows in notes to indicate cause and effect. For example, X → Y means that X causes Y. In other words, X is the cause and Y is the effect.

Examples with Cause First

Because of/due to robots, the number of factory jobs has decreased.
Because/since robots are cheaper than human workers, factories are using more robots.
Human workers cannot work 24 hours a day; **as a result,/therefore**, more and more factories are using robots.
Labor costs are cheaper in Asia, **so** many American factories are moving there.

Examples with Effect First

The number of factory jobs decreased **because of/due to** robots.
Factories are using more robots **because/since** they are cheaper than human workers.
The (first, second, main, etc.) **cause of/reason for** unemployment is automation.

---

3 **Taking Notes on Cause-and-Effect Statements** Take notes on each sentence from the Strategy Box above. Remember to abbreviate, use symbols, and write key words only. Compare notes with a classmate.

1. _____

2. _____

3. _____

4. _____

5. _____

6. _____

7. _____

4 **Creating Abbreviations** In the chart below are key words from the lecture. Create abbreviations or symbols for them before you listen.

Words	Abbreviations
economy	
manufacturing	
service	
technology	
approximately	
million	
medical	
computer	
percent	
bachelor of arts	

5 **Listening and Taking Notes on Causes and Effects** Listen to cause-and-effect statements from the lecture and take notes. You will hear each statement twice.

Example

You hear: "In many cases, automation causes unemployment."

You write: *automation → unemp.*

1. _machines insteand of human workers_
2. _1000s of manufacturing jobs don't exist anymore._
3. _We need more medical services because people live longer_
4. _Medical technology givs serious illnesses live longer_
5. _Most married women now work outside at home._

6 **Taking Notes on Statistics** Review "Taking Notes on Statistics" on page 38. Listen to sentences from the lecture and take notes. You will hear each sentence twice.

1. _____
2. _____
3. _____
4. _____
5. _____

Exchange notes with a partner. Try to repeat the sentences by using your partner's notes.

7 **Taking Notes** Listen to the lecture and take notes in the best way you can. Use your own paper. Listen specifically for the following information:

Part 1

- How has the U.S. job market changed?
- Why?

Part 2

- What are three categories of fast-growing occupations between 2002 and 2012?
- What should people do in order to get high-paying jobs?

8 **Outlining the Lecture** Complete the outline with the information from Activities 3 through 7. Listen again if necessary.

The Changing U.S. Job Market

Part 1

I. 2 questions this lec. will answer:

A. _What are the best jobs going to be?_

B. _How can I prepare myself to get one of_
those good jobs?

II. History: Last 100 yrs., change in U.S. labor market: from _manufacturing_ to
service economy

A. Definitions

1. _In a manufacturing economy people_
e.g.: _make things (furniture, clothes)_

2. _In a service economy people do_
e.g.: _things (cut your hair, fix your shoe_
cell computers, restorant
workers.

III. Reasons for ↓ in manuf. jobs

A. _automation,_

B. _Foreign comtitaon, most manufacturing i_
done outside the US.

1. stat: _↓ 5 miellien manu-ng jobs have_ ← since 2001
disappered
The service jobs is going to grow by more then 20 million just in the 10 years.

IV. _____

_(2×8×52)_

A. Stat: _____

Part 2

V. Fastest growing service jobs *1. health care,*

    A. _____

        1. e.g.: _____

        2. Reasons

          – _____

          – _____

    B. *new jobs related with computers*

        1. e.g.: _____

        2. Stat: _____

    C. *personal care services,*

        1. e.g.: _____

        2. Reason: _____

VI. Educ. requirement for good jobs: *bachelor of arts degree*

After You Listen

9 **Discussing the Lecture** Use your notes and experience to discuss the following questions.

1. What is the difference between a service economy and a manufacturing economy? Give examples of jobs in each category.

2. How has the American job market changed? What are two reasons for this change?

3. Why will there be more healthcare jobs in the future?

4. How much will the computer industry grow in the next ten years? What kind of jobs will there be?

5. What are examples of jobs in the category of personal care services? Why is the number of these jobs increasing?

6. Look at the list of Fastest Growing Occupations, 2002–2012 on pages 82–83. Which of these jobs would you like to have? What do you need to do to prepare yourself for this job?

10 Reviewing Vocabulary Use vocabulary from the box to complete the summary of the lecture.

automation	competition	labor costs	service
bottom line	economy	manufacturing	trend
categories	health care	salary	

A   One hundred years ago, the United States had a _manufacturing_ [1] economy. This meant that most people made things by hand or machine. In contrast, today the United States has a _service_ [2] economy, in which workers provide services instead of making products. The United States has lost a lot of manufacturing jobs, and it is certain that this _automation_ [3] will continue in the future.   5

B   There are several reasons for this important change in the U.S. _economy_ [4]. The first is _labor costs_ [5]. It is cheaper to use machines than human workers in factories. Another reason is _bottom line_ [6] from foreign countries where _competition_ [7] are   10 lower than in the United States. Therefore, many products that used to be manufactured in the United States are now made overseas.

C   What will the good jobs of the future be? Over the next ten years, the fastest growing occupations will be in three _categories_ [8]: _health care_ [9], computers, and personal care and services. Many of   15 these jobs will not pay very well, however. If you want to get a good job with a high _salary_ [10], the _trend_ [11] is this: Get a good education.

11 **What Would You Do?** Read the situation and follow the instructions.

> ### Situation
>
> A new supermarket is opening in your neighborhood. The company needs to hire four people for job openings immediately. The jobs are: manager, checker,[1] stock clerk,[2] and butcher.[3] You are going to role-play job interviews for these people.

1. Choose four people to be interviewers. Each interviewer will interview the applicants for one of the jobs available.

2. All other students will play the role of job applicants. The teacher will tell you which position you are applying for.

3. Go to page 260 to find the information you need for your role. Learn it well so that you don't have to read it during your interview. You can add information during your interview if you want to.

4. Your teacher will divide the class into four groups. Each group will consist of an interviewer and all the interviewees for that job. The interviewers will interview each interviewee for five minutes. The four groups should have their interviews at the same time. (You can listen to other groups while you wait to be interviewed. Don't listen to your own group's interviews.)

5. After all the interviews are finished, the interviewers will report to the class. They will tell which applicant they picked for the job and why they chose that person.

▲ A checker and shoppers at a supermarket

[1]A checker is the same thing as a cashier or a checkout clerk.
[2]Stock clerks put new merchandise on the shelves of a supermarket. They often work at night.
[3]A butcher cuts and prepares meat.

Getting Meaning from Context

1 Prelistening Questions Look at the pictures below and the list of occupations in the Focus on Testing box on page 91. For each job, answer these questions:

1. What does each person do? If you are not sure, guess.

2. What education or training is needed for each job?

3. Would you enjoy doing this job? Why or why not?

FOCUS ON TESTING

TOEFL® iBT

Using Context Clues

Many tests such as the TOEFL® iBT measure your academic listening and speaking abilities. This activity, and others in the book, will develop your social and academic conversation skills, and provide a foundation for success on a variety of standardized tests. The following conversations take place at work.

1. Listen to the first part of each conversation.

2. After each conversation, stop the recording. Write the letter of each speaker's job in the blank.

3. In the **Clues** column, write the words that helped you choose your answer.

4. Listen to the next part of the conversation to hear the correct answer.

Occupation		
a. architect	d. restaurant host	g. receptionist
b. computer programmer	e. dentist	h. tailor
c. accountant	f. police officer	i. electrician

Questions	Clues
_f_ 1. What's the woman's job?	*police officer*
_g_ 2. What's the woman's job?	*receptionist*
_d_ 3. What's the man's job?	*restaurant host*
_e_ 4. What's the man's job?	*accountant*
_h_ 5. What's the man's job?	*tailor*

---

2 Game: Twenty Questions In this game, one person thinks of a job but does not tell the class what it is. The class tries to guess by asking a maximum of 20 *Yes* or *No* questions.

Examples

"Can you do this job outdoors?"

"Is a college education necessary for this job?"

"Is this job often done by women?"

The student who correctly guesses the occupation wins. If no one guesses after 20 questions, the same person leads another round.

Focused Listening

F🔍CUS

Understanding the Intonation of Tag Questions

When people need information or don't know something, they normally ask a question; for example, "Are you from China?" However, when English speakers *think* they know the answer to a question, but they *aren't sure*, they often form tag questions with *rising intonation:*

You're from China, aren't you?   You speak Chinese, don't you?

The rising intonation means that the person is asking for information.

In contrast, it is also possible to form tag questions with *falling intonation*, like this:

It's nice weather, today, isn't it?   That test was hard, wasn't it?

Tag questions with falling intonation are not real questions. When people ask these kinds of questions, they expect agreement. The tag is a way of making conversation or small talk.

3 **Recognizing the Intonation of Tag Questions** Listen to these ten tag questions. Decide if they are real questions (if the speaker is really asking for information) or if the speaker is just looking for agreement. Put a check (✓) in the correct column.

Question	Real Question	Expecting Agreement
1.	✓	
2.		✓
3.		✓
4.	✓	
5.	✓	
6.		✓
7.	✓	
8.		✓
9.		✓
10.	✓	

Using Language Functions

Answering Negative Tag Questions

In Activity 3, the main verb in each sentence was affirmative, and the verb in the tag question was negative.* Here is the proper way to *answer* such questions:

Tag with rising intonation:

A: You're from China, aren't you?

B: Yes, I am.

A: We have homework tonight, don't we?

B: No, we don't.

Meaning of answer:

Speaker A is correct. Speaker B *is* from China.

Speaker A is mistaken, so Speaker B corrects him.

Tag with falling intonation:

A: It's really cold today, isn't it?

B: Yes, and I don't have a jacket.

Meaning of answer:

Speaker B agrees with Speaker A.

Beth: Ali, you know Alicia, don't you?

Ali: Yes, I do. Hi Alicia!

*You will practice tag questions with affirmative verbs ("You're not a student, are you?") in Chapter 10.

4 **Asking and Answering Negative Tag Questions** Work in pairs. Student A should look at page 248. Student B should look at page 256. Complete the statements in your list and add negative tag questions. Decide if the intonation should rise or fall. Then, ask your partner the questions and listen for your partner's answers.

Example

A: This is your cell phone, isn't it?

B: No, it's Kathy's.

A Homemaker's Typical Day

Before You Listen

1 Prelistening Discussion Answer the questions with a small group.

1. Do you think managing a house and children is a job? Why or why not?

2. It is estimated that homemakers work as many as 60 hours a week. Is (or was) your mother or father a full-time homemaker? How many hours does/did she or he work each week?

3. Make a list of skills that a homemaker needs to have, such as cooking and financial planning.

2 Previewing Vocabulary Listen to these idioms related to work in the home. Discuss their meanings. Write the meaning of each item. (The words *make* and *do* are often used in these kinds of idioms.)

Idiom	Meaning
to make (breakfast, lunch, dinner)	
to do the dishes	
to make the beds	
to balance the family budget	
to do the laundry	
to water the lawn (garden)	
to shop for groceries	

3 Predicting The pictures in Activity 4 on page 95 show a typical day in the life of an American "househusband." The pictures are not in the correct order. With a partner, look at each picture and use the vocabulary from Activity 2 to describe what is happening. Then try to predict the order of the pictures.

4 **Sequencing Events** Listen to the man describe his day. Write numbers under the pictures to show the order in which each activity occurred. If two things happened at the same time, give them the same number. Pay attention to time words (*before, after, during*, etc.) and verb tenses. (Note: Only *some* of the activities are shown in the pictures.) Then compare answers with a partner.

5 **Discussion** Discuss the following questions in small groups.

1. Which tasks does the man do? Who does or did these things in your family?
2. Which tasks does the man's wife do? How does this compare to your family?
3. Would you like to have this man's life? Why or why not?

Strategy

Graphic Organizer: Matrix Diagram

A matrix diagram organizes information about two or more characteristics of two or more topics. You can use a matrix diagram to compare these characteristics or to show them clearly so that you can study or discuss them easily. You will use a matrix diagram in Activity 6.

6 **Talking About "Men's" and "Women's" Jobs**

1. The chart below shows a list of jobs. Put a check (✓) in the column that describes the *traditional* thinking of people from your culture. Put an X in the column that describes *your* thinking.

Job	Men	Women	Both
computer programmer			
nurse			
architect			
college professor			
bus driver			
film director			
police officer			
computer software salesperson			
mail carrier			
lawyer			

Job	Men	Women	Both
pilot			
administrative assistant			
manager of a company			
telephone repairperson			
firefighter			
diplomat			
farmer			

2. Work in small groups and compare your charts. Discuss the differences between attitudes in different countries. Also, explain differences between your opinion and the traditional opinion of people from your culture.

3. While traveling or living in different countries, have you been surprised to see women doing what were traditionally men's jobs or vice versa? Where? What kinds of jobs?

▲ Is being a chef traditionally a man's job or a woman's job?

7 **Interview** Interview someone outside of class about his or her work experience. Work in small groups. Add to the list of the following interview questions.

1. What do you do?
2. How long have you been working at your present job?
3. How many jobs have you had in your life?
4. What was the worst or strangest job you've ever had?
5. _____
6. _____
7. _____
8. _____
9. _____

Prepare a short oral report about your interview. Talk about the person you interviewed and the most interesting things you learned about him or her.

You may begin your report like this:

> "I interviewed Mr. Richard Baldwin. He works as the student advisor at the English Language Center. He has worked in this job for eight years. Mr. Baldwin had many other jobs before this one. The worst job was in college, when he worked as a dishwasher in the cafeteria..."

▲ "Here's a photo of Mr. Richard Baldwin."

Self-Assessment Log

Check (✓) the words you learned in this chapter.

Nouns

- automation
- bottom line
- category
- competition
- economy
- health care
- illness
- job market
- labor costs

- manufacturing
- rank
- salary
- service
- trend

Verbs

- complain
- grow by X%

- spend time
- support

Expressions

- in the mood
- the worst

Check (✓) the things you did in this chapter. How well can you do each one?

	Very well	Fairly well	Not very well
I can hear and use stress and reductions.	☐	☐	☐
I can use phrases for apologizing.	☐	☐	☐
I can talk about jobs and careers.	☐	☐	☐
I can read and understand a table.	☐	☐	☐
I can ask for and give advice.	☐	☐	☐
I can take notes on causes and effects using an outline.	☐	☐	☐
I can guess meanings from context.	☐	☐	☐
I can participate in interviews.	☐	☐	☐
I can use tag questions.	☐	☐	☐

Write what you liked and what you learned in this chapter.

In this chapter,

I learned _____

_____

I liked _____

_____

5 Lifestyles Around the World

> "It takes a village to raise a child."
>
> African proverb

In this
CHAPTER

Conversation A Single Mother

Lecture Changes in the American Family

Getting Meaning from Context Talking About Lifestyles

Real-World Task Using Numbers, Percentages, and Graphs

 Connecting to the Topic

1. Describe the relationship of the man and the boy.

2. Where are they? What is the man doing? What is the boy doing?

3. Imagine a typical day for this man. How is it different from a typical day for your parents when you were a child?

A Single Mother

Before You Listen

In the following conversation, a neighbor comes over to ask Jeff for a favor.

1 Prelistening Questions Discuss these questions with your classmates.

1. What does it mean to "ask someone for a favor"? Give an example.
2. What is a single mother or a single father?
3. What kinds of challenges do you think single parents face?

◀ Sharon

2 Previewing Vocabulary Listen to the underlined expressions from the conversation. Then use the context to match them with their definitions.

Sentences

1. __d__ I will <u>look into</u> your problem as soon as I have time.

2. __c__ If I don't <u>take off</u> right this minute, I'm going to miss my bus.

3. __b__ My mother is very <u>old-fashioned</u>. She doesn't like new ideas.

4. __e__ Time is <u>running out</u> for me to finish this paper. It's due tomorrow!

5. __a__ My mother is sick. I want to <u>check up on</u> her on my way home from work.

Definitions

a. to see if someone is OK

b. traditional; not modern

c. to find out information about something

d. to end

e. to leave

Listen

3 Comprehension Questions Close your book and listen to the conversation. Listen for the answers to these questions. After you listen, discuss your answers with a partner.

1. What does Sharon want from Jeff? Why? *She had a computer problem*

2. What surprised Mari about Sharon?

3. What was Nancy thinking about doing before she got married? *singl mother.*

4. How does Mari feel about what Nancy says? Why?

Stress

FOCUS

Two- and Three-Word Verbs

Many verbs in English consist of two or three words. The first word is a verb and the second and third words are usually prepositions. In most of these verbs, the second word receives the stress. Listen to these examples:

The plane **took off** at seven o'clock.

John **checked up on** his mother.

Please **drop me off** at the corner.

4 Listening for Stressed Words (Part I) Listen to the following sentences from the conversation. They contain two- and three-word verbs. During each pause, repeat the sentence; then fill in the missing stressed words.

1. Come on ___*in*___.

2. They want me to look ___*into*___ a computer problem right away.

3. If he wakes ___*up*___, just give him a bottle.

4. Listen, I've got to take ___*off*___.

5. Thanks so much, Jeff, for helping me ___*out*___.

6. I take ___*care*___ of him from time to time when Sharon's busy.

7. I worried that time was running ___*out*___.

8. I could never bring ___*up*___ a baby by myself.

9. I'd better check ___*up*___ on Joey.

Compare answers and discuss the meaning of the two- and three-word verbs with a partner. Then take turns reading the sentences using the correct stress.

5 Listening for Stressed Words (Part II) Now listen to part of the conversation again. Some of the stressed words are missing. During each pause, repeat the phrase or sentence. Then fill in the missing stressed words.

Mari: Hey, Jeff, I didn't know you liked ___*babyes*___.

Jeff: Well, Joey is ___*spacial*___. I take care of him from time to time when Sharon's ___*busy*___. And then ___*she*___ does favors for ___*me*___ in return. Like last week she lent me her ___*car*___.

Mari: And her ___*hasband*___? Is he...

Jeff: She's not ___*merried*___. I don't think she ___*ever*___ was, actually.

Mari: Never?

Jeff: ___*Nop*___, ___*never*___. I think she's ___*happy*___ being a ___*single*___ mother.

Mari: Oh. Is that pretty ___*common*___ in America?

Jeff: Well, it's ___*certenaly*___ becoming more and more common. Even ___*Nancy*___ used to talk about it. You know, before she got ___*married*___.

Nancy: Hi, guys.

Mari/Jeff: Hi.

Nancy: Uh, _what_ were you saying about me?

Jeff: That you _used_ to talk about having a _baby_ by yourself before you _met_ Andrew.

Nancy: Oh yeah, I _worried_ that _time_ was running out. You know, like, what if I _never_ got married?

Mari: Maybe I'm _____ - _____, but I could _____ bring up a baby by _____. I think it would be so difficult…

Nancy: Yeah, raising a _____ is tough. I'm really _____ I met Andrew.

Mari: And, if you have a baby, you'll have _____ here to help you with _____.

Jeff: We'll see. Speaking of babysitting, I'd _____ check up on Joey.

Check your answers using the listening script on pages 279–280. Then read the conversation with two classmates. Pronounce stressed words louder, higher, and more clearly than unstressed words.

Reductions

FOCUS

Sometimes the letter *h* is not pronounced at the beginning of English words.

Example give him ⟶ give im
Where has he been? ⟶ Where as e been?

The letter *h* is often not pronounced when;

- a word is unstressed (such as **him, her, has**) **and**
- it doesn't come at the beginning of a phrase or sentence.

Compare:

1. Unreduced: Is he asleep?
   Reduced: Is e asleep?

2. Unreduced: The children have gone.
   Reduced: The children uv gone.

3. Unreduced: Here's the newspaper.
   The *h* is not dropped because it is at the beginning of the sentence.

In a few words, like *honest* and *hour,* the *h* is never pronounced.

6 **Listening for Reductions** Listen to the following sentences from the conversation. Repeat them after the speaker. Draw a slash (/) through any *h* sounds that are dropped.

Example

Is h̸e asleep?

1. If h̸e wakes up, just give h̸im a bottle.

2. Thanks so much, Jeff, for helping me out.

3. I take care of h̸im from time to time when Sharon's busy.

4. And h̸er husband?

5. Hi, guys.

6. You'll have Jeff here to help you with babysitting.

After You Listen

7 **Using Vocabulary** Work in pairs to practice the new vocabulary. Student A should look at page 249. Student B should look at page 257.

Discuss your answers to the following questions with a partner.

1. Do you sometimes argue with your parents because you think their ideas are old-fashioned? Give examples.

2. At what age does a woman's time to have a baby run out?

3. Would you look into raising a baby by yourself? Why or why not?

Using Language Functions

F⊙CUS

Asking for Help or a Favor

In the conversation, Sharon asks Jeff for a favor, and Jeff agrees.

Sharon: Can you do me a big favor? Would you mind watching Joey until I get back?

Jeff: Sure, no problem.

Sometimes it is necessary to say no when someone asks for help or a favor. In that case, we usually apologize and give a reason why we cannot help. For example, Jeff might have said, "I'm really sorry, Sharon, but I have to go to work now."

The following expressions are used for talking about favors.

Asking for a Favor	Responding	
Expressions	**Yes**	**No**
Can/could you do me a (small/big) favor?	Sure./Yes./OK./	I'm sorry, but…
		I'd like to, but…
Can/could I ask you for a favor?	Yeah./Of course.	
		I wish I could, but…
Will/can/could you + verb?	Sure, what do you need?	
Could you give me a hand (with something)?		Let me think about it.
	I'd be glad to.	
Can/could you help me with (something)?		I really can't.
Would you mind verb + *-ing*?	No, not at all.*	

*The answer "No, not at all" means that the speaker *doesn't mind doing* something. In other words, the speaker agrees to do it.

8 Asking for a Favor Work in pairs to practice asking for help and responding. Student A should look at page 249. Student B should look at page 257.

9 Role-Play Work in pairs to practice asking for help and responding. Take turns, using the situations below. Then role-play one of the situations for the class.

1. Ask a classmate if you can copy his or her lecture notes because you were absent.
2. You want to ask out a girl or guy from your biology class. Ask his or her best friend to introduce you.
3. Ask your neighbor if she can feed your cat for three days while you are out of town.
4. Ask a co-worker if you can borrow five dollars until you have a chance to get some cash.
5. Ask your brother if you can live with him and his wife for the next three months so that you can save some money to go on vacation with your friends.
6. Ask a friend if you can borrow his or her favorite sweater to wear on a very special date.
7. In a crowded movie theater, ask the person sitting next to you if he or she will change seats with you because the person sitting in front of you is very tall.

In groups, discuss whether you would feel comfortable asking for favors in the above situations.

Changes in the American Family

Before You Listen

This lecture is about changes in the American family, and how some businesses are responding to these changes.

 1 **Prelistening Discussion** Discuss these questions in small groups.

1. Look at the photos of the two families. Describe the family members and their lifestyles. When do you think each photo was taken?

2. Based on the photos, how do you think the "typical" American family has changed since the 1950s?

3. How are families changing in your community? Why?

2 **Previewing Vocabulary** You will hear the following words and phrases in the lecture. Check (✓) the words you don't know. Discuss the meanings with a partner.

Nouns		Verbs	Adjective
▦ cost of living	▦ maternity leave	▦ benefit	▦ flexible
▦ daycare center	▦ opportunity	▦ can/can't afford	
▦ flexibility	▦ policy	▦ transfer	
▦ homemaker		▦ volunteer	

Listen

Strategy

Taking Notes on Examples
In English there are many expressions to signal examples. Here are a few:

> For example,…
> For instance,…
> As an example,…
> … such as …
> To give (one) example,…

In notes, people often use the abbreviation *e.g.* to indicate an example.

homework

3 **Taking Notes on Examples** You will hear statements supported by examples. Notes for the statements are below. Listen and take notes on the missing examples. Be sure to indent the examples and use abbreviations, symbols, and key words. You will hear each item twice.

1. *Today women are wrking. in profs. not open 30–40 yrs. ago* *Today*

   _____

2. *Now most Am. homes no full-time homemaker → new probs*

   _____

   _____

3. *Some co's. give new parents pd. vacation*

   _____

   _____

Exchange notes with a classmate. Use your partner's notes to try to restate the information you heard.

4 **Taking Notes (Part I)** Listen to the first part of the lecture and take notes in the best way you can. Use your own paper. Listen specifically for this information:

1. How has the American family changed? What is the biggest change?

2. What's the main reason for this change?

5 **Outlining the Lecture** Below is a sample outline of the first part of the lecture. Use your notes from Activities 3 and 4 to fill in the missing information. Remember to use abbreviations and symbols. Listen again if necessary.

▲ Children coloring pictures at a daycare center

Topic: Changes in the American Family

I. "Typical" Am. fam

   A. 1950s: _____

     _____

     _____

   B. Changes today:

     1. _____

       _____

     2. _____

       _____

     3. _____

     Stats: _____

     _____

     Reasons: _____

     _____

     New problems: _____

     _____

6 Taking Notes (Part II) Listen to the second part of the lecture. Continue taking notes on your own paper. After listening, use your notes to fill in the missing information below.

II. Company policies/programs:

A. _Policy paid maternity leave for mother or father, or both (12 week)_

B. If co. transfers worker, co. finds job for husb./wife

C. _Another policy that many companies now offer is called "flex time"_

D. _4. is telecommuting or we called teleworking_

E. _Some companies have a day care centers at the office where trained people take care of the employers' children_

concl.: _In my opinion, our government and our society need to do a lot more to help working parents and their children._

After You Listen

7 Discussing the Lecture Discuss the following questions about the lecture and your own experiences. Refer to your notes as necessary.

1. In the U.S., why are more and more mothers in two-parent families working these days? (Give two reasons.) How does this compare with what is happening in your home country?

2. With both mothers and fathers working, what new problems do families in the U.S. have?

3. Review the five programs and policies that some U.S. businesses have introduced to help working parents. For each program or policy, talk about the advantages and disadvantages for the workers and the employers.

4. Why don't *all* U.S. companies offer these programs to their employees?

5. Of the five programs and policies, which one would be the most useful for you and your family?

8 Reviewing Vocabulary Work in small groups. Look back at the vocabulary list in Activity 2 on page 109. Quiz each other on the terms and their meanings.

9 **What Would You Do?** Read the following story from the *Washington Post* newspaper. In small groups, discuss the questions that follow.

Husband Sues Wife over Housework

Tokyo—A 33-year-old Japanese woman divorced her husband after he demanded that every day she cook him breakfast, iron his pants, and clean the house. The woman worked full-time, but the husband said it was the wife's job to do all the housework.

The husband, a 35-year-old public servant, filed a lawsuit demanding that the wife pay him about $38,000 because she did not live up to her end of the marriage arrangement.[1]

1. If you were the judge in this case, what would you decide? Do you agree with the wife or the husband? Why? (To find out what really happened, turn to page 261.)

The newspaper article continues:

Increasingly, young [Japanese] women delay marriage, or even refuse to get married, because of the long-established expectations that women alone should raise the children and take care of the housework. Surveys show the average age at which Japanese women marry has risen to 27, with an increasing number now deciding not to tie the knot[2] at all.

[1]She did not do the things that her husband expected her to do.
[2]to get married

2. Compare the situation of Japanese women and women in other countries. Are women in other countries getting married later? Do some women refuse to get married? Why?

3. In your opinion, whose job is it to take care of children and do housework? Why?

Median age of tying knot in the US

1900		2009	
22	26	26	28
Women	Men	Women	Men

Source: U.S. Census Bureau

Focused Listening

F⦶CUS

Linking

In writing, words are separated by spaces. In speech, words are usually separated by pauses. However, sometimes words don't have pauses between them. The words are *linked*, or connected.

Example Please put it in a box. ⟶ Please **pudidinabox.**

Words are linked according to the following rules:

1. In a phrase, when a word ends in a consonant sound and the next word starts with a vowel sound, the two words are linked.

   For example:
   an⏝eye   where⏝are   run⏝out⏝of   put⏝it⏝in⏝a box

2. If a word ends in the vowel sounds /iy/ as in *me,* /ey/ as in *say,* /ay/ as in *eye,* or /oy/ as in *boy,* and the next word starts with a vowel, the words are linked with the sound /y/.

   For example:
   the⏝end of   say⏝it   my⏝aunt   enjoy⏝it

3. If a word ends in the vowel sounds /uw/ as in *you,* /ow/ as in *show,* or /aw/ as in *how,* and the next word starts with a vowel, the words are linked with the sound /w/.

   For example:
   you⏝are late   show⏝us   how⏝are you

Note: Don't try to memorize these rules. If you practice listening to English a lot, you will learn the rules naturally.

▲ **Teacher:**
What⏝are you coloring⏝in today, Anna?

1 Pronouncing Linked Phrases Listen and repeat the linked phrases.

Rule 1: Consonant sound + vowel

1. fifty dollars a month
2. the check is late
3. care about
4. in an apartment
5. get a job

Rule 2: Vowel + vowel

6. the end of (the month)
7. people my own age
8. come see us
9. no way out
10. the toy is broken

Rule 3: Vowel /uw/, /ow/, or /aw/ + vowel

11. grow up
12. go on
13. who is it
14. now it's ready
15. new art

2 Pronouncing Sentences Listen and repeat these sentences. Notice the stress, intonation, linking, reductions, and pauses.

1. I usually get up at 7 A.M., but today my alarm clock didn't go off.
2. At 8 A.M., I woke up in a panic. My first class was at 8:30! I couldn't be absent because we were having a test.
3. I jumped out of bed and got dressed in two minutes.
4. Then I ran out of the house, jumped in my car, and drove off.
5. Luckily, I found a parking spot and made it to class by 8:40.
6. I was out of breath and sweating.
7. A few people looked at me curiously.
8. Luckily, no one noticed that I wasn't wearing any shoes.

With a partner, take turns reading the sentences again. Pay attention to stress, intonation, linking, reductions, and pauses.

Getting Meaning from Context

FOCUS ON TESTING

Using Context Clues

Many tests such as the TOEFL® iBT measure your academic listening and speaking abilities. This activity, and others in the book, will develop your social and academic conversation skills, and provide a foundation for success on a variety of standardized tests. You're going to hear several people talking about their lifestyles.

1. Listen to the beginning of each passage.

2. Listen to an incomplete statement. Stop the recording and choose the best way to complete the statement.

3. In the **Clues** column, write the words that helped you choose your answer.

4. Listen to the last part of each passage to hear the correct answer.

Answers	Clues
1. Ⓐ a factory worker Ⓑ a retired person Ⓒ a landlord Ⓓ a fashion model	
2. Ⓐ the police Ⓑ her teachers Ⓒ her friends Ⓓ her parents	
3. Ⓐ is a daycare worker Ⓑ has never been married Ⓒ is divorced Ⓓ is married now	
4. Ⓐ with his parents Ⓑ in a college dormitory Ⓒ alone Ⓓ with roommates	
5. Ⓐ a retirement home Ⓑ a house with friends Ⓒ an apartment Ⓓ her son's house	

3 **Discussing Lifestyles** Do you know any people like those in the recording you listened to in the Focus on Testing activity? If yes, talk about their lifestyles and their problems or difficulties. Talk about the following people and answer the questions below:

- a retired man living on Social Security (money that retired people receive each month from the U.S. government)
- a teenage girl who feels that her parents treat her like a baby
- a divorced parent raising his or her children alone
- a young man who lost his job and moved back into his parents' house
- an elderly person living in a retirement home

1. As a teenager, how is/was your relationship with your parents? Do/Did you ever feel that your parents treat/treated you like a baby?

2. In your opinion, is it the government's responsibility to take care of people when they retire? If not, whose responsibility is it?

▲ Senior citizens playing pool at a retirement home

Using Numbers, Percentages, and Graphs

In this section you are going to compare lifestyles in different countries. In Chapter 2, page 38, you practiced taking notes on statistics. Review the vocabulary from that page. In this section you will continue learning how to talk about numbers and percentages.

Before You Listen

FOCUS

Numbers and Percentages

Read the following sentences with numbers and percentages. Pay close attention to prepositions.

1. Seventy-five percent **of** U.S. women are married by age 30.

2. By age 30, 75 percent **of** women in the United States have been married.

3. By 2020, the percentage **of** elderly people in Japan will grow **from** 19 percent **to** 25 percent.

4. The number **of** unmarried Korean women in their 30s rose **from** 0.5 percent **to** 10.7 percent.

5. China's divorce rate went up **by** 21.2 percent in 2004.

6. The number **of** children declined **to** 1.6 (pronounced "one point six") **per** family.

1 **Prelistening Discussion** Discuss the following questions about *your* community.

1. In the last 50 years, has the number of working women increased, decreased, or stayed the same?

2. Is the divorce rate increasing or decreasing?

3. With whom do older people usually live?

Strategy

Graphic Organizer: Line Graph

A line graph can help you understand change or growth. For example, it can show changes in things like divorce rates or salaries over a period of time.

2 **Completing Line Graphs**

1. Here are three incomplete line graphs. Listen to the information and complete the graphs. The first item is done for you.

2. Work with a partner and compare graphs.

Population of Working Women in the U.S.

%
65
60
55
50
45
40
35
30
25
20

1960 1980 1990 2003
Year

U.S Divorce Rate, 1960–2003 (per 1,000 people)

Rate

12
11
10
9
8
7
6
5
4
3
2
1

1960 1970 1980 1990 2003

Year

People in the U.S. over Age 65 Living Alone,1970–2000

%

60
55
50
45
40
35
30
25
20
15
10
5

1970   1980   1990   2000

Year

3 **Talking About Statistics** Write five true or false statements based on the information in the graphs. Then take turns saying your statements to one or more partners. If a statement is false, your classmate(s) should correct it.

Example

A: In 2000, 20 percent of elderly women lived alone.

B: That's false. In 2000, 40 percent of elderly women lived alone.

Discuss your answers to the following questions with a partner.

1. Are you surprised by the information you learned from the graphs? Why or why not?

2. What are some possible reasons for the decrease in divorce rates since the 1990s?

3. Why do you think more elderly women than elderly men live alone?

Talk It Over

4 **Comparing Lifestyles in Different Countries** The charts on page 121 and 122 are from *The World Factbook*. They contain information about lifestyles in different countries. However, the charts are not complete. Work in groups of three. Each student should look at one chart. Take turns asking and answering questions about the information in your chart. Fill in the missing information as your group members answer your questions.

Examples

Q: What was the average life expectancy in France?

A: The life expectancy in France was 79.44 years (or "almost 80 years").

Q: What was the GDP in Russia?

A: The GDP in Russia was $8,900.

Q: How many children did the average woman have in Mexico?

A: The average woman in Mexico had 2.49 children (or "between 2 and 3 children").

Chart A

Country	# Children per Woman	Life Expectancy	TV Sets per Person	Per Capita GDP[1]
Korea	1.5	75.5	.4	$17,800
United States	2.07	77.43		37,800
Argentina	2.24	75.7	.3	11,200
France	1.84	79.44	.6	27,600
Senegal		56.56	.08	1,600
Thailand	1.89	71.41	.5	7,400
Mexico	2.49	74.94	.3	9,000
Italy	1.27	79.54	.5	26,700
Saudi Arabia	4.11	75.23	.3	11,800
China (PRC)	1.69	71.96	.3	5,000
Egypt	2.95	70.71	.2	4,000
Iran	1.93	69.66	.1	7,000
Russia		66.39	.5	8,900
Japan	1.38		.8	28,200
Turkey	1.98	72.08	.4	

Chart B

Country	# Children per Woman	Life Expectancy	TV Sets per Person	Per Capita GDP[1]
Korea	1.5	75.5	.4	
United States	2.07		1.00	$37,800
Argentina	2.24	75.7	.3	11,200
France	1.84	79.44	.6	27,600
Senegal	4.84		.08	1,600
Thailand	1.89	71.41	.5	7,400
Mexico	2.49	74.94	.3	9,000
Italy	1.27	79.54	.5	26,700
Saudi Arabia	4.11	75.23	.3	11,800
China (PRC)		71.96	.3	5,000
Egypt	2.95	70.71	.2	4,000
Iran	1.93	69.66		7,000
Russia	1.26	65.12	.5	8,900
Japan	1.38	81.04	.8	28,200
Turkey	1.98	72.08	.4	6,700

[1]GDP means "gross domestic product." This number refers to the total value of goods and services produced by a country over a certain period of time. Per capita GDP is this number divided by the number of people living in the country.

Chart C

Country	# Children per Woman	Life Expectancy	TV Sets per Person	Per Capita GDP[1]
Korea	1.5	75.5	.4	$17,800
United States	2.07	77.43	1.00	37,800
Argentina	2.24	75.7	.3	
France	1.84	79.44	.6	27,600
Senegal	4.84	56.56	.08	1,600
Thailand	1.89		.5	7,400
Mexico	2.49	74.94	.3	9,000
Italy	1.27	79.54	.5	
Saudi Arabia	4.11	75.23	.3	11,800
China (PRC)	1.69	71.96	.3	5,000
Egypt		70.71	.2	4,000
Iran	1.93	69.66	.1	7,000
Russia	1.26	65.12		8,900
Japan	1.38	81.04	.8	28,200
Turkey	1.98	72.08	.4	6,700

Source: *The World Factbook*

5 Discussion Discuss the questions below with your group.

1. Based on the information in the charts, which five countries have the highest GDP?

2. Which five countries have the lowest GDP?

3. Compare the number of the children per woman, the life expectancy, and the TV sets per person for the countries you named in questions 1 and 2. What general statements can you make, based on this information? Use complete sentences.

Example

The countries with the lowest GDPs usually have the largest number of children per woman, and the countries with the highest GDPs have the smallest number. For example, in Japan, the average woman has 1.38 children, but in Senegal, the average woman has more than 4 children.

Self-Assessment Log

Check (✓) the words you learned in this chapter.

Nouns	Verbs	Adjectives
▨ cost of living	▨ benefit	▨ flexible
▨ daycare center	▨ can/can't afford	▨ old-fashioned
▨ flexibility	▨ check up on	
▨ homemaker	▨ look into	
▨ maternity leave	▨ run out	
▨ opportunity	▨ take off	
▨ policy	▨ transfer	
	▨ volunteer	

Check (✓) the things you did in this chapter. How well can you do each one?

	Very well	Fairly well	Not very well
I can hear and use stress and reductions.	☐	☐	☐
I can ask for and respond to requests for favors.	☐	☐	☐
I can take notes on examples using an outline.	☐	☐	☐
I can talk about lifestyles and company policies.	☐	☐	☐
I can guess meanings from context.	☐	☐	☐
I can complete graphs.	☐	☐	☐
I can talk about statistics.	☐	☐	☐

Write what you learned and what you liked in this chapter.

In this chapter,

I learned _____

_____

I liked _____

_____

6

Global Connections

The question is no longer IF the Internet can transform learning in powerful ways. "

The Web-Based Education Commission

In this **CHAPTER**

Conversation Taking Classes Online

Lecture Body Language Around the World

Getting Meaning from Context Customs and Traditions

Real-World Task Participating in a Survey

Connecting to the Topic

1 Look at the photo. What are the students doing?

2 How can students use the Internet to help with school?

3 What is distance learning? What kinds of classes can you find online?

Taking Classes Online

Before You Listen

In the following conversation, Mari and Jeff talk about taking courses online.

1 **Prelistening Questions** Discuss these questions with your classmates.

1. Have you ever taken a course online? If not, why not?
2. What are the advantages of taking an online class?
3. Do you think it is possible to study a language online? Why or why not?

▲ What are some things you can learn online? What devices can you use to learn?

2 Previewing Vocabulary Listen to sentences with words and expressions from the conversation. Then use the context to match them with their definitions.

Sentences

1. __e__ It takes a long time to <u>get to know</u> a new city.

2. __g__ Sarah <u>stays in touch</u> with her family by phone and Skype.

3. __e__ Please don't <u>interrupt</u> me; wait until I finish talking.

4. __f__ I don't know if my essay was good or not because the teacher didn't give me any <u>feedback</u>.

5. __b__ Computers and smart phones make communication very <u>convenient</u>.

6. __d__ Yvonne was sick for two weeks, so she has to <u>catch up on</u> all the homework she missed.

7. __h__ You knew about the test for a week. <u>How come</u> you didn't study?

8. __a__ The <u>deadline</u> for paying our credit card <u>bill</u> is July 26.

Definitions

a. time limit, the last date to finish something

b. easy to do or to use

c. start to be familiar with

d. do something you didn't have time to do before

e. stop someone from continuing an action

f. reaction, suggestion, opinion about someone's work

g. communicate with someone regularly

h. why

Listen

3 Comprehension Questions Listen to the conversation. You don't need to understand all the words. Just listen for the answers to these questions. After you listen, discuss your answers with a partner.

1. Why is Jeff taking Chinese online?

2. What does he like about this class?

3. Who are his classmates?

4. How does his teacher give Jeff feedback?

5. What does Jeff advise Mari to do?

Stress

4 Listening for Stressed Words Listen to the conversation with pauses. Some of the stressed words are missing. During each pause, repeat the phrase or sentence. Then fill in the missing stressed word.

Jeff: [saying some words in Chinese]

Mari: Oh, sorry, am I _____?

Jeff: No, that's okay. I'm just _____ _____

on my Chinese homework.

Mari: Oh, I didn't know you were taking _____.

Jeff: Yeah, I'm taking it _____.

Mari: Online? Doesn't the college offer _____ classes?

Jeff: They do, but the regular _____ to _____ classes were full. I like _____ class better anyway.

Mari: Really? How _____?

Jeff: Well, for one thing, it's so _____. I mean, I don't need to _____ about fitting it into my schedule. I can just go online _____ I want and do my work.

Mari: Whenever? Don't you have _____?

Jeff: Yeah, we have to _____ the homework and _____ in group discussions by a certain date. But I don't feel _____, you know, the way I do in a regular class.

Mari: I see what you _____. I'm not always _____ to participate in class.

Jeff: Uh-huh. And _____ thing I like: the _____ in the class. My classmates are from _____ over the States and even from _____. There's someone from Canada and people from _____ and Brazil.

Mari: Wow. That's a lot of different _____ zones! Seems like the _____ world wants to learn Chinese these days.

Jeff: Yup. And get this: the instructor is in _____.

Mari: That's so cool. But how does he correct your _____? Don't you need the face-to-face _____?

Jeff: No, he listens to our _____ recordings and gives us _____. And once a week we talk on Skype.

Mari: So you know what everyone _____ like?

Jeff: Sure. We've all become _____ and chat on Facebook all the time, too. And we've all agreed to stay in _____ after the course ends and meet next year in _____!

Mari: Oh, so you'll get some face-to-face contact _____ all!

Jeff: Of course. You _____ really get to know a culture without _____ there.

Mari: True. That's _____ why I came here. Not just to learn

_____ but also to get to know the _____

and customs.

Jeff: Right. But anyway, you should _____ try an online class

some time. Almost all American _____ and universities

offer them, you know.

Mari: I probably will. You certainly got me _____.

Check your answers using the listening script on page 283. Then read the conversation with a classmate. Pronounce stressed words louder, higher, and more clearly than unstressed words.

Intonation

FOCUS

Intonation in Questions and Requests

Information questions have a rising-falling intonation pattern:

- Where do you live?   • What's your name?

Yes/No questions and requests have a rising intonation pattern:

- Are you ready to go?   • Could you please repeat that?

5 **Practicing Intonation of Questions** Listen to the following questions and repeat them after the speaker.

Yes/No questions

1. Am I interrupting?

2. Don't you have deadlines?

Requests for help or permission

3. Could you show me how to sign up online?

4. Can we come in?

Information Questions

5. How come?

6. How does he correct your pronunciation?

6 Identifying Intonation Patterns Listen to the following sentences. Repeat each sentence after the speaker; then circle the up arrow for rising intonation, or the down arrow for rising-falling intonation.

1.   ↗   ↘   4.   ↗   ↘   7.   ↗   ↘

2.   ↗   ↘   5.   ↗   ↘   8.   ↗   ↘

3.   ↗   ↘   6.   ↗   ↘

Listen

 7 Reviewing Vocabulary Discuss the following questions with a partner. Use the underlined vocabulary in your answers.

1. How can teachers of large classes <u>get to know</u> their students?

2. Do you <u>stay in touch</u> with friends from elementary or high school? Why or why not?

3. In your culture, is it polite to <u>interrupt</u> when someone is speaking? What can you say if you don't want to be interrupted?

4. Give examples of negative and positive <u>feedback</u> you have recently received about your English.

5. What's more <u>convenient</u>: living at home with your parents or living in a dormitory on campus?

6. When was the last time you stayed up all night to <u>catch up on</u> school work? Why were you behind schedule?

7. <u>How come</u> some people never miss a <u>deadline</u> and others often do?

Using Language Functions

F⊙CUS

Interrupting Politely

At the beginning of the conversation, Mari enters Jeff's room and says, "Oh, sorry. Am I interrupting?" In many cultures it is impolite to interrupt a person who is speaking or working. However, most Americans are accustomed to interruptions and don't mind them. Here are some expressions that English speakers use to interrupt politely.

Expressions for Interrupting Politely

Am I interrupting?	I'm sorry to interrupt, but…
Can/May I interrupt?	Pardon me, but…
Excuse me (for interrupting), but…	Sorry, but…
I'd like to say something.	Wait (a minute). (I have a question.)

8 **Role-Play** Work in groups of three. Two people are talking and a third person interrupts. Take turns being the interrupter.

Situation 1

Two students are discussing a movie they plan to see. A third student interrupts and tells them that they shouldn't see the movie because it's terrible.

Situation 2

Two friends are looking at photos on a tablet computer. A third friend interrupts to ask where they bought the tablet and whether they recommend the brand.

Situation 3

An employee is complaining to the manager about long working hours. Another employee interrupts to say that he or she agrees with the complaint.

9 **The Interrupting Game** Work in groups of four to five students. Your teacher will give each student in the group a topic to discuss.

1. When it is your turn, start speaking about your topic.

2. Your classmates will interrupt you often, using the expressions from page 130.

3. When you are interrupted, answer the person who interrupted you, but then return to your topic. Follow the example.

Example

Speaker: Last night I went to the gym and…

Student 1: Excuse me for interrupting, but which gym do you go to?

Speaker: It's Total Fitness, just two blocks from my house. Anyway, I usually exercise there by myself, but last night I took a class.

Student 2: Sorry, but why did you decide to do that?
And so on.

4. The game ends when the speaker finishes the story.

▲ "I'm sorry to interrupt, but is this room free at 3 o'clock?"

10 Survey: Find Someone Who...

1. Ask your classmates about ways they connect to the global community. Find a person who answers "Yes" and write his or her name in the space.

Example

Do you have more than 10 international Facebook friends who live in another country?

Find someone who...	Name
has more than 10 international Facebook friends	
has lived (or plans to live) abroad for at least a year	
has worked or plans to work for a multinational company	
has taken an online course	
thinks everyone in the world should learn English	
speaks three or more languages	
has visited more than five countries	
would marry someone from another country	

2. Make sentences about your classmates. Your teacher will say the name of a student. Say what you learned about this person.

Example

Teacher: Peter

Class: He has taken an online course. / He has visited more than five countries.

Body Language Around the World

Before You Listen

The lecture in this chapter is about the ways that people in different cultures use "body language" to communicate without words.

1 Prelistening Discussion Discuss the questions in small groups.

1. Look at the photos. What are the people in each picture doing? Is their body language common in your culture? Is it polite?

2. Have you ever been surprised by the nonverbal behavior of a visitor to your country?

3. While traveling outside your country, have you been surprised by people's body language, or have you made a "mistake" by using the wrong body language? Explain.

2 Previewing Vocabulary Listen to these words and phrases from the lecture. Check (✓) the ones you don't know. Discuss their meanings with a partner.

Nouns	Verbs	Adjectives	Adverbs
authority	convey *show*	affectionate	harmoniously
gestures	hug	horrified	unintentionally
overview		invisible	*planned*
potential		offended	
		offensive	

Listen

Strategy

Taking Notes on Similarities and Differences

Taking notes on differences

The following sentence is from the lecture:

"In Arab cultures, for instance, you will also notice that men sit and stand very close to each other. On the other hand, in East Asia, people usually stand farther apart than Americans do."

Here are sample notes for this sentence. Notice the use of indenting, key words, abbreviations, and symbols:

> Standing
> Arabs: men stand & sit close
> E. Asia: Ppl stand farther than Amer

Taking notes on similarities

Read the sentences from the lecture, followed by sample notes.

"In some parts of Africa and the Caribbean, for example, children are taught to look down when they're talking to a person with greater authority, such as a parent or a teacher. Similarly, in Japan an employee would not make direct eye contact with an employer."

> Africa, Carib, + Japan: no eye contact w/ person in authority, e.g. tchr, boss

Expressions signaling similarity and difference

The following expressions appear in the lecture. These expressions signal a similarity or a difference.

Differences	Similarities
differ from	similarly
in contrast	also
on the other hand	be similar
the opposite	
be different	

3 **Taking Notes on Similarities and Differences** Listen to sentences with similarities and differences. Complete the notes. You will hear each sentence twice.

1. _a general_ rule: people stand arm's length (=70 cm) apart when talking.

   Latin Americans: _usually stand much closer to each other,_

2. Arab culture: _men sit and stand very close to each other._

   E. Asia: _people stand farther apart then Americans do._

3. U.S.: _You should look at a person's eyes when ...._

   Africa, Carib: _the children are taught to_

4. _look down when they thokink._ : no eye contact w/ _in Japan no eye contact with employee_

5. Mexico/Italy: it's normal to _____

   France: everybody _____

   Japan: _____

4 **Taking Notes (Part 1)** Listen to the first part of the lecture and take notes in the best way you can. Use your own paper. Listen for similarities and differences in two areas of nonverbal communication.

5 **Outlining the Lecture** Here is a sample outline of the first part of the lecture. Use your notes from Activities 3 and 4 to fill in the missing information. Remember to use abbreviations and symbols. Listen again if necessary.

Part 1

Topic: _About nonverbal comun-n or body lang._

Intro: _morment, dectance, eye contaket touching._

A. Movement (gestures, _of the hend and arms even) the feet_

   1. U.S. "OK" gesture = _good_ in Russia, _zero_
      in Brazil _offensive._

   2. Pointing: OK in U.S., _well._

   3. Show bottom of shoe: _____

B. Distance

    1. Every culture people have _____

    2. Standing:

        a. U.S. + _____: arm's length (=70 cm) when talking

        b. Latin Cultures: _____

              _____

        c. Arab (men): _____

        d. East Asia:

              _____

6 Taking Notes (Part 2) Listen to the second part of the lecture. Continue taking notes on your own paper. After listening, use your notes to fill in the missing information below.

C. _____

    1. U.S.: _____

    2. Africa, Carib: _____

    3. Japan: _____

D. _____

    1. Latin: _____

        a. E.g. France: _____

    2. Japan: _____

Conclusion: _____

_____

_____

7 **Discussing the Lecture** Discuss the following questions about the lecture and your own experiences. Refer to your notes as needed.

1. Demonstrate the "OK" gesture that former President Clinton used. Does this gesture have a different meaning in your culture? Which gesture or gestures do you use to mean that something is OK or good?

2. How much personal space do people in your culture typically require? What do you do if someone steps inside your personal space?

3. What are the "rules" for making or avoiding eye contact in your culture?

4. In your culture, what body language do people use when they greet a) people they know and b) people they don't know?

5. In your culture, what body language do you use to convey the following meanings:

be quiet	go away	you're crazy
something smells bad	I don't know	good luck
who, me?	come here	stop
boring	something is good	I can't hear you.
someone talks too much	something is bad	yes / no

8 **Reviewing Vocabulary** Work in small groups. Look back at the vocabulary list in Activity 2 on page 134. Quiz each other on the terms and their meanings.

PART 3 Strategies for Better Listening and Speaking

Focused Listening

Blending Consonants

When one word ends in a consonant sound and the next word begins with the same consonant sound, the two sounds are *blended*, or combined, to form one longer sound.

Examples

hot + tea = hot̓tea

bad + dog = bad̓dog

listen + now = listen̓now

1 Pronouncing Names with Blended Consonants Here are some typical English names. Listen and repeat them after the speaker. Blend the consonants so that each name sounds like one word.

1. Margaret Thompson
2. Louis Sachs
3. Bill Landers
4. Ann Norton
5. Rick Cates
6. Phillip Patterson

7. David Dees
8. Judith Thayer
9. Steve Volker
10. Peter Rainer
11. Jacob Branson
12. Craig Gray

2 Listening for Blended Consonants Listen to the sentences and circle the blended sounds.

1. Jamil lives in a small town.
2. Yesterday Linda had a really bad day.
3. Michelle texted her mother eight times.
4. Susanna's birthday is August tenth.
5. Let's see the movie at the Friss Cinema.
6. Would you like some hot tea and cookies?
7. Kevin needs a tall ladder to reach that high window.
8. Malik Khan hosts a popular radio show.

3 Pronouncing Sentences Circle the blended consonants and mark the linked sounds in the sentences below. Then practice saying these sentences with correct blending, linking, stress, reductions, and intonation. Finally, listen to the audio to check your pronunciation.

Example

She bought an expensive vase.

1. Whose black car are you driving?
2. Pat told me to have a good day.
3. The yard was full of fall leaves.
4. Chris said, "We're ready to take a walk."
5. This story is so sad.
6. I forgot to write down Ned's phone number.
7. I received a letter with three stamps on it.
8. Did you forget to make our dinner reservations?

FOCUS ON TESTING

TOEFL® iBT

Using Context Clues

Many tests such as the TOEFL® IBT measure your academic listening and speaking abilities. This activity, and others in the book, will develop your social and academic conversation skills, and provide a foundation for success on a variety of standardized tests. You are going to hear short conversations about different ways to travel.

1. Listen to each conversation.

2. Listen to the question for each conversation. Stop the recording and choose the best answer to each question.

3. In the **Clues** column, write the words that helped you choose your answer.

Answers	Clues
1. Ⓐ best for families with children. Ⓑ popular among young people. Ⓒ expensive. Ⓓ great if you want privacy.	
2. Ⓐ They're popular mostly in Europe. Ⓑ They help people find a cheap place to rent. Ⓒ You can trade homes only with friends. Ⓓ A company helps you make the exchange.	
3. Ⓐ people who want to help others. Ⓑ people who want to travel comfortably. Ⓒ people who want to visit famous places. Ⓓ people who enjoy seeing museums.	

Answers	Clues
4. (A) famous cities (B) the economy (C) the environment (D) teaching	
5. (A) both travelers and hosts (B) people who don't trust strangers (C) people who move to a new country (D) tour guides	

Using Language Functions

FOCUS

Expressing Pros and Cons

Pros and cons are the good (pros) and bad (cons) sides of something. Many situations, decisions, or choices have both pros and cons.

Example

What are the pros and cons of staying at a youth hostel? **One disadvantage** is that several people have to share one bathroom. But the low cost **is a big plus**.

Study these common expressions:

Pros	Cons
One advantage is… The biggest advantage is… Another good point is… … has some good points, too. … is a big plus.	One disadvantage is… The biggest disadvantage is… Another drawback is…. … is a big drawback. The downside of… is…

4 Comparing Different Ways to Travel Work in groups. Compare the five ways of travel in the photos. In the chart on page 142, take notes on the pros and cons of each type of travel. Use the expressions in the Focus box on page 140 and expressions of similarity and difference in Part 2, page 134.

Example

A: One good thing about youth hostels is that they're inexpensive.

B: Yes, but on the other hand, a big drawback is that you don't have any privacy.

▲ youth hostel

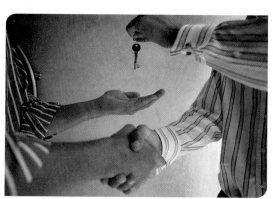

▲ house exchange

couch surfing ▲

▼ ecotourism

Pros	Cons
youth hostel	
house exchange	
volunteer travel	
eco-tourism	
couch surfing	

Compare your list of pros and cons with the lists of your classmates.

5 Discussion Discuss the questions in small groups.

1. Do you know anyone who has traveled in one of these ways?
2. Which of these travel choices do you like best? Why?

Participating in a Survey

You are going to listen to a telephone survey about helping people. Look at the following words and expressions. Use them to talk about the pictures.

Example

A: Do you do any kind of volunteer work?

B: Yes, I help out at the homeless shelter once a month.

Nouns	Verbs
charity	give to charity
donation	donate, make a donation
volunteer	volunteer (your time)
	do volunteer work
help	help out

1 **Prelistening Questions** Discuss the following questions with your classmates.

1. Have you ever participated in a phone survey? What was the topic?

2. Why do people choose to do volunteer work?

3. Who has the greatest obligation to help poor people: the government, rich people, or everybody?

Listen

2 **Listening to a Phone Survey** Fill in the questionnaire with the information you hear. If the answer to a question is not given, leave the space blank.

SURVEY QUESTIONNAIRE

Respondent's Name: _____

Respondent's Age: _____ 20–30 yrs _____ 40–50 yrs _____ 60–70 yrs
_____ 30–40 yrs _____ 50–60 yrs _____ 70–80 yrs
_____ over 80

Yearly Income: _____ $20,000–40,000
_____ $40,000–60,000
_____ $60,000–80,000
_____ $80,000–100,000
_____ above $100,000

1. Donated money: _____ YES _____ NO
2. Volunteered: _____ YES _____ NO
3. Helped a stranger: _____ YES _____ NO
4. Country with most generous people: _____
5. Life satisfaction
   Range: 1 2 3 4 5 6 7 8 9 10

3 **Discussing the Survey Questions**

1. Compare your answers to Activity 2 with a classmate. Then give your own answer to each survey question. How do your responses compare to the woman's answers in Activity 2?

2. The chart below gives information about charitable giving in selected countries. Use the chart to answer the questions on page 146. Is your country on the list? If not, do an Internet search for "charitable giving by country".

Charitable Giving by Select Countries				
Country	% of population giving money to charity	% of population who volunteered	% of population who helped a stranger	Total average
Australia	70%	38%	64%	57%
Switzerland	71%	34%	60%	55%
United States	60%	39%	65%	55%
Hong Kong	70%	13%	50%	44%
Thailand	73%	18%	36%	42%
Italy	62%	16%	45%	41%
Chile	48%	16%	49%	38%
Indonesia	45%	27%	35%	36%
Mexico	25%	20%	50%	32%
Tunisia	19%	12%	61%	31%
Brazil	25%	15%	49%	30%
Korea	27%	22%	38%	29%
Saudi Arabia	27%	12%	45%	28%
Japan	17%	23%	25%	22%
China	11%	4%	28%	14%
Greece	8%	5%	28%	14%

Source: World Giving Index 2010 by Charities Aid Foundation

3. Which country has...

- the highest percentage of people who volunteered?
- the highest percentage of people who gave money to charity?
- the highest percentage of people who helped a stranger?

4. Does anything surprise you about the information in the chart?

5. In your opinion, what is the most effective way to help people in need:

    a. by giving money to charity organizations

    b. by volunteering your time with community or religious organizations

    c. by helping people individually

    d. other: _____

Talk It Over

4 **Conducting a Survey** Design a survey to find out about your community's generosity. Use the questionnaire on page 144 as a model, but feel free to add other questions.

Step 1: Write 5-10 questions. Be sure they can be answered with yes / no or short answers.

Step 2: Prepare a chart or blank survey form to use for recording people's answers. For example:

Question	Speaker 1	Speaker 2	Speaker 3
Have you given money to charity in the last month?	No	No	Yes

Step 3: Select a group of people to survey. If you can't find English speakers, survey people in your own community.

Step 4: Practice your introductory sentences. For example,

"Hello. My name is _____. I'm conducting a survey for my English class. Do you have a few minutes to answer some questions?"

Step 5: With your class, summarize the results of your survey.

Example

I surveyed ten people. Forty percent regularly volunteer, but only ten percent have donated money recently.

Self-Assessment Log

Check (✓) the words you learned in this chapter.

Nouns	Verbs	Adjectives	Adverbs
▦ authority	▦ catch up on	▦ affectionate	▦ harmoniously
▦ deadline	▦ convey	▦ convenient	▦ unintentionally
▦ feedback	▦ get to know	▦ horrified	
▦ gestures	▦ hug	▦ invisible	Expression
▦ overview	▦ interrupt	▦ offended	▦ How come...?
▦ potential	▦ stay in touch	▦ offensive	

Check (✓) the things you did in this chapter. How well can you do each one?

	Very well	Fairly well	Not very well
I can hear and use stress and reductions.	☐	☐	☐
I can use intonation in questions and requests.	☐	☐	☐
I can use phrases for interrupting politely.	☐	☐	☐
I can take notes on similarities and differences using an outline.	☐	☐	☐
I can talk about customs in different countries.	☐	☐	☐
I can guess meanings from context.	☐	☐	☐
I can write and conduct a survey.	☐	☐	☐

Write what you learned and what you liked in this chapter.

In this chapter,

I learned _____

_____

I liked _____

_____

7 Language and Communication

"To have another language is to possess a second soul."

Charlemagne,
King of the Franks,
Emperor of the West

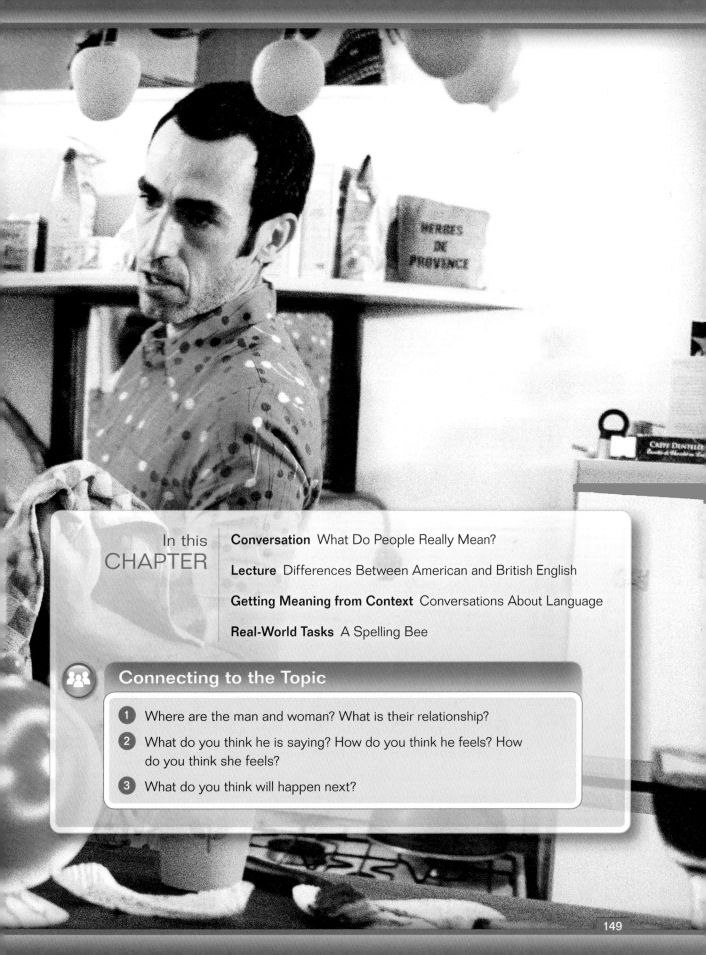

In this
CHAPTER

Conversation What Do People Really Mean?

Lecture Differences Between American and British English

Getting Meaning from Context Conversations About Language

Real-World Tasks A Spelling Bee

Connecting to the Topic

1. Where are the man and woman? What is their relationship?

2. What do you think he is saying? How do you think he feels? How do you think she feels?

3. What do you think will happen next?

What Do People Really Mean?

In the following conversation, Nancy and Mari talk about friendliness and friendship in the United States.

▲ Nancy, Mari, and Yolanda

 1 **Prelistening Questions** Discuss these questions with your classmates.

1. What do you think is happening in the photo on page 150?

2. What is the difference between "friendliness" and "friendship"?

3. Have you ever had a friend from another culture? Was it difficult to communicate with this person at first? In what way?

4. Look at the photo on page 151. Which people look the friendliest to you? Why?

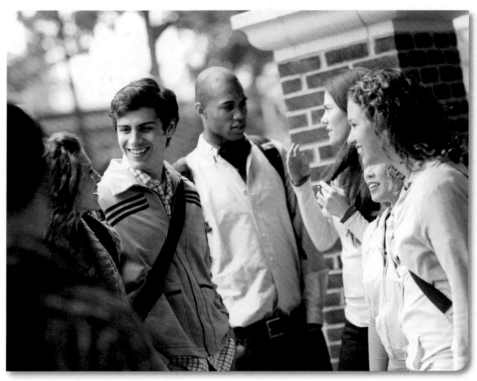

▲ Friends on campus

2 **Previewing Vocabulary** Listen to the underlined words and expressions from the conversation. Then use the context to match them with their definitions.

Sentences

1. _____ Nobody is using this chair. Have a seat and rest.

2. _____ **A:** I don't like Kathleen. She's so two-faced!

   B: Yeah, she's nice when she's with you, but she says bad things about you behind your back.

3. _____ The student from Brazil was popular because of her friendliness.

4. _____ If a good friend lied to me, I would end my friendship with her.

5. _____ It's hard to make friends with people if you don't speak their language well.

6. _____ After the teacher explained the math problem five times, the students finally began to catch on.

7. _____ I don't understand what our teacher wants us to do. I am completely in the dark.

8. _____ It's hard to say if he likes me because he never talks about his feelings.

Definitions

a. a close, trusting relationship

b. "Sit down."

c. understanding or knowing nothing about a particular thing

d. to begin to understand

e. "I can't be sure."

f. a warm and open way of behaving with people

g. to become friendly with someone

h. dishonest

3 Comprehension Questions Listen to the conversation. You don't need to understand all the words. Just listen for the answers to these questions. After you listen, discuss your answers with a partner.

1. What is the relationship between Yolanda and Mari?
2. Why is Mari confused?
3. What does Nancy say about friendship and friendliness in the United States?
4. Do Yolanda and Mari go to the movies together often?
5. According to Nancy, what does "How are you?" mean?

Stress

4 Listening for Stressed Words Now listen to part of the conversation again. Some of the stressed words are missing. During each pause, repeat the phrase or sentence. Then fill in the missing stressed words.

Mari: I don't understand Americans.

Nancy: Huh?

Mari: Did you _hear_ what she said? "I'll call you, we'll go to a _____." But every time I try to pick a _____ day or time, she says she's _____, she has to check her _____. And then she _____ call.

Nancy: Mm hmm...

Mari: Why do Americans say things they don't _____? They _____ so nice, like they _____ say, "How are you," but then they keep on _____ and don't even wait for your _____. They're so... how do you say it... _____-faced?

Nancy: I know it _____ that way sometimes, Mari. But it's _____ _____. It's just that for Americans, friendliness and friendship _____ always the same thing.

Mari: What do you _____?

Nancy: Well, as you know, Americans can be very _____ and friendly. Like, they _____ you to sit down, they _____ you questions, they _____ you all about their families. So naturally you think they're trying to make

_____ with you. But actually, friendship,_____

friendship, doesn't happen so _____.

Mari: So, when people say "How are you," they're just being _____?

They don't really _____?

Nancy: Not exactly. The thing you have to _____ is that "How are

you" isn't a _____ question. It's more like a

_____, a way of saying hello.

Mari: Aha, I _____ it! And "Have a nice day" is just a

_____ _____ way to say good-bye?

Nancy: Exactly. _____ you're catching on.

Mari: But I'm _____ in the dark about Yolanda. Does she

_____ to be my friend or _____?

Nancy: It's _____ to say. Maybe she's just too _____

these days. I guess you'll just have to be _____.

Mari: Hmm. That's good _____, I guess. Thanks.

Check your answers using the listening script on pages 288–289. Then read the conversation with a partner. Pronounce stressed words louder, higher, and more clearly than unstressed words.

Intonation

Statements with Rising Intonation

You heard the following exchange in the conversation:

Mari: So when people say "How are you," they're just being polite?
They don't really care?

Nancy: Not exactly.

Note that Mari's questions are actually statements—"They're just being polite?" "They don't really care?"—with rising intonation. This way of talking is often used in rapid, informal English, especially when the speaker is surprised or expects an affirmative answer.

5 **Understanding Statements with Rising Intonation** Listen to the following "statement questions" and rewrite them as "true" questions in the spaces.

Example

You hear: "You're going to work?"

You write: *"Are you going to work?"*

1. _____

2. _____

3. _____

4. _____

5. _____

After You Listen

6 **Using Vocabulary** Work in pairs to practice the new vocabulary. Student A should look at page 250 Student B should look at page 258.

Using Language Functions

FOCUS

Contradicting Politely

To contradict means "to say the opposite of what someone has just said." For example:

Mari: Why do Americans say things they don't mean? They're so … how do you say it… two-faced?

Nancy: I know it seems that way sometimes, Mari. But it's not true.

In her answer, Nancy contradicts Mari and corrects her wrong idea.

There are polite and impolite ways to contradict people. Here are some common expressions that are used for this purpose:

Polite	Well, you might think… but actually…
	Well, actually…
	It's true that… but…
	It seems… but…
	That's not completely true.
Impolite/Rude	You're wrong.
	What are you talking about?
	That's ridiculous.

7 **Contradicting Stereotypes** Discuss stereotypes with your classmates and practice contradicting each other politely.

Language Tip

stereotype (noun) A too-general, overly simplified, and often negative idea about *all* members of a group or culture.

Example
"Americans are rich and care only about money." This description is a stereotype because it is too general and not true about all Americans.

1. Look at the picture. Describe this couple. Guess their nationality and explain your guess. Have you ever met people like this?

2. Complete the following sentence with adjectives or nouns. Share your sentences with your classmates and write your adjectives and nouns on the board.

   Americans are _____, _____,
   _____, and _____.

3. With your class and teacher, discuss the following questions:

   a. Which of the words listed on the board are stereotypes? Which ones are facts? Remember, a stereotype is an idea that is too simple, too general, and cannot possibly be true for all members of a group or culture.

   b. How can you change your statements so that they are not stereotypes?

4. Work with a partner. Take turns stating stereotypes about these groups and then politely correcting those stereotypes. Use the expressions from the list on page 154.

   Americans are...
   Movie stars are...
   Athletes are...
   Women/Men are...

   People from _____ are...
   (your culture)

▲ Stereotypical tourists

Example

Student 1: Americans are only interested in money.

Student 2: I know it seems that way, especially if you don't know many American people personally. But actually, Americans can be very generous. They donate a lot of food and money to charities.

8 What Is Friendship? Look at the list of situations in the box. Then, in small groups discuss the questions that follow.

Situations

- take care of you when you are sick
- lend you money
- take you to or pick you up from the airport during school or work hours
- give you a gift on your birthday
- help you with your homework
- disagree with you
- tell you secrets
- help you move to a new house or apartment
- always tell you the truth
- take care of your pets or your children if you go away on vacation
- invite your relatives to his or her home
- other _____

Questions

1. Which of the things from the list above would you expect a friend to do for you? Which would you not expect? Why?

2. Which of the things from the list above would you do for a friend? Which wouldn't you do? Why?

▲ A group of friends on campus preparing balloons for a birthday party.

Differences Between British and American English

Before You Listen

This lecture is about some differences between British and American English.

An "elevator" in ▶
American English
is a "lift" in
British English.

◀ "Do you have an
elevator?"

"Have you got a lift?" ▶

 1 **Prelistening Discussion** Discuss these questions in small groups.

1. Which English-speaking countries have you visited (if any)?

2. What special ways of speaking English did you notice there?

3. Which accent of English is easiest for you to understand: American, British, Australian, or something else? Why?

 2 **Previewing Vocabulary** Listen to these words from the lecture. Check (✓) the words you don't know. Discuss the meanings of the words with a partner.

Nouns		Adjectives	Adverbs
▨ category	▨ sample	▨ identical	▨ while
▨ dialect	▨ standard	▨ noticeable	▨ whereas
▨ majority		▨ unique	

Listen

Strategy

Classifying and Taking Notes on Classification
Lectures are often organized by classification. That is, the lecture topic is classified, or divided, into several smaller topics. These smaller topics are called *subtopics*. A well-organized lecturer will announce these topics in the introduction. You should listen for this information because it helps you plan and organize your notes.

A graphic organizer like the one below can help you organize topics and details. Use this type of graphic organizer when you're taking notes on a lecture about several topics, or when you're organizing your own thoughts or research.

3 Classifying Lecture Organization Listen to the introductions from three lectures. Write the subtopics in the spaces under each topic.

homework

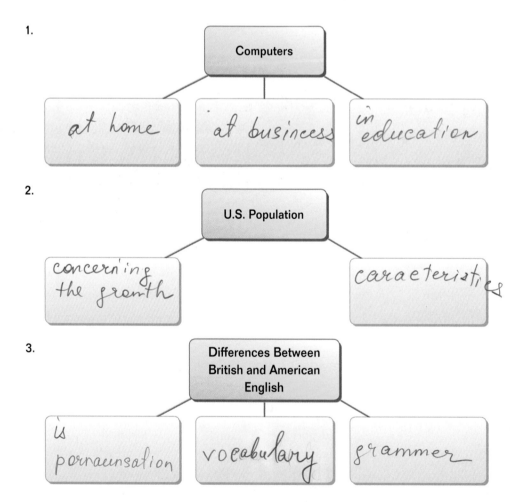

1.

Computers

at home | at business | in education

2.

U.S. Population

concerning the growth | caraeteristies

3.

Differences Between British and American English

is pornaunsation | vocabulary | grammer

Some Vocabulary Differences Between American and British English

American English	British English
apartment	flat
bathroom	loo
garbage can	dustbin
soccer	football
raincoat	mackintosh
quotation marks (punctuation)	inverted commas
lawyer	solicitor
pharmacist	chemist
truck	lorry
elevator	lift
cookie	biscuit
dessert	sweet

4 Taking Notes (Part I) Listen to the first part of the lecture about British and American English. Take notes in the best way you can. Use your own paper.

5 Outlining the Lecture Here is a sample outline of the first part of the lecture. Use your notes from Activity 4 to fill in the missing information. Remember to use abbreviations and symbols. Listen to the lecture again if necessary.

Differences Between American and British English

I. _There are 3 categores of differences 1. pornunsation 2. vocabulary 3 grammer_

Examples:

Sound	Am.E.	B.E.
1. "a"	/ae/	/a/
2. _kent fort_	،little، trenty-one	"New Yok" – for _pfypulcceyf_
3. _kant duiyo_	"liddle," "twenny-one"	_Nerr York_ for _unbffsuyf_

pfypulyf

quf – boat → uobffuyf
pwp   boat → pflypulceryf

6 Taking Notes (Part II) Listen to the second part of the lecture. Continue taking notes on your own paper. After listening, use your notes to fill in the missing information below.

II. _____

_____

_____ S. _____

_____

_____

   A. Eng. has over _____ *one million* _____ words

   B. # of vocab diffs between Am.E. and B.E.:

   _____

   _____

   Examples:

   <u>Am.E.</u>   <u>B.E.</u>

   _____   _____

   _____   _____

   _____   _____

III. _____

_____

_____

   A. Am.E. almost = B.E.

   B. few diffs.:

<u>Grammar</u>	<u>Am.E.</u>	<u>B.E.</u>
1. Verbs	*get*	
2.		
3.		

IV. _____

_____

7 **Discussing the Lecture** Discuss the following questions about the lecture and your own experience. Refer to your notes as necessary.

1. What is meant by standard English? How is the standard different in the United States or Canada and Great Britain?

2. Why are most speakers of American and British English able to understand one another with little difficulty?

3. In what category can you find the biggest difference between American and British English: pronunciation, vocabulary, or grammar? Where do you find the smallest variation? Give a few examples of differences between them. Use the words *while* and *whereas* to state the contrast.

    Example

    In standard American English, people use the verb *have*, whereas speakers of British English use *have got* to mean the same thing.

4. What language or languages are spoken by the majority of people in your community?

5. Do you speak a dialect of your first language? What are the unique characteristics of this dialect, and how is it different from the standard language? Use *while* or *whereas* to explain the differences.

6. If you ever have children, do you want them to be bilingual? Why is this important or useful?

8 **Summarizing Your Discussion** Write a summary of your discussion in Activity 7.

_____

_____

_____

_____

_____

_____

_____

_____

9 **Reviewing Vocabulary** Work in small groups. Look back at the vocabulary list in Activity 2 on page 157. Quiz each other on the terms and their meanings.

9 Comparing American and British English Read the following sentences with a partner. Decide together if they are written in American or British English. Check your answers by using an American-British–British-American dictionary online.

▲ Famous British cultural icons: Big Ben, a double-decker bus, and a red telephone booth.

▲ New York City: Times Square, pedestrians, and yellow cabs

	American	British	
1.		✓	A lorry hit my car on the motorway.
2.			Can you help me lift this garbage can?
3.			Hundreds of people queued up at the cinema.
4.			Please open the trunk so I can put in these suitcases.
5.			Ask the chemist if this medicine is safe.
6.			I need a new rucksack, but I'm not sure what color to get.
7.			My family and I will be on holiday next week.
8.			You can hang your raincoat in the closet.

Getting Meaning from Context

FOCUS ON TESTING

TOEFL® iBT

Using Context Clues

Many tests such as the TOEFL® iBT measure your academic listening and speaking abilities. This activity, and others in the book, will develop your social and academic conversation skills, and provide a foundation for success on a variety of standardized tests. The following conversations are about language.

1. Listen to each conversation.
2. Listen to the question for each conversation. Stop the recording and choose the best answer to each question.
3. In the **Clues** column, write the words that helped you choose your answer.

Answers	Clues
Conversation 1	
1. (A) a city (B) a language (C) a country (D) a religion	
2. (A) from the television (B) from the radio (C) from a book (D) from a magazine article	
3. (A) It's easy to learn. (B) It has no native speakers. (C) The woman wants to learn it. (D) It sounds like Polish.	
Conversation 2	
4. (A) to buy more bees (B) to kill the bees (C) to repair the roof (D) to learn more about bees	
5. (A) direction (B) distance (C) quantity (D) taste	

Answers	Clues
6. (A) the study of language (B) the study of insects (C) the study of dancing (D) the study of communication	
Conversation 3 7. (A) to improve her pronunciation (B) to save time (C) to practice typing (D) to finish her term paper	
8. (A) try Rita's software (B) finish his term papers (C) buy his own software (D) borrow the woman's computer	
9. (A) You have to type fast to use it. (B) It can save your life. (C) It's useful for students and writers. (D) It's expensive.	

Focused Listening

FOCUS

Interjections

Interjections are sound combinations that have specific meanings in spoken English. They are not real words, so they are not usually written. Listen to these interjections.

Interjections	Meanings
Uh-huh.	Yes
Uh-uh.	No
Uh-oh.	I made a mistake. Something is wrong.
Huh?	What?
Oops.	I dropped something. I made a mistake.
Ouch!	That hurts!
Aha!	I finally understand.
Hmm.	I'm not sure; let me think.

1 **Understanding Interjections** Listen to the short conversations. Write the meaning of the *second* speaker's interjection in each blank.

Conversation 1: _____

Conversation 2: _____

Conversation 3: _____

Conversation 4: _____

Conversation 5: _____

Conversation 6: _____

2 **Using Interjections** Work in pairs to practice using interjections. Student A should look at page 250. Student B should look at page 258.

Using Language Functions

F☉CUS

Guessing

To show that you are unsure about something, use the following expressions:

| I guess | I suppose | It might | It looks like |
| I think | I'd say | It could | |

Example

A: What language is this? I don't recognize it.

B: Hmm. I suppose it's something Scandinavian. It looks like Swedish, but it might be Danish.

3 **Guessing Meanings of Slang Expressions** The chart on page 166 contains American slang expressions. Read the sentences with your classmates. Guess what the underlined slang words mean. Use expressions from the list above. Then turn to page 261 to check your answers.

Example

"That movie was a real bomb."

Student 1: I think it means the movie was terrible.

Student 2: Yeah, but it could also mean that the movie was great.

Student 3: I guess it means that the movie was long and boring.

Slang Expressions	Possible Meanings
1. Jenna <u>freaked out</u> when she saw her boyfriend on a date with another girl.	
2. On Saturday afternoon, I like to go to the park and <u>shoot some hoops</u> with my brothers.	
3. The clothing in this store is really <u>cheesy</u>. I would never wear it.	
4. Teenage boys always act <u>goofy</u> when they're around girls.	
5. I really need a break. If I don't take a vacation soon, I'm going to <u>lose it</u>.	
6. To celebrate his birthday, we <u>pigged out</u> on pizza and ice cream.	
7. I told my dad about my bad grade, but he was totally <u>chill</u> about it.	
8. Kyle was <u>bummed out</u> when he got a D on his chemistry test.	
9. We were <u>wiped out</u> after playing two hours of basketball.	
10. I was going to ask my boss for a raise, but at the last minute I <u>chickened out</u>.	

Spelling Bee

Before You Listen

One common contest in American schools is called a spelling bee. In a spelling bee, competitors are given words to spell out loud. They remain in the game as long as they spell the words correctly, but if they make a mistake they must leave the game.

1 Prelistening Questions

1. Are you a good speller in your native language?
2. Do you spell well in English?
3. Give examples of words that are hard to spell in English.
4. How can a person become a better speller?

▲ A school spelling bee champion

2 **Identifying Spellings** Listen to a spelling bee in a U.S. middle school class. The words are taken from a list of commonly misspelled words. As you listen, choose the spelling you hear *even if it is wrong!* During the pause, check (✓) whether you think the spelling is right or wrong. Continue listening, and you will hear the correct spelling. The first one has been done as an example.

Spelling	Right	Wrong	Spelling	Right	Wrong
1. Ⓐ tryes Ⓑ tires Ⓒ tries	✓		**6.** Ⓐ ninty Ⓑ ninety Ⓒ ninnty	✓	
2. Ⓐ chose Ⓑ choose Ⓒ choise		✓	**7.** Ⓐ analyze Ⓑ analize Ⓒ analise	✓	
3. Ⓐ effect Ⓑ affect Ⓒ effete	✓		**8.** Ⓐ possibility Ⓑ possibilety Ⓒ possibilty	✓	
4. Ⓐ quizes Ⓑ kwizzes Ⓒ quizzes			**9.** Ⓐ misterious Ⓑ mysterious Ⓒ mesterious		✓
5. Ⓐ suceed Ⓑ succede Ⓒ succeed			**10.** Ⓐ lightening Ⓑ litening Ⓒ lightning		

3 **Class Spelling Bee** Have a spelling bee in your English class. Use words that you have learned in Chapters 1 through 6 of this textbook.

④ Creating Dialogues Look at the photos on this page and on page 170. Use your imagination to create a dialog for each photo. What are the people saying in each photo? Use as many of the expressions in the box as you can. Read or perform your dialog for the class.

Aha!	Huh?	Ouch!
catch on	I guess	That's not completely true.
chicken out	I suppose	two-faced
friendship	I think	Uh-oh
goofy	in the dark	Well, actually
Have a seat.	It's hard to say	wipe out
Hmmm.	make friends	

1.

▲ Alicia and Lee

_____

_____

_____

_____

_____

_____

_____

2.

▲ Lee, Beth, and Alicia

_____

_____

_____

_____

_____

3.

▲ Lee and Ali

_____

_____

_____

_____

_____

Self-Assessment Log

Check (✓) the words you learned in this chapter.

Nouns
- category
- dialect
- friendliness
- friendship
- majority
- sample
- standard

Verbs
- catch on
- make friends

Adjectives
- identical
- in the dark
- noticeable

- two-faced
- unique

Adverbs
- whereas
- while

Expressions
- Have a seat.
- It's hard to say.

Check (✓) the things you did in this chapter. How well can you do each one?

	Very well	Fairly well	Not very well
I can use phrases for contradicting politely.	☐	☐	☐
I can talk about stereotypes.	☐	☐	☐
I can take notes on a lecture using an outline.	☐	☐	☐
I can classify information.	☐	☐	☐
I can talk about American and British English.	☐	☐	☐
I can guess meanings from context.	☐	☐	☐
I can participate in a spelling bee.	☐	☐	☐

Write about what you learned and what you liked in this chapter.

In this chapter,

I learned _____

_____

I liked _____

_____

CHAPTER 8

Tastes and Preferences

"Markets change, tastes change, so the companies and the individuals who choose to compete in those markets must change."

Dr. An Wang
Chinese-American inventor,
co-founder of Wang Laboratories

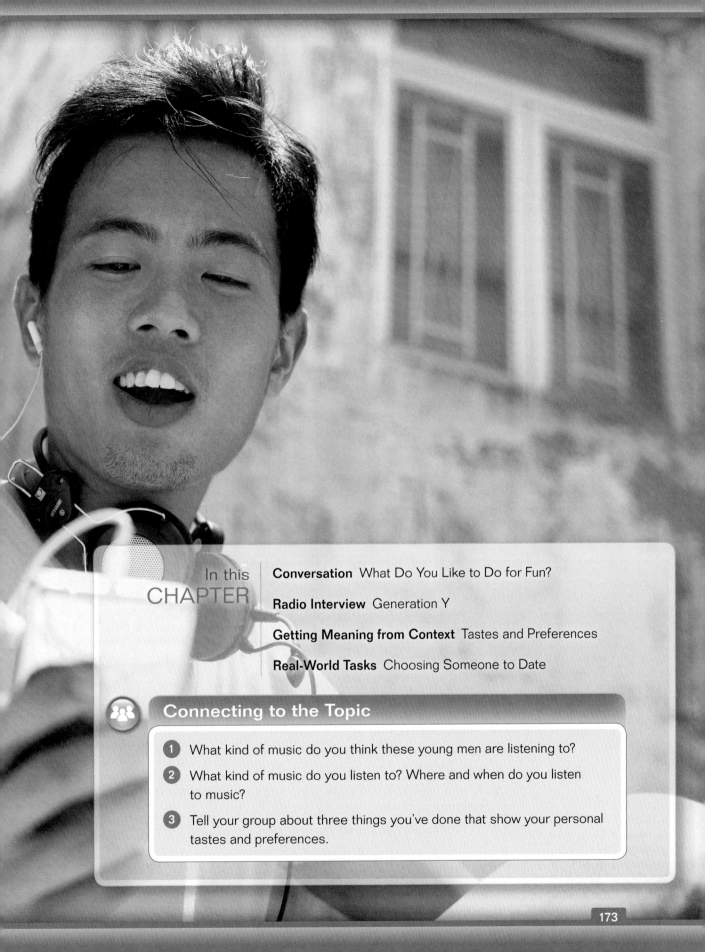

In this
CHAPTER

Conversation What Do You Like to Do for Fun?

Radio Interview Generation Y

Getting Meaning from Context Tastes and Preferences

Real-World Tasks Choosing Someone to Date

Connecting to the Topic

1. What kind of music do you think these young men are listening to?

2. What kind of music do you listen to? Where and when do you listen to music?

3. Tell your group about three things you've done that show your personal tastes and preferences.

What Do You Like to Do for Fun?

> Jeff and his friend Dan play in a rock band. Last night, Mari went to a club to hear them play. Today Dan has stopped by the house for a visit.

▲ Jeff, Dan, and Mari

1 Prelistening Questions Discuss these questions with your classmates.

1. What do you think is happening in the photo?

2. Do you like to listen to music? What kind of music do you prefer? Do you like to go to clubs to listen to music?

3. In your opinion, is it important for two people to have the same tastes in order to be happy together?

4. What are some ways of asking about people's likes and dislikes in English?

2 Previewing Vocabulary Listen to the underlined words and phrases from the conversation. Then use the context to match them with their definitions.

Sentences

1. _____ **A:** Did you <u>have a good time</u> last night?
   B: Not really. The concert was boring.

2. _____ **A:** What do you think of this song?
   B: <u>I'm crazy about it!</u>
   A: I really like it, too.

3. _____ **A:** What is this delicious <u>dish</u>?
   B: It's vegetable lasagna. Carmen made it.

4. _____ **A:** <u>I can't stand</u> that old hat. When are you going to throw it out?
   B: Sorry, I like it.

5. _____ Harry and Renata don't <u>see eye to eye</u> on anything, but they are very happily married.

6. _____ Ahmed <u>doesn't care for</u> sports. He prefers to read and listen to music.

Definitions

a. to dislike a little

b. to dislike strongly; to hate

c. to enjoy oneself

d. to agree

e. "I love it!"

f. food cooked or prepared in a special way

Listen

3 Comprehension Questions Close your book as you listen to the conversation. Listen for the answers to these questions. After you listen, discuss your answers with a partner.

1. Do Mari and Dan like most of the same things?

2. At the end of the conversation, what do Dan and Mari agree to do together?

3. Fill in the chart with details about Dan's and Mari's tastes and preferences. If information is not given, fill in the box with an *X*.

	Dan Likes	Mari Likes
Music	rock	jazz
Food	mexican food	japanese food
Art	modern art	19 th century Monet, Vangog, Renoir.
Sports	football	Bascetball
Movies	Science fiction.	

Stress

4 **Listening for Stressed Words** Now listen to part of the conversation again. Some of the stressed words are missing. During each pause, repeat the phrase or sentence. Then fill in the missing stressed words.

Dan: What did you think of our _____?

Mari: Well, your music is _____ for _____, but to tell you the truth, it was kind of _____. I guess I really prefer _____.

Dan: Do you go to _____ much?

Mari: No, not very often. I _____ _____ them. They're ___*so*___ expensive!

Dan: Yeah, I know what you ___*meen*___. Well, what do you like to do for ___*fun*___?

Mari: I ___*loved*___ to ___*eat*___! I love going to different ___*atnic*___ restaurants and trying new ___*dishes.*___

Dan: What's your ___*favorite*___ kind of food?

Mari: Well, ___*japanece*___, of course. What about you?

Dan: Well, I'm ___*not*___ ___*crazy*___ about sushi or sashimi. But I really like ___*mexican*___ food.

Mari: Ooh, I ___*can*___ ___*not ctend*___ beans, and I don't like ___*chees*___. Uh… What about _____ food?

Dan: I don't ___*cary*___ for it. Too ___*speacy*___. Um… do you like ___*american*___ food? You know, hamburgers, hot dogs, French fries…

Mari: ___*Yaak*___! All that fat and salt and sugar… We don't see eye to eye on _____, do we?

Dan: Well, let's see. What's your opinion of ___*moden*___ art? There's a ___*wonderful*___ show at the county _____ right now.

Mari: To be _____, I don't ___*get*___ the modern stuff. I prefer ___*19th*___ century art, you know, Monet, van Gogh, Renoir.

Dan: Hmm. How do you feel about ___*sports*___? Are you interested in _____?

Mari: _____ football? I _____ it!

Dan: Basketball?

Mari: It's OK.

Dan: How about tall musicians with _____ hair?

Mari: It _____.

Dan: OK, I got it. How about _____ musicians with
_____ hair who invite you to a _____?

Mari: Science fiction?

Dan: Sounds _____!

Mari: _____ we agree on _____!

Check your answers using the listening script on page 293. Then read the conversation with a partner. Pronounce stressed words louder, higher, and more clearly than unstressed words.

Reductions

FOCUS

The following exchange is from the conversation:

Dan: Are you interested in football?

Mari: American football? I hate it!

Dan: Basketball?

Note the form of Dan's second question. The complete question should be "Do you like basketball?" However, Dan drops the subject and the verb because his meaning is clear to Mari from the context of the first question. This kind of reduction is common in rapid, informal speech.

5 Listening for Reductions Listen to the following short exchanges. Write the full questions instead of the reduced ones.

1. _____

   _____

2. _____

   _____

3. _____

   _____

4. _____

   _____

5. _____

   _____

6 **Reviewing Vocabulary** Work in pairs to practice the new vocabulary. Student A should look at page 251. Student B should look at page 259.

Using Language Functions

FOCUS

Talking About Likes and Dislikes

Like Very Much

It's fantastic/terrific/cool*/
 super*/awesome.*

I love it.

I'm crazy about it.

Cool!*

Like a Little

It's nice/all right/ not bad.

I like it.

Neutral

It's OK.

It's so-so.

I can take it or leave it.

Dislike Very Much

It's terrible/horrible/awful/gross.*

It stinks.*

I can't stand it.

I hate it.

Yuck!*

Dislike a Little

I don't care for it.

I don't like it.

I'm not crazy about it.

*These expressions are slang.

7 **Asking About Likes and Dislikes** Read the conversation on page 176. Complete the questions that Dan asks to find out about Mari's likes and dislikes.

1. _____*What did you think of*_____ our band?

2. _____ kind of food?

3. _____ American food?

4. _____ modern art?

5. _____ sports?

6. _____ football?

7. _____ tall musicians with brown hair?

Work with a partner. Use expressions from Using Language Functions above to answer the questions.

8 Talking About Likes and Dislikes Here is a list of the topics and examples mentioned in the conversation. Work with a partner. First, add other examples of each topic. Then take turns asking and answering questions about each other's likes and dislikes. Use the language from Activity 7 and from the Using Language Functions box on page 178.

Examples Q: How do you feel about heavy metal?

A: I don't care for it much.

Topics	Examples
Music	rock, hip-hop
Food	Italian
Art	modern
Sports	baseball
Movies	science fiction

Talk It Over

9 Giving an Impromptu Speech

1. Write one specific question about people's tastes and preferences. Use language from Activity 8. You may choose a topic from the following list or pick your own, but be sure your question is specific.

    Too general: How do you feel about sports?

    Specific: Are you interested in golf?

Topics		
animals	foods	sports
cars	music	things to do on a Saturday night
cities	places to be alone	times of the day
colors	places to eat	TV shows
days of the week	places to take	writers, artists, actors, singers
flowers	a vacation	seasons

2. Your teacher will collect all the questions and put them in a box.

3. Students will take turns picking a question from the box and speaking about it for about one minute. In your speech, you can:

    • give your opinion about the topic, using expressions for talking about likes and dislikes

    • give reasons for your opinion

    • talk about your experience with the topic

Generation Y

Before You Listen

You are going to hear a radio interview with Dr. Stuart Harris, a professor of marketing, about a part of the U.S. population known as Generation Y.

1 Prelistening Discussion Discuss these questions in small groups.

1. What do you know about the three generations in the photos on this page?

2. Into which generation do you fit? What are some characteristics of your generation in your native country?

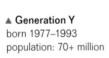

◀ **Baby Boomers**
born 1946–1964*
population: 72 million

Generation X
born 1964–1976
population: 40–45 million ▶

▲ **Generation Y**
born 1977–1993
population: 70+ million

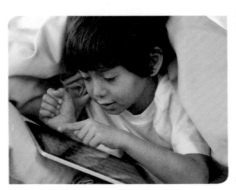

◀ What will the next generation be labeled? And how many of them are there?

*Numbers and dates are approximate.

2 Previewing Vocabulary Listen to these words and phrases from the interview. Check (✓) the ones you don't know. Discuss the meanings of new words with a partner.

Nouns
- ▓ brand
- ▓ conflict
- ▓ consumer
- ▓ developed country
- ▓ income
- ▓ phenomenon
- ▓ standard of living

Verb
- ▓ identify with

Adjectives
- ▓ Caucasian
- ▓ confident
- ▓ diverse
- ▓ hip (informal)

- ▓ loyal
- ▓ optimistic
- ▓ significant
- ▓ tolerant

Culture Note

The word **hip** describes something or someone that is cool, modern, and in fashion. A person, city, restaurant, book, or clothing can be hip. A **hipster** is a cool, modern, and fashionable man or woman.

Listen

Strategy

Recognizing Paraphrases

To paraphrase means to say something again with different words. Speakers paraphrase often in order to make sure their listeners understand what they are saying or to emphasize something important.

When you are taking notes, you need to recognize paraphrases so that you don't write the same idea or information twice in your notes. The following phrases signal that a speaker is paraphrasing:

> In other words…
> That is… (abbreviated as *i.e.*)
> That is to say…
> I mean
> To put it another way…

Paraphrase signals can connect two complete sentences, a sentence and a phrase, or a phrase and another phrase. They can be at the beginning of a sentence or in the middle.

3 **Practicing Paraphrase Signals** Match each sentence on the left with a paraphrase on the right. Then add a paraphrase signal from the Strategy box on page 181 and write or say complete sentences.

Example

*Generation Y refers to people who were born between the late 1970s and the early 1990s, **in other words**, between 1977 or 1978 and 1993 or 1994.*

1. __b__ Generation Y refers to young Americans who were born between the late 1970s and the early 1990s.

2. _____ One-fourth of the people in this generation grew up in single-parent homes.

3. _____ One-third of Generation Y-ers are not Caucasian.

4. _____ These young people want to be modern.

5. _____ Three-fourths of the members of Generation Y have mothers who work.

a. seventy-five percent

b. between 1977–78 and 1993–94

c. one in four

d. This is the most diverse generation in U.S. history.

e. They're not interested in the traditional way of life.

4 **Predicting Note Organization** In this chapter you are going to hear an interview, not a lecture. An interview consists of questions and answers. With your teacher and classmates, discuss the form your notes might have.

5 **Taking Notes (Part I)** Listen to the first part of the interview about the characteristics of Generation Y. Take notes in the best way you can. Use your own paper.

6 **Rewriting Your Notes** Look at the sample notes on page 183. They are in the form of two columns. Use your notes from Activity 5 to fill in the missing information. Remember to use abbreviations and symbols. Listen to the interview again if necessary.

Generation Y	
Questions/Topics	Answers
A. Meaning of Gen Y?	1. Young Am. born late 1970s– early 1990s, i.e. 1977–1994
	2. Number = _____ _____ _____
B. Number—significant?	Yes. Reason: _____ → _____ → _____ _____ _____
C. _____ _____ _____ _____	1. _____ _____ _____ 2. _____ _____ _____ 3. ⅓ not Caucasian
D. Tolerant?	_____ _____ Also _____ _____ _____ _____
E. _____ _____ _____ _____	Stats: 1. Total income/yr: _____ _____ _____ 2. Spend: _____ _____ _____

7 **Taking Notes (Part II)** Listen to the second part of the lecture. Continue taking notes on your own paper. After listening, use your notes to fill in the missing information below.

F. _____

_____

_____

_____

G. Preferred brands?

H. _____

_____

I. _____

Fashion, fast food, _____

_____

_____

_____

1. have grown up w/ media → smart

    shoppers

2. Don't like trad. advert.

3. _____

4. _____

Not only U.S. Internat'l, but diff. in other

countries, e.g.:

1. _____

2. _____

After You Listen

8 **Discussing the Lecture** Discuss the following questions about the interview and your own experiences. Refer to your notes as necessary.

1. Who are the members of Generation Y in the United States?
2. How old are they now?
3. What are some characteristics of this group?
4. What are some adjectives to describe Generation Y?
5. How much money do Generation Y-ers have?
6. What do they spend their money on?
7. How do Generation Y-ers feel about brand-name items?
8. What are some characteristics of Generation Y in other countries?

9 **Reviewing Vocabulary** Work in small groups. Look back at the vocabulary list in Activity 2 on page 181. Quiz each other on the terms and their meanings.

10 **Talking About Fads** In the interview, Dr. Harris mentioned graphic T-shirts and flip-flops as examples of fads that were popular with Generation Y-ers in the first decade of this century. Look at the chart on page 186. Work in small groups. Answer the following questions.

1. For each category, give other examples of Generation Y fads that you know about.

2. Are these fads popular with young people in your country, community, or school?

3. Who follows them? Do you?

▲ What fads can you identify in these photos?

Current Fads	
Categories	Example
Clothing	*Flip-flops, graphic tees, skinny jeans*
Hair	
Body decoration and jewelry	
Food	
Electronics	
Musicians	
Cars	
Sports	
Entertainment	
Activities	
Books	

Strategies for Better Listening and Speaking

Focused Listening

F🔍CUS

Yes/No Questions with *Do, Does,* or *Did*

It can be difficult to understand present and past *yes/no* questions with pronoun subjects. Such questions are often reduced and linked, so it can be hard to hear the difference between *do/does* and *did.* For example:

Long	**Short**
Do I look tired?	du‿wi look tired?
Did he own a car?	did‿ee‿own‿a car?

It may be almost impossible to hear the difference between *Do we* and *Did we* or between *Do they* and *Did they.* In those cases, you may need to listen to the context to tell if the question is in the present or past.

---

1 *Yes/No* **Questions with** *Do, Does,* **or** *Did* Listen for the difference between unreduced and reduced pronunciation. Repeat both forms after the speaker.

Unreduced Pronunciation	**Reduced Pronunciation**
1. Do I look tired? *Yes, I do*	du-wi look tired? ✓
2. Did I look tired? *No, I did*	did-ay look tired?
3. Do you live with your parents?	d'yuh live with your parents?
4. Did you live with your parents?	didjuh live with your parents?
5. Does he own a car?	duzee own a car? ✓
6. Did he own a car?	didee own a car? ✓
7. Does she need any help?	dushee need any help?
8. Did she need any help?	ditshe need any help?
9. Do we have any homework?	duwee have any homework?
10. Did we have any homework?	diwee have any homework?
11. Do they live together?	d'they live together?
12. Did they live together?	di-they live together?

homework (handwritten note)

2 Distinguishing Among *Do*, *Does*, and *Did* You will hear one sentence from each pair that follows. Listen and choose the sentence you hear.

1. Ⓐ Do you have time to eat lunch? ✓

   Ⓑ Did you have time to eat lunch?

2. Ⓐ Does he play the piano? ✓

   Ⓑ Did he play the piano?

3. Ⓐ Do they need help?

   Ⓑ Did they need help? ✓

4. Ⓐ Do I look like my sister? ✓

   Ⓑ Did I look like my sister?

5. Ⓐ Does she understand the instructions?

   Ⓑ Did she understand the instructions? ✓

6. Ⓐ Did we sound good?

   Ⓑ Do we sound good? ✓

7. Ⓐ Do they own a house?

   Ⓑ Did they own a house? ✓

8. Ⓐ Did we need to rewrite the composition?

   Ⓑ Do we need to rewrite the composition? ✓

3 *Do*, *Does*, and *Did* in Questions Listen to the questions and write the missing words.

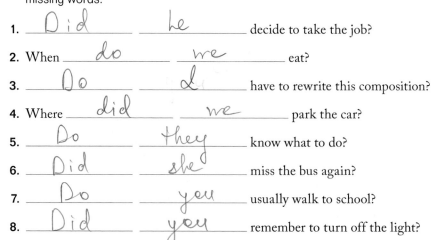

1. _____Did_____ _____he_____ decide to take the job?

2. When _____do_____ _____we_____ eat?

3. _____Do_____ _____I_____ have to rewrite this composition?

4. Where _____did_____ _____we_____ park the car?

5. _____Do_____ _____they_____ know what to do?

6. _____Did_____ _____she_____ miss the bus again?

7. _____Do_____ _____you_____ usually walk to school?

8. _____Did_____ _____you_____ remember to turn off the light?

FOCUS ON TESTING

Using Context Clues

Many tests such as the TOEFL® iBT measure your academic and speaking abilities. This activity, and others in the book, will develop your social and academic communication skills, and provide a foundation for success on a variety of standardized tests. The following conversations are about people's tastes and preferences.

1. Listen to the beginning of each conversation.
2. Listen to the question for each conversation. Stop the recording and choose the best answer to each question.
3. In the **Clues** column, write the words that helped you choose your answer.
4. Listen to the last part of each conversation to hear the correct answer.

Answers	Clues

1. (A) a car
   (B) a painting ✓
   (C) a television set
   (D) a movie
	modern, cost, not a liziss 5000 dollars for that painting

2. (A) a T-shirt ✓
   (B) a tie
   (C) a suit
   (D) a wallet
	black, mait, brown

3. (A) ice-skating
   (B) snow skiing
   (C) water-skiing
   (D) snowboarding ✓
	cold, flying snoboarcling isn't for me

4. (A) She likes it.
   (B) She does not like it. ✓
   (C) She thinks it's funny.
   (D) She's angry.
	You look so deferent I am not crerry about it, sorry

5. (A) She likes it. ✓
   (B) She is not sure.
   (C) She thinks it's funny. ✓
   (D) She's angry.
	you colored your hiar, I love it, it is so cool

Using Language Functions

Expressing Approval and Disapproval

To approve means "to believe that someone or something is good or acceptable."
Disapprove has the opposite meaning. As an example, many people approve of tattoos
these days, but they probably disapprove of them for children.

The following expressions are used to express approval and disapproval.

Approval	**Disapproval**
I approve of + (noun/verb + ing)	I disapprove of + (noun/verb + ing)
I'm in favor of + (noun)	I'm against + (noun)
I'm for + (noun)	

4 **Practicing Expressions of Approval and Disapproval** Complete each
statement with an expression of approval or disapproval. Then work with a partner
and discuss your answers.

1. I _____ laws that forbid smoking in restaurants.

2. I _____ speed limits on highways.

3. I _____ uniforms for high school students.

4. I _____ unmarried couples living together.

5. I _____ women working as police officers and firefighters.

On the Spot!

5 **What Would You Do?** The chart on page
191 lists behaviors and fashions that are popular
among many young people. In the "You"
column, write a plus (+) sign if you approve
of these things or a minus (−) sign if you
disapprove. Think about what your parents would
approve or disapprove of. Complete the column
marked "Your Parents" with plus or minus signs.

Body piercing ▶

Activity/Product	You	Your Parents
pierced ears		
body piercing (nostril, lips, tongue, eyebrows)		
tattoos		
smoking		
rap music		
Internet dating		
living with roommates of the opposite sex		
dating a person from a different race or religion		
a couple living together before marriage		
downloading songs from the Internet (without paying)		
online forums		

Discuss the following questions in small groups. Use expressions from Using Language Functions on page 190.

1. Why do you approve or disapprove of each item?
2. In which cases do you agree with your parents? In which cases do you disagree?
3. Do your opinions about any particular activities depend on whether a male or female does it? Which activities?

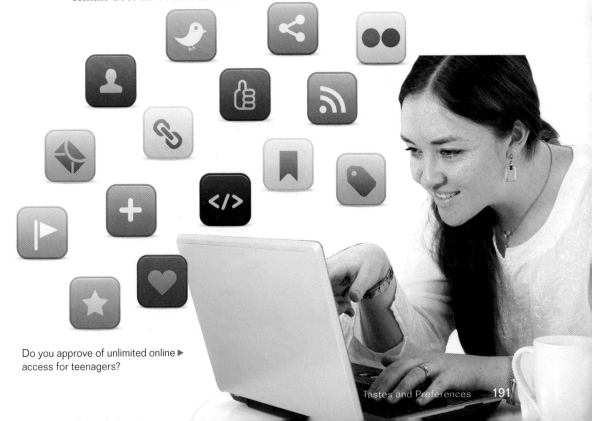

Do you approve of unlimited online ▶ access for teenagers?

Choosing Someone to Date

In this section you will hear about David, a 22 year old Business Administration student. For the past year he has been occasionally dating two women, Katherine and Jean. He likes both of them very much. David would like to settle down with one girlfriend so he feels it's time to choose one woman and "get serious." Both women are interested in him, but David is having a hard time choosing between them.

Before You Listen

1 **Describing Your Ideal Partner** On a piece of paper, list at least five qualities you value in a romantic partner. Then share your list with one or more classmates.

Examples

Unmarried people
"My ideal wife would be intelligent."
"My ideal partner would have a good job."

Married people
"The qualities I admire most in my husband are his intelligence and sense of humor."

Listen

2 **Comparing People's Qualities** Listen as David describes Katherine and Jean. Take notes on their positive and negative qualities in the chart on the next page.

◀ David tries to choose between two women.

enteresting talk with her
went sam high-school
she laught

	Katherine	Jean
Positive Qualities	*intelligent, my parents get crazy with him, she like, politets, books*	*smart, intelligent too. she not essy talk to you, she like sports she has a sense of humor.*
Negative Qualities	*sensitive, not good menerging many, not respon seply*	*great with mony don't want children don't shure about ?*

loves kids, but she has a bad temprowry.

After You Listen

3 **Discussion** Compare your answers from Activity 2 with a partner. Then discuss the following questions:

1. Are Jean's and Katherine's positive qualities important to you too?
2. What other positive qualities do you want in a partner?
3. Would Jean's and Katherine's negative qualities bother you?
4. What other qualities would you want to avoid in a partner?
5. What do you think David should do? Why?

Talk It Over

4 **Reading Personal Ads** Read the ads. Then choose the ad that sounds most interesting to you. Tell the members of your group which ad you chose and why.

FROM WOMEN:

TALL, attractive brunette, enjoys music, dancing, hiking, travel. Looking for good-looking, honest, secure man with sense of humor for friendship, possible relationship. Box 192.

ELEGANT, petite grad student, marriage-minded, looking for professional man to share tennis, skiing, reading, sailing, opera. Box 120.

ARTISTIC, bookish elementary school teacher, vegetarian. Looking for marriage with witty man who loves classical music, kids, pets. Box 239.

EUROPEAN grad student, 5'6", looking for fun-loving man to achieve perfect relationship. Box 923.

BRAINY REDHEAD, financially independent looking for ski companion with refined taste and great sense of humor. Box 329.

FROM MEN:

EASYGOING GUY, 33, college grad, good-looking, mature; looking for woman, slim, educated, for romance & more. Box 385.

WANT TO LAUGH? Talkative male, 24, looking for partner for dating fun. I'm smart, handsome, educated & hip.

Into rock music, dancing & partying. Box 127.

STOCKBROKER, 5'11", attractive, spontaneous, traveler; looking for attractive, fit, honest female. Box 383.

FIREFIGHTER, athletic, attractive, 28, looking for woman for companionship & adventure. Must enjoy life. Race/ religion/age not important. Box 472.

POETIC, marriage-minded professional pilot, 6'3", looking for non-smoking, energetic, adventurous woman for serious relationship. Box 489.

5 **Writing an Online Profile** In this activity, you will write an online profile. Read the information in the boxes and follow the directions.

How to Write an Interesting Profile

1. Begin your profile by describing yourself. You may choose to include some of the following information:
   - your age
   - nationality
   - profession
   - religion
   - what you look like ("tall, nice-looking man")
   - what you enjoy doing ("loves intelligent conversation")
   - what kind of person you are ("honest, caring")
   - something unique about you ("bird lover")

2. In the second part of the profile, write about the person you would like to meet. List the characteristics that are important to you.

3. State what you want from a relationship: Marriage? Fun? A serious relationship? Friendship? Someone to share a hobby with? A tennis partner?

The Language of Profiles

1. Do not write complete sentences. Notice that the ads on page 193 begin with adjectives or descriptive phrases.

2. Use the phrase *looking for* when you describe the person you would like to meet.

3. Use commas to separate a series of adjectives ("honest, attractive, funny guy").

4. Use adjective clauses ("looking for woman who loves golf") and prepositional phrases ("lawyer with a great sense of humor").

Write a profile for yourself. Follow the instructions in the boxes above. Don't write your name on your profile. Your teacher will collect all the profiles and post them on the bulletin board.

Read all the profiles and try to guess which classmate wrote each one. Finally, each person in the class should say which profile he or she wrote.

Self-Assessment Log

Check (✓) the words you learned in this chapter.

Nouns
- brand
- conflict
- consumer
- developed country
- dish
- income
- phenomenon
- standard of living

Verb
- identify with

Adjectives
- Caucasian
- confident
- diverse
- hip (informal)
- loyal
- optimistic

- significant
- tolerant

Expressions
- can't stand
- don't/doesn't care for
- have a good time

- I'm crazy about it!
- see eye to eye

Check (✓) the things you did in this chapter. How well can you do each one?

	Very well	Fairly well	Not very well
I can hear and use stress and reductions.	☐	☐	☐
I can talk about my likes and dislikes.	☐	☐	☐
I can give a one-minute speech.	☐	☐	☐
I can recognize paraphrases.	☐	☐	☐
I can take notes on an interview using an outline.	☐	☐	☐
I can talk about fads.	☐	☐	☐
I can distinguish between *do, does*, and *did*.	☐	☐	☐
I can use phrases to express approval and disapproval.	☐	☐	☐
I can guess meanings from context.	☐	☐	☐
I can talk about my ideal partner.	☐	☐	☐

Write what you learned and what you liked in this chapter.

In this chapter,

I learned _____

_____

I liked _____

_____

9 New Frontiers

"Man cannot discover new oceans unless he has the courage to lose sight of the shore."

Andre Gide
French writer, humorist, and moralist

Ma

ON

C

ON

ON

ON

Connecting to the Topic

1. Describe what you see in the photo. What is a "smart house?"
2. What are the pros and cons of a smart home?
3. Tell about five ways that technology makes our lives easier.

House
Bedroom

date Status

g lights   OFF

lamps   FF

apes

lights

Living in a "Smart" House

Before You Listen

In the following conversation, Andrew, Nancy, and Mari talk about technology in the home. Look at the photos and answer the questions in the captions.

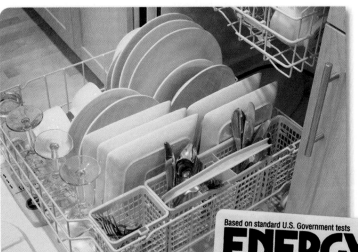

What are some ▶
ways to save
energy when
doing the dishes?

▼ Read this label. What
kind of appliance is this
label for? How does the
appliance save energy?

Based on standard U.S. Government tests

ENERGYGUIDE

Clothes Washer
Capacity: Standard
Top Loading

Model(s)   WHSB9000B

Compare the Energy Use of this Clothes Washer with Others Before You Buy.

This Model Uses	ENERGY STAR
686 kWh / year	A symbol of energy efficiency

Energy use (kWh/year) range of all similar models

Uses Least Energy		Uses Most Energy
177		1298

kWh/year (kilowatt-hours per year) is a measure of energy (electricity) use.
Your utility company uses it to compute your bill. Only standard size, top loading
clothes washers are used in this scale.

**Clothes washers using more energy cost more to operate.
This model's estimated yearly operating cost is:**

$55	$23
when used with an electric water heater	when used with a natural gas water heater

Based on eight loads of clothes a week and a 1999 U.S. Government national average cost
of 8.22¢ per kWh for electricity and 68.8¢ per therm for natural gas. Your actual operating
cost will vary depending on your local utility rates and your use of the product.

Important: Removal of this label before consumer purchase violates the Federal Trade Commission's Appliance Labeling Rule
(16 C.F.R. Part 305).

DWG NO: 175D3516P10

▲ What are other ways to save energy
in the home? Name five ways.

1 Prelistening Questions Discuss these questions with your classmates.

1. How do people use technology to help save energy in their homes?

2. What is a "smart" house? Do you know anyone who lives in one?

3. What can you control remotely with your smart phone?

2 Previewing Vocabulary Listen to the underlined words and phrases from the conversation. Then use the context to match them with their definitions.

Sentences

1. _d_ We used our air conditioning every day last month, so our <u>utility bill</u> was over $200.

2. _j_ Janet, I haven't seen you <u>for ages</u>! You look so different.

3. _b_ Fifty years ago, televisions couldn't be operated <u>remotely</u>. You had to change channels by walking to your TV.

4. _a_ Three of my <u>appliances</u> broke recently; I had to get a new refrigerator, toaster, and washing machine.

5. _e_ Buying things online is a <u>convenient</u> way to shop. You don't need to go anywhere or wait in line.

6. _g_ My boss performs her job fast and well; she is very <u>efficient</u>.

7. _h_ The doctor will be here soon. <u>In the meantime</u>, please have a seat.

8. _i_ The old factory was <u>turned into</u> an apartment building.

9. _f_ Leave the TV <u>on</u>; I want to hear the basketball results.

10. _c_ I can't <u>install</u> our new dishwasher by myself; I need a plumber to do that.

Definitions

a. machines used in people's homes

b. from far away

c. to put in or connect a machine and make it work

d. payment for gas or electricity service

e. useful because it's easy to use

f. not turn off

g. not wasting time, money or energy

h. a period between now and a future event

i. change something to another thing

j. in a long time

3 Comprehension Questions Listen to the conversation. Listen for the answers to these questions. Then compare answers with a partner.

1. What's the problem with Andrew and Nancy's utility bill?
2. What makes a smart house more efficient than a regular house?
3. Can you guess why Andrew and Nancy don't have a smart house yet?
4. What good habits did Mari learn in Japan?
5. What does Nancy suggest at the end?

Stress

4 Listening for Stressed Words Listen to the conversation again. Some of the stressed words are missing. During each pause, repeat the phrase or sentence. Then fill in the missing stressed words.

Andrew: Nancy!

Nancy: Yeah?

Andrew: Look at this ___utility___ bill. We're spending ___may___ too much on ___electricity___.

Nancy: Ugh, I know. It's because ___seme___ people in this house never remember to turn off ___lights___.

Mari: Um, ___I___ turn off lights all the ___time___. In Japan, we're very ___careful___ about saving energy.

Andrew: Well, if we had a ___smart___ house, we wouldn't have to ___worry___ about this so much.

Mari: A smart house?

Nancy: Yeah, we've been talking about that for ___ages___. Go ahead, Andrew, explain what it ___is___.

Andrew: Well, a ___smart___ house is a house that has ___automatic___ systems for controlling the lights, ___temperature___, windows and doors...

Mari: You mean the lights turn off by ___themselves___?

Andrew: Yes, they can turn on or off at a ___specific___ time that you decide.

Nancy: Or the ___system___ can tell if someone is in the ___room___ or not. If the room is empty, the lights go ___off___.

homework

Andrew: And the heating and _air_ _conditioning_ work the same way.

Mari: That's very cool.

Andrew: And you can program other _appliances_ to do stuff too.

Mari: Like which _ones_? How?

Andrew: Like your security system _recognizes_ you and opens your door, your _music_ turns on when you enter a _room_, your refrigerator tells you when you _run_ out of food…

Mari: So it's all _computerized_, right?

Nancy: Right. And get this, you control everything _remotely_ from your phone or _tablet_.

Andrew: So let's say you're on _vacation_ or at work, but don't remember if you turned off your _stove_. It's all very _convenient_

Nancy: And _efficient_!

Mari: You just need an _app_ on your phone and that's it?

Andrew: Well, yes, an _app_, but you also have to _install_ a control system, you know, the hardware, then some _software_.…

Nancy: Yeah, it can get a little _complicated_ And expensive!

Andrew: But we will _definitely_ turn this house into a _smart_ one eventually…

Nancy: OK, but in the _meantime_, let's all be smart about _saving_ energy. Um, who left the TV on in the _bedroom_?

Andrew: Oops.

Check your answers using the listening script on pages 296–297. Then read the conversation with a partner. Pronounce stressed words louder, higher, and more clearly than unstressed words.

5 **Using Vocabulary** Work in groups. Look at the pictures. Choose one of them and tell a story about it using all the vocabulary in the box. The group that uses the most vocabulary from the list wins!

appliances	efficient	install	leave on	turn into
convenient	for ages	in the meantime	remotely	utility

Example Veronica has had the same washing machine <u>for ages</u>, and it finally broke down. Now she is shopping for a new, high-tech one and wants to know…

Example Paul works for his company <u>remotely</u> so he can stay home with his daughter. It's very <u>convenient</u> because…

Pronunciation

Pronouncing *TH*

The English language has two sounds that are written with the letters *th*. The two sounds are almost the same, but one of them is voiced and the other is voiceless.

Example

Voiced: *there*   Voiceless: *think*

To pronounce both sounds, follow these steps:

1. Place the tip of your tongue between your teeth.
2. Keep your lips relaxed.
3. Exhale air from your lungs.
4. Be sure to do steps 1 to 3 *all at the same time*.

To produce the voiced /th/ sound, make your vocal cords vibrate as you exhale.

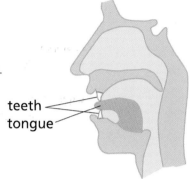

teeth
tongue

---

6 Pronouncing Voiced and Voiceless *th* Listen to two lists of words. Repeat the words after the speaker.

Voiceless *th*	Voiced *th*
thick	this
bath	that
third	then
thirty	themselves
bathroom	bathe
monthly	father
throw	weather
health	breathe

7 Distinguishing Between Voiced and Voiceless *th* Now listen to the following sentences. Repeat them after the speaker. Underline every voiceless *th* you hear. Circle every voiced *th*.

Example

I think there is someone at the door.

1. That's going to happen on October third.
2. Breathe out when you pronounce the /th/ sound.
3. Next Thursday is my birthday.
4. The weather is getting warmer on Earth.
5. Elizabeth takes a bath every night.
6. There's something to think about.
7. Tom's brother gave him a new toothbrush.

Using Language Functions

Introducing Surprising Information

To introduce surprising or unexpected information, speakers often use special phrases such as:

Believe it or not,...

Get this...

It's weird/ strange/ funny, but...

Surprisingly,...

You're not going to believe this, but...

Example

Believe it or not, instead of teachers, remote-controlled robots teach in some elementary schools in Korea.

▲ A teaching robot leads an elementary school class.

8 Fact or Fiction Game

1. Your teacher will hand out a card to each student in the class. The card will say "fact" or "fiction." Don't show your card to anyone.

2. Use one of the expressions from the list above to tell something surprising or unexpected about yourself. If your card says "fact," your story must be completely true. If it says "fiction," you must invent a story, but it should sound true.

3. Take turns telling your stories. After you are finished, the class should vote on whether you told the truth or not. Your purpose, of course, is to fool your classmates.

Facial Recognition Software

Before You Listen

You are going to hear a student presentation about a kind of technology called facial recognition software. The student explains what it is, how it can be used, and why it is important to have laws that control the use of this technology.

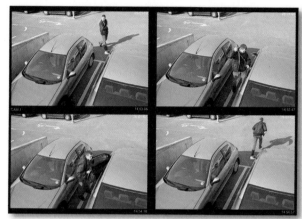

◀ A thief breaks into a car.

A security guard ▶ captures the theft on camera and sends his team to the parking lot. Police may be able to identify the thief using Facial Recognition Software.

 1 Prelistening Discussion Discuss the questions in small groups.

1. In your country, are there cameras in public areas? What are they used for?

2. Are there pictures of you on the Internet? Do you worry that someone could use them to get private information about you?

3. Have you ever had your identity stolen? How did it happen? How did you fix the problem?

2 **Previewing Vocabulary** Listen to these words and phrases from the lecture. Check (✓) the ones you don't know. Discuss their meanings with a partner.

Nouns		Verbs	Adjectives
▦ antidepressant	▦ potential	▦ display	▦ essential
▦ aspect	▦ privacy	▦ match	▦ facial
▦ billboard	▦ riot	▦ scan	
▦ display	▦ width		
▦ impact			

Listen

Strategy

Recognizing Persuasive Language

Persuading (or *convincing*) means using information and language to try to change people's thinking or get them to change their behavior. To build a persuasive argument, you need to know how to a) convince listeners that a problem exists and b) persuade them to change their mind or take action.

Convincing people that a problem exists

_____ Here's the issue.

_____ Why is that bad? It's bad because…

_____ What's wrong with that? Well,…

_____ There is a big/ huge problem with…, and that is…

_____ You might think this is a good thing, but actually / in reality / in fact…

_____ Some people say… / but the truth is…

Persuading people to take action

You have to / ought to / should / need to…

It's important / necessary / essential / crucial to…

Here's what you can do.

I want to persuade you to…

Unless (people) (verb)… (something bad will happen).

3 **Listening for Persuasive Language** Listen to short passages with persuasive language. Write P if the speaker's purpose is to show a problem. Write A if the purpose is to persuade listeners to take action.

Context	Problem or Action?
1. News report	P
2. Public service announcement	A
3. Friends talking	A or P
4. Student speech	A
5. Lecture in urban planning class	P

4 Taking Notes and Outlining (Part I) Listen to the first part of the lecture and take notes in the best way you can. Use your own paper. After listening, use your notes to fill in the missing information in the outline. Remember to use abbreviations and symbols.

Part I

I. Intro

  A. Situation: You're walking _in a shopping moll_, see digital advertising displays w/ ads for _shoes followed by deodorant_

  B. Billboard "knows" _How age you are_. Uses computer software to _scanned your face_, match ads to _your age, sex, body. It is called_

  C. Lecture topic: facial recognition software (FRS)

    1. _negative_

    2. positive uses

    3. _software_

    4. argument: _negative impact on privacy._

II. Two kinds of facial recognition software

  A. Recognizes _human feaces._

    1. used in _your face but couldn't indentefy_

    2. used in bars to _in Cicago, when to inestefy the nember of men or woman at the one fire_

  B. _recognis how you are !_

    1. measures _distance between you eyes sape your noise_

    2. useful for _are you criminal or terrorist potencial_

      a. e.g. _In England can analize people faces who enrolved in riots._

stetion Tokio

are you criminal person or no

New Frontiers   **207**

homework

5 Taking Notes and Outlining (Part II) Listen to the second part of the lecture. Continue taking notes on your own paper. After listening, use your notes to fill in the missing information below.

III. Problem with FRS: ___to take a away your prilvee'___

IV. Explanation

   A. Your name & photo on ___internet, FB___

   B. Public camera takes a photo of you > someone can match that photo

      w/ your Internet photo > get ___your name, age, addresse all kinds of privete infor.___

V. Dangerous

   A. Strangers can know ___enploiment history, shoe size___

   B. Can get ___your medical history___

   C. "Smart" billboards can display _____

     > embarrassing

un Germany control your dath dasic.

VI. What to do ___limit photos with photos___

   A. ___don't let tag people your fotos in FB___

   B. ___to support law to protet people information obut you goverment should take___

After You Listen

6 Discussing the Lecture Discuss the following questions about the lecture and your own experiences. Refer to your notes as needed.

1. According to the lecture, how do "smart" billboards work to identify people?

2. What are two kinds of facial recognition software? How is each kind used?

3. What is the speaker's opinion about facial recognition software? What reasons does he give?

4. Do you agree or disagree with the speaker?

5. What actions does the speaker want listeners to take? After hearing the lecture, do you plan to take either of these actions?

7 Reviewing Vocabulary Work in small groups. Look back at the vocabulary list in Activity 2 on page 206. Quiz each other on the terms and their meanings.

Strategy

Signposting

Signposting at the beginning of your speech means telling your audience what you are going to say and what your purpose is. For example, in Activity 4 you heard:

"Today I'm going to explain what facial recognition technology is and tell you about some of the positive ways that we can use it. But then, in the second part of my speech, I'm going to tell you about the negative aspects of this technology. Especially the negative impact on privacy. And I'm going to try to persuade you that this technology is something that we and the government need to control very carefully."

Signposting tells your listeners the important points they should listen for and helps them get ready to take notes. Be sure to include signposting whenever you give a speech.

8 Giving a Speech to Persuade

1. You are going to give a speech in which you describe an issue and persuade your listeners to take action. Brainstorm topics for your speech.

   Examples
   - Everyone should be a vegetarian.
   - There should be strict fines for spitting in public places.
   - Social networking sites like Facebook are a waste of time.
   - Private cars should be forbidden in downtown areas.
   - This is not a good time to invest in the stock market.

2. Do research and take notes about the issue you selected.

3. Prepare an outline of your speech. Be sure to include these parts:

   I. Introduction
      A. Background
      B. Statement of the issue
      C. Your plan for this speech (signposting)

   II. Body
      A. Explanation of the issue using reasons, facts, etc.
      B. Actions you want your listeners to take about this issue

4. Include language for stating the issue and encouraging action from the box on page 206.

5. Practice your speech once with a partner. Have your partner offer suggestions for improvement.

6. Give your speech in front of the class.

Getting Meaning from Context

FOCUS ON TESTING

TOEFL iBT

Signal Words for Guessing the Correct Answer

Many tests such as the TOEFL @iBT measure your academic listening skills. The items in this exercise will help you develop one of these important skills - the ability to guess ("infer") information or draw conclusions from information you hear. The following vocabulary is often used in this type of question.

infer	What can you <u>infer</u> from the story?	
imply	What does the speaker <u>imply</u>?	
conclude	What can you <u>conclude</u> from this information?	

Using Context Clues

You are going to hear five short talks about recent inventions, discoveries, or trends in science.

1. Listen to each passage.

2. Listen to the question at the end of each passage. Stop the recording, read the answer choices below, and choose the best answer to each question.

3. In the **Clues** column, write the words that helped you choose your answer.

Answers	Clues
1. (A) Driverless cars are safer than cars driven by humans. (B) Driverless cars were invented in 2010. (C) Disabled people are not allowed to drive. (D) Driverless cars will never have accidents. ✓	
2. (A) cleans better than traditional machines. (B) costs less to buy than traditional machines. (C) reduces the amount of water people use each month. ✓ (D) is bad for the environment.	

Answers	Clues
3. (A) Steven Chu is a professor of geo-engineering. (B) Human activity can help reduce global warming. ✓ (C) In Greece, all buildings must be painted white. (D) In the U.S. there are plans to remove 11 million cars from the roads.	
4. (A) It is not yet possible to create <u>artificial meat</u> in a laboratory. (B) People in Holland and Britain are already eating artificial meat. (C) Artificial meat does not taste good. (D) By the year 2050, all the meat we eat will be artificial. ✓	⇒ *[handwritten note]*
5. (A) price (B) <u>efficiency</u> (C) safety (D) fun	✓ *[handwritten note]*

1 Talking About New Frontiers The following inventions and trends were discussed in the listening passages. What are the advantages and disadvantages of each? What role, if any, do you think they might play in your life?

1. a driverless car
2. a "dry" washing machine
3. geo-engineering
4. artificial food
5. a car that flies
6. government rules (such as laws about the colors of buildings)

▲ Houses painted white in a Greek village

Focused Listening

Pronunciation of –*ed* Endings

The –*ed* ending indicates the past tense or past participle of regular verbs. For example:

- Tom wash**ed** his car last weekend. (Past tense verb)
- Kai is interest**ed** in becoming a nurse. (Past participle used as adjective)
- Several houses were destroy**ed** by the storm. (Past participle used in passive voice)

Pay attention to the correct pronunciation of –**ed** endings. They are pronounced in three different ways:

1. /**id**/ in words ending in /t/ or /d/

   Examples

   need ⟶ needed   decide ⟶ decided

2. /**t**/ in words ending in a voiceless consonant

   Examples

   help ⟶ helped   rush ⟶ rushed

   cook ⟶ cooked   watch ⟶ watched

3. /**d**/ in words ending in a voiced sound

   Examples

   burn ⟶ burned   hire ⟶ hired

   rob ⟶ robbed   live ⟶ lived

---

2 **Practicing –*ed* Endings** Listen and repeat the following words after the speaker.

/t/	/d/	/id/
ripped	changed	accepted
looked	questioned	invented
based	played	started
asked	mentioned	corrected
guessed	interviewed	tweeted

homework

3 **Distinguishing Among −ed Endings** Listen to the past tense verbs and check the pronunciation that you hear. You will hear each word twice.

	/t/	/d/	/id/
1.	✓		
2.		✓	✓
3.			✓
4.	✓	✓	
5.		✓	
6.			✓
7.	✓		
8.		✓	
9.			✓
10.	✓		
11.		✓	
12.			✓
13.	✓		
14.		✓	
15.		✓	

4 **Pronouncing −ed Endings** With a partner, decide on the −ed pronunciation of these words. Write /t/, /d/, or /id/ in the blanks. Then say the words. Finally, listen to check your pronunciation.

1. _____ emptied   /d/
2. _____ used   /d/
3. _____ stayed   /d/
4. _____ worked   /t/
5. _____ passed   /t/

6. _____ waited   /id/
7. _____ benefited   /id/
8. _____ judged   /d/
9. _____ identified   /d/
10. _____ drummed   /d/

Using Language Functions

Expressing Interest or Surprise

English speakers show that they are interested and paying attention by making eye contact, nodding their heads, and using words and expressions for showing interest. For example:

That's really interesting.

That's an interesting/great/nice story.

Really?

Wow!

If you are surprised by something you hear, you can say:

(That's) incredible / unbelievable / amazing!

I can't believe it!

I'm shocked!

5 Talking About Discoveries We discover things that are already there, just waiting for us to find them. Most discoveries are quite ordinary. For example, think of the way you felt the first time you tasted a delicious new food.

Work in small groups and tell your classmates about discoveries that you have made in your life. Use expressions from the box above to show interest or surprise. See the chart below for examples of discoveries.

Example

Student A: I recently discovered that there were four sets of twins in my father's family.

Student B: Wow. That's amazing! Were you shocked?

Student A: Yeah, I couldn't believe it!

Personal Discoveries	
Categories	Examples
A place	a park, a new shop
A new activity or form of entertainment	snowboarding, playing the saxophone
Something you never noticed before about something familiar	the smell of a common flower, the purring of a cat
Something unusual about another country or another group of people	The world's tallest building is in Dubai. Oranges originally came from Asia.
A skill you found you have	the ability to make perfect coffee, the ability to grow plants

Tracking a Journey on a Map

Before You Listen

1 Prelistening Questions

1. What is the young man in the picture doing? Do you know who he is?

2. What is the most adventurous thing you have done in your life?

3. Discuss the meanings of these words with a partner: journey, voyage, trip, travel, sail, sailboat, pirate, destination.

▲ Zac Sunderland: the youngest American to sail solo around the world

2 **Reading Background Information** Read the paragraph about Zac Sunderland.

Sailing Around the Globe

Zac Sunderland, an American teenager, used to dream about traveling around the world. In 2009, he made his dream come true. He saved his money, bought a sailboat and became the first person under 18 to sail around the world alone.

3 **Following a Journey on a Map** Look at the map below. Find Zac's starting point: Marina del Rey, California. Then listen and circle the different stops on Zac's voyage. Connect the points to mark his route from start to finish.

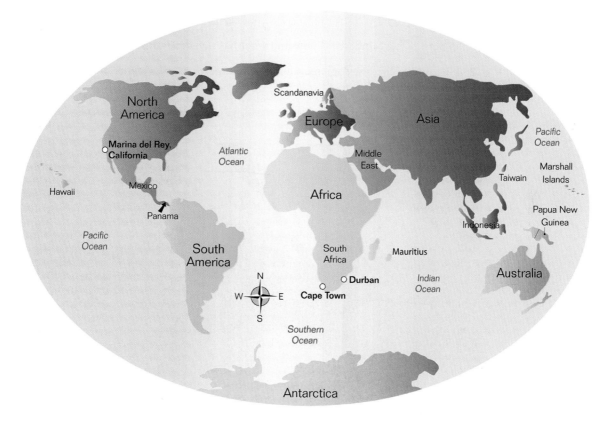

4 **Discussion** Compare your map and the stops you marked with a classmate. Then discuss the following questions:

1. What kind of person do you think Zac is? What characteristics would a person have to have in order to sail around the world alone?

2. Zac was only 16 years old when he began his voyage. Do you think this is too young to sail around the world alone?

3. Many people said Zac's parents were crazy for allowing him to go on his voyage. Zac's parents supported him and said it was Zac's decision. What do you think? Should a teenager have the right to make a decision like this for himself?

4. Have you ever dreamed of going on a dangerous adventure by yourself? Do you think your parents would support you? What would other people say? How would you answer them?

5 **Presentation** Do an Internet search and find information on one of the following topics. Then present your findings to your class:

1. Where is Zac Sunderland now and what has he been doing since 2009?

2. Has anyone broken Zac's record as the youngest person to sail around the world alone? Explain.

3. List five other types of adventure travel. What are the dangers of each?

▲ What other kinds of adventure travel can you think of?

Self-Assessment Log

Check (✓) the words you learned in this chapter.

Nouns
- antidepressant
- appliances
- aspect
- billboard
- display
- impact
- potential
- privacy
- riot
- utility bill
- width

Verbs
- display
- install
- leave on
- match
- scan
- turn into

Adjectives
- convenient
- efficient
- essential
- facial

Adverb
- remotely

Expressions
- for ages
- In the meantime

Check (✓) the things you did in this chapter. How well can you do each one?

	Very well	Fairly well	Not very well
I can hear and use stress and reductions.	☐	☐	☐
I can use phrases to introduce surprising information.	☐	☐	☐
I can talk about advances in technology.	☐	☐	☐
I can take notes on a lecture using an outline.	☐	☐	☐
I can recognize and pronounce -*th* sounds.	☐	☐	☐
I can distinguish between -*ed* endings.	☐	☐	☐
I can use phrases to express interest and surprise.	☐	☐	☐
I can guess meanings from context.	☐	☐	☐
I can recognize signposting in a speech or lecture.	☐	☐	☐
I can recognize persuasive language.	☐	☐	☐
I can talk about my dreams and plans.	☐	☐	☐
I can follow a journey on a map.	☐	☐	☐

Write what you learned and what you liked in this chapter.

In this chapter,

I learned _____

_____

I liked _____

_____

10 Ceremonies

> There is nothing like a ritual for making its participants think beyond their own appetites, and for making them feel that they belong to something greater, older and more important than themselves."

Tom Utley
British journalist

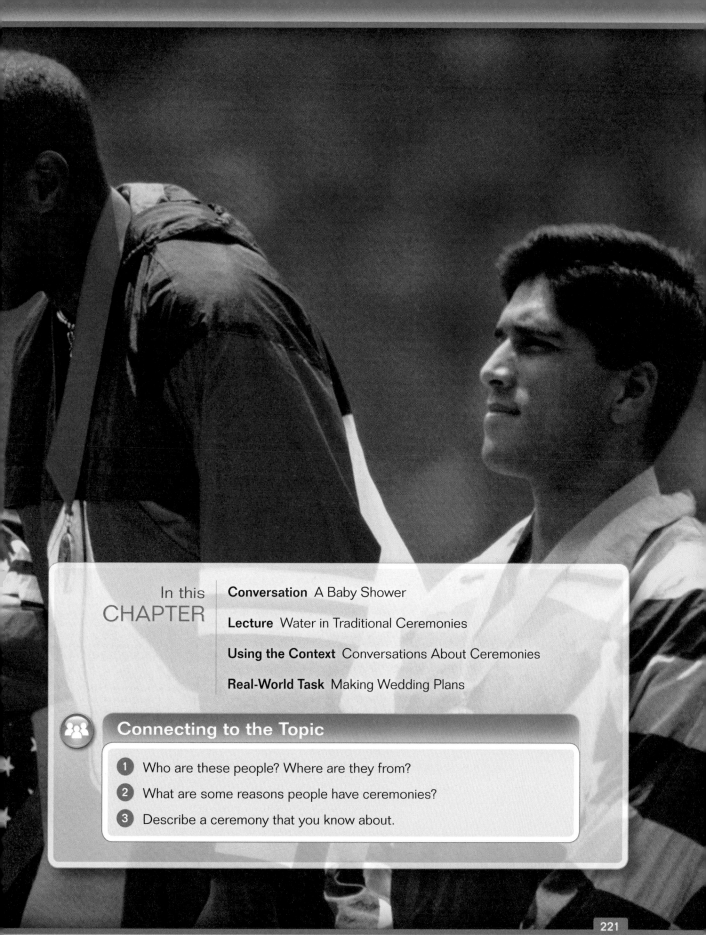

In this
CHAPTER

Conversation A Baby Shower

Lecture Water in Traditional Ceremonies

Using the Context Conversations About Ceremonies

Real-World Task Making Wedding Plans

Connecting to the Topic

1. Who are these people? Where are they from?

2. What are some reasons people have ceremonies?

3. Describe a ceremony that you know about.

A Baby Shower

Before You Listen

In the following conversation, Mari, Jeff, and Sharon talk about an invitation to a baby shower.

▲ A baby shower

1 **Prelistening Questions** Discuss these questions with your classmates.

1. What are the women in the picture doing? What kind of celebration is this?
2. How do people in your culture celebrate the birth of a baby?

2 Previewing Vocabulary Listen to the underlined words and expressions from the conversation. Then use the context to match them with their definitions.

Sentences

1. _d_ The Olympic Games were <u>hosted</u> by China in 2008.

2. _a_ My family members <u>shower</u> each other <u>with</u> dozens of gifts every Christmas.

3. _f_ In some cultures, couples are not <u>allowed</u> to see each other before the wedding ceremony.

4. _g_ My sister's new baby is <u>due</u> next week, so we are all very excited.

5. _c_ When Jane was <u>pregnant</u> with her first baby, she gained 15 kilos in nine months.

6. _b_ Everyone laughed at the <u>silly</u> costumes worn by the guests at the Halloween party.

7. _h_ That store sells everything a <u>mother-to-be</u> could possibly need.

8. _i_ When the bride came in wearing her long white dress, everyone <u>went ooh and aah</u>.

9. _e_ You will need to <u>register</u> at the store's website before you can buy gifts online.

Definitions

a. to give someone a lot of things

b. not serious, childish

c. expecting to have a baby

d. to offer a place and arrange everything necessary for a special event such as a party

e. to sign up for an online service, organization, mailing list, etc.

f. permitted

g. expected to happen or arrive at a specific time

h. a woman who is going to have a baby

i. informally expressing joy and surprise

Listen

3 Comprehension Questions Listen to the conversation. Listen for the answers to these questions. After you listen, compare answers with a partner.

1. What kind of invitation did Mari receive?

2. Who are the hosts?

3. Is Jeff invited too? Why or why not?

4. When is Nancy and Andrew's baby due?

5. What are three things people do at baby showers?

6. How is gift-giving different in Japan and in the United States?

7. Where is Mari probably going to buy a gift for the baby?

Stress

4 **Listening for Stressed Words** Now listen to part of the conversation again. Some of the stressed words are missing. During each pause, repeat the phrase or sentence. Then fill in the missing stressed words.

Mari: Hmm. But isn't Nancy and Andrew's baby due at the end of

_____? And this invitation says April

_____.

Sharon: Well, yes. The custom is to have a shower _____

the baby is born, when the woman is seven or eight months

_____.

Mari: Very interesting. And everybody brings a _____?

Sharon: Right. Something for the baby: You know, _____ or

clothes or something for the baby's _____.

Mari: OK. The _____ says it's for lunch, so...

Sharon: Yeah, we'll have lunch, and _____ we'll play

_____.

Mari: Games? What _____ of games?

Jeff: _____ games.

Sharon: _____ games like bingo, or guessing games, or baby

trivia games. And the _____ get small prizes.

Mari: It _____ like fun.

Sharon: It is. And then, at the _____ of the party, there's

usually a cake with _____ decorations, and then the

mother-to-be opens her _____.

Mari: While the _____ are still there?

Sharon: Sure. That's my _____ part! Everybody gets to see

the gifts.

Jeff: And go "oooh, aaah..."

Sharon: And see how _____ the woman is.

Mari: Wow. That's so _____ from our custom. In Japan

we usually _____ _____ a gift in

front of guests.

Sharon: Really? That _____ different.

Mari: Well, what kind of gift do you think I should _____ for her?

Sharon: She's registered _____, so you can see what she's already _____ and what she still needs. Would you like me to write down the _____ address for you?

Mari: Sure. _____ would be great.

Check your answers using the listening script on pages 300–301. Then read the conversation with a partner. Pronounce stressed words louder, higher, and more clearly than unstressed words.

After You Listen

5 Using Vocabulary Discuss the following questions with a partner. Use the underlined vocabulary in your answers.

1. Discuss a recent event that you were invited to. Who hosted it? What did the hosts do to make the event successful?

2. When was the last time your family showered you with advice? Examples: after graduation, before getting married, before traveling abroad, and so on.

3. What are some real activities in your life that you have to complete before a specific date? For example, when are the following due?
   - a rented DVD
   - a borrowed library book
   - a telephone bill
   - the rent
   - homework

4. What kinds of things were you not allowed to do when you were a child?

5. In your culture, is it a custom to give a pregnant woman and her husband gifts before the baby is born?

6. What advice do people in your culture traditionally give to a mother-to-be?

7. In what situation do you feel comfortable acting silly?

8. Would you go "ooh and aah" if you met your favorite movie star? Why or why not?

9. What do you think of the modern custom of couples registering online for wedding or baby shower gifts they want?

Pronunciation

Stress in Compound Phrases

Compound phrases combine two nouns or an adjective and a noun.

- **Stress in Noun + Noun Combinations**

  The first word of the phrase is normally stressed.* For example:

  baby + shower = baˈby shower

- **Stress in Adjective + Noun Combinations**

  In most cases both words are stressed equally. For example:

  silly + games = silˈly gamesˈ

*This is true whether the compound is spelled as one word (e.g. *bridesmaid*) or two words (e.g. *baby shower*).

---

6 **Pronouncing Noun + Noun Combinations** Listen to the following noun + noun combinations. Notice where the stress is placed and repeat each phrase after the speaker.

baˈby decorations	dinˈner party	graduˈation gift
welˈcoming ceremony	wedˈding invitation	floˈwer arrangement

7 **Pronouncing Adjective + Noun Combinations** Listen to the following adjective + noun combinations and repeat them after the speaker. Remember to stress both words equally.

female relative	favorite part	instant message
traditional ceremony	white dress	funny hat

8 **Predicting Stress** Read the examples of compound nouns and adjective + noun combinations. Based on the rules above, mark the stressed word(s) in each item. Then listen to check your answers.

1. young mother	stepmother
2. coffeepot	large pot
3. nice place	fireplace
4. flashlight	green light
5. wedding cake	delicious cake
6. hair dryer	dry hair
7. busboy	tall boy
8. fast reader	mind reader

Using Language Functions

Offering to Do Something

At the end of the conversation, notice the expressions Mari and Sharon use to offer each other help:

Sharon: Would you like me to write down the Internet address for you?

Mari: Sure. That would be great.

Mari: Is there anything I can do to help with the party?

Sharon: Thanks, but it's not necessary.

Study these expressions commonly used in English to offer, accept, or decline help:

Offer

Would you like me to...?

Is there anything I can do to...?

May I...?

Could I...?

What can I do to...?

Accept

Sure.

Yes.

I'd appreciate it.

If you wouldn't mind.

Decline

No, that's OK, thanks.

No, but thanks anyway.

Thanks, but it's not necessary.

No, but thanks a lot for asking.

▲ Can I help you figure out that design problem for your website?

9 Role-Play Work with a partner. Create a conversation about each photo. Use some of the expressions from the list on page 227 to offer, accept, or decline help.

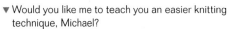

▼ Could I help you load the car for the trip?

▼ Would you like me to teach you an easier knitting technique, Michael?

◄ Can I help you choose the best laptop for your needs?

▲ Is there anything I can help you with, Grandma?

Water in Traditional Ceremonies

Before You Listen

You are going to hear a talk about the uses of water in ceremonies and celebrations around the world.

▲ Young people celebrating the New Year in Thailand

▲ A baptism

Washing with water before prayer ▶

1 **Prelistening Discussion** Discuss this question in small groups.

1. What are some symbolic meanings that water has? Check the ones you know about:

☐ purity

☐ danger

☐ fertility

☐ death

☐ change

☐ wealth

☐ good luck

☐ other _____

2 **Previewing Vocabulary** Listen to these words and phrases from the lecture. Check (✓) the ones you don't know. Discuss the meanings of new words with a partner.

Nouns	Verbs		Adjectives
prayer	cleanse	pour	fascinating
priest	focus on	pray	pure
ritual	involve	purify	
sin	narrow (something) down	sprinkle	
symbol		symbolize	
symbolism	play a part in		

Listen

Strategy

Digressing from (Going off) and Returning to the Topic

Lecturers often include personal stories, jokes, or other information not directly related to the main topic. When speakers "go off the subject" (digress) like this, do not take notes. Start taking notes when the speaker signals a return to the main subject.

Study the expressions below:

Going off the Topic	**Returning to the Topic**
By the way	As I was saying
That reminds me	Anyway
Before I forget	Back to our topic
	Where was I?

3 **Recognizing Digressions** Listen to part of the lecture. Listen carefully for the place where the speaker goes off and then returns to the topic. After you listen, look at the following notes and cross out any unnecessary information.

A. Thailand

    Speaker's experience

      — April: hottest time of year

      — Thail. doesn't have four seasons.

      — dry season: Nov.–Feb.

      — hot season: March–June

      — rainy season: July–Oct.

      — spkr was walking down street & teens threw water on him

      — reason: April 13th = Songkran

    Songkran = water festival

      — people throw water on each other

      — wash hands of elders w/scented water

      — belief = water will wash away bad luck

4 **Taking Notes** Listen to the whole lecture. Take notes in the best way you can. Use your own paper.

5 **Outlining the Lecture** Use your notes from Activity 4 to fill in the missing information in the outline on page 232. Remember to use abbreviations and symbols. Listen to the lecture again if necessary.

Culture Note

The Peace Corps

The Peace Corps is a U.S. government organization that tries to help developing countries by sending volunteers (people who work without payment), especially young people, to teach skills in education, health, farming, and so on.

I. Intro

Speaker: _____

General Topic: _____

II. Specific Topic: _____

A. _____

_____

_____

_____

_____

_____

_____

_____

B. _____

_____

_____

_____

_____

_____

C. Christian ceremony: baptism

_____

_____

_____

_____

_____

III. Conclusion _____

6 **Discussing the Lecture** Discuss the following questions about the lecture. Refer to your notes as necessary.

1. What is the speaker's background?

2. What similarity did he find among different cultural celebrations?

3. What role does water play in each of the ceremonies that the speaker described?

4. Does water play a role in any of the major celebrations or festivals in your culture?

 7 Reviewing Vocabulary Work in small groups. Look back at the vocabulary list in Activity 2 on page 230. Quiz each other on the terms and their meanings.

Talk It Over

Strategy

Graphic Organizer: Multi-Column Chart
A multi-column chart can help you organize different characteristics of one or more items, events, people, and so on. You can use a multi-column chart to organize facts or your thoughts about a topic.

 8 Interview Choose a ceremony or celebration that is found in most cultures, for example, New Year's Eve, a birthday, a wedding, and so on. Interview a classmate or a friend from a different culture, community, or religion and ask about his or her way of celebrating these events. Take notes in the chart below. Note any similarities between their customs and yours in the last column.

Celebration	Country	What People Do	Reason for Celebration	Other Notes
Baby shower— 1 or 2 mos. before baby's birth	United States	Women give party and bring gifts for mother-to-be	Welcome new baby, shower baby and mother with gifts and good wishes	

Choose the most interesting or unusual ceremony from your chart and share the information with your class in a short presentation.

Getting Meaning from Context

FOCUS ON TESTING

TOEFL® iBT

Using Context Clues

Many tests such as the TOEFL® iBT measure your academic listening and speaking abilities. This activity, and others in the book, will develop your social and academic conversation skills, and provide a foundation for success on a variety of standardized tests. You are going to hear five short conversations about ceremonies.

1. Read the list of ceremonies below. Define the unfamiliar items with the help of your teacher.

2. Listen to the conversations.

3. Stop the recording after each conversation. In each blank, write the letter of the ceremony that the conversation is about.

 g ceremaf

1. _g_ Conversation 1
2. _c_ Conversation 2
3. _d_ Conversation 3
4. _a_ Conversation 4
5. _f_ Conversation 5

    a. anniversary   **e.** promotion
    b. baptism   **f.** retirement
    c. funeral   *pujw*   **g.** wedding
    d. graduation

---

1 **Talking About Ceremonies** Which of the ceremonies in the activity above have you attended in the last year? Work in groups. Describe your experiences.

Focused Listening

FOCUS

Affirmative Tag Questions

In affirmative tag questions, the main verb is negative, and the tag is affirmative.

Example

George isn't married, is he?

This question can have different meanings, depending on the intonation.

Falling Intonation

Purpose: to start a conversation, to make an observation. The speaker already knows the answer.

Example

George isn't married, is he?

Rising Intonation

Purpose: to get information. The speaker doesn't know the answer.

Example

George isn't married, is he?

Speakers also use affirmative tag questions with rising intonation to express a hope. For example, in Focus on Testing: Using Context Clues, Conversation 5, you heard:

Mother: You and Robert aren't going to shove cake in each other's faces,

are you?

Daughter: No, Mom, don't worry.

The mother hopes that the bride and groom will not shove cake in each other's faces. We can infer that she disapproves of this custom.

---

2 **Recognizing the Meaning of Affirmative Tag Questions** Listen to the tag questions and decide the speaker's meaning.

Question   **The Speaker...**

1.
(A) is sure Alia bought flowers.
(B) isn't sure if Alia bought flowers.

2.
(A) thinks the ceremony wasn't long.
(B) isn't sure the ceremony was long.

3.
(A) is sure he needs to bring a present.
(B) isn't sure if he needs to bring a present.

4.
(A) hopes the listener is not going to wear that shirt to the party.
(B) knows the listener is not going to wear that shirt to the party.

5.
(A) is asking a question.
(B) is making an observation.

6.
(A) is certain the listener is not bringing a dog.
(B) hopes the listener is not bringing a dog.

7.
(A) is not sure if the wedding has started.
(B) knows the wedding has started.

8.
(A) is asking a question.
(B) is sure the listener didn't like the party.

Answering Affirmative Tag Questions

Many English learners get confused about the correct way to answer affirmative tag questions. Look at these examples:

Question	Answer	Meaning of Answer
1. It's not your birthday today, is it?	No, it's not.	The speaker was correct. It's not the listener's birthday.
2. It's not your birthday today, is it?	Yes, it is.	It is the listener's birthday. The speaker was wrong.

3 **Asking and Answering Affirmative Tag Questions** Work in pairs to ask and answer affirmative tag questions. Student A should look at page 251. Student B should look at page 259.

Using Language Functions

Offering Congratulations and Sympathy

It is polite to offer congratulations on happy occasions such as anniversaries, graduations, promotions, and birthdays. In contrast, we offer sympathy in cases of death, injury, illness, accident, unemployment, or bad luck.

	Congratulations	Sympathy
Offering	Congratulations! Congratulations on… I'm very happy for you. It's great that…	Please accept my sympathy. (formal) I was so sorry to hear (that/about)… I'm (so) sorry. It's (really) (awful, terrible) that…
Accepting	Thank you (very much). Thanks (a lot).	Thank you for your concern. (formal) You're very kind. (formal) I appreciate it. Thank you.

4 **Role-Play** Prepare conversations with a partner for the following five situations. Add details to each situation. Take turns offering and expressing congratulations and sympathy. Then role-play one of the situations for the class.

1. One of your classmates had a serious car accident and spent two weeks in the hospital. He or she is now at home recovering. Call your classmate, express sympathy, and offer to help.

2. You have just been accepted to a university. You call your friend to tell him or her about it. Your friend congratulates you.

3. You run into an acquaintance you haven't seen in a while. She tells you that she quit smoking and hasn't had a cigarette in six months. Offer your congratulations.

4. Your good friend tells you he or she was promoted and is moving to a new city for work. He or she is excited about the new job but sorry about moving. Express both congratulations and sympathy to your friend.

5. Your teacher announces that he will be absent from the next class because he has to go to his aunt's funeral. Offer your sympathies.

WITH DEEPEST
Sympathy

▲ A sympathy card

Making Wedding Plans

Katsu and Sandra are engaged to be married. He is a first-generation Japanese-American. She is a fourth-generation American. They met at college. Although Katsu and Sandra were both raised in the United States, their backgrounds are very different. For that reason they have decided to hire a professional wedding consultant to help them plan their wedding. In this section, you will hear each of them talking to the consultant.

Sandra Bennett ▶
Age 28
Dallas, TX

◀ **Katsuhiro Mata**
Age 30
San Francisco, CA

Culture Note

Participants in Traditional North American Weddings
- Justice of the peace: A nonreligious official who performs a wedding ceremony.
- Bridesmaid: A female friend or relative who helps the bride and stands by her during the wedding ceremony.
- Groomsman: A male friend or relative who helps the groom get ready for the wedding, usher wedding guests to their seats, and escort bridesmaids during the wedding ceremony.
- Flower girl: A young girl who walks down the aisle before the bride and groom carrying flowers or scattering flower petals.

1 **Comparing Wedding Preferences** Imagine that you are planning your wedding ceremony. Read the questionnaire. Take notes on your preferences. Then sit in groups and compare your preferences.

My Wedding Preferences	
Location	
Date/time of year	
Type of service/ceremony (e.g., religious, traditional, modern)	
Number of guests (approx.)	
Number and types of attendants (bridesmaids, groomsmen, etc.)	
Role of parents/grandparents	
Clothing	
Music	
Colors	
Other details	

Listen

2 **Taking Notes on Wedding Preferences** Listen as Katsu and Sandra talk separately to the wedding consultant. Divide into two groups. Each group will listen to one of the conversations and take notes. If a detail is not mentioned, leave it blank.

american   *japan*

	Sandra	Katsu
Location	*garden* *big treodishenal* *wedding in church*	*garden* *done the doors*
Date/time of year	*agre* →	*April or* *may*
Type of service/ceremony (e.g., religious, traditional, modern)	*huuge*	*smoll,* *and close frend*
Number of guests (approx.)	*everbode* *her family not* *riligen*	*only family* *close frends*
Attendants (bridesmaids, groomsmen, etc.)	*couson* *flourgel*	*their parents*
Role of parents/ grandparents	*very*	*not o*
Clothing	*suit not* *formal*	*wath dress*
Music	*clussical* *citar and* *flut*	*vilion* *soft*
Colors	*airs is* *she liks.*	*purpal a color* *loves* *flors*
Other details		

y nyo - ynuyyns

3 **Discussion** Work with a student who listened to the other conversation. Tell each other about the conversation you heard and fill in the chart on page 240 with the information your partner gives you. Pay attention to the similarities and differences between Katsu and Sandra.

▲ A wedding on a golf course

4 **Role-Play**

1. Work in groups. Imagine that you are wedding planners. Look at your chart of Katsu's and Sandra's preferences and make recommendations regarding each of the details below. Give reasons for your decisions in cases where Sandra and Katsu disagree.

   Example

   "I recommend that Katsu's and Sandra's parents walk down the aisle with them. That way Sandra gets her wish to walk with her father, and Katsu gets his wish to walk with his parents. And Sandra's mother will also feel included."

   - Location
   - Date/time of year
   - Type of service/ceremony
   - Number of guests
   - Number and types of attendants
   - Role of parents/grandparents
   - Clothing
   - Music
   - Colors
   - Other details

2. Role-play a conversation between Katsu, Sandra, and the wedding planner. Discuss two or three details that Sandra and Katsu don't agree on. The wedding planner should:

   - congratulate Katsu and Sandra on their engagement
   - offer his or her recommendations

   Sandra and Katsu should respond by asking questions, discussing, and finally making decisions about the details of their ceremony.

Self-Assessment Log

Check (✓) the words you learned in this chapter.

Nouns	Verbs		Adjectives
▨ mother-to-be	▨ cleanse	▨ pour	▨ allowed
▨ prayer	▨ focus on	▨ pray	▨ due
▨ priest	▨ host	▨ purify	▨ fascinating
▨ ritual	▨ involve	▨ register	▨ pregnant
▨ sin	▨ narrow	▨ shower	▨ pure
▨ symbol	(something)	▨ sprinkle	▨ silly
▨ symbolism	down	▨ symbolize	
	▨ play a part in		**Expression**
			▨ go "ooh and ah"

Check (✓) the things you did in this chapter. How well can you do each one?

	Very well	Fairly well	Not very well
I can hear and use stress and pronunciation.	☐	☐	☐
I can use expressions to make and respond to offers.	☐	☐	☐
I can recognize digressions.	☐	☐	☐
I can take notes on a lecture using an outline.	☐	☐	☐
I can talk about celebrations and ceremonies.	☐	☐	☐
I can use and answer tag questions.	☐	☐	☐
I can use expressions to offer congratulations and sympathy.	☐	☐	☐
I can guess meanings from context.	☐	☐	☐
I can compare preferences.	☐	☐	☐

Write what you learned and what you liked in this chapter.

In this chapter,

I learned _____

_____

I liked _____

_____

Chapter 1 Part 4

5 Describing Map Locations page 24

Ask your partner for the locations of the places listed under your map. Ask "Where is _____?" Your partner will use expressions of location. Then ask your partner to repeat the description. Write the name of the place on the map. When you are finished, your two maps should be the same.

Example

Student A: Where is the University Library?

Student B: It's on University Avenue, up the street from the Administration Building.

Student A: Is it north or south of Short Avenue?

Student B: North.

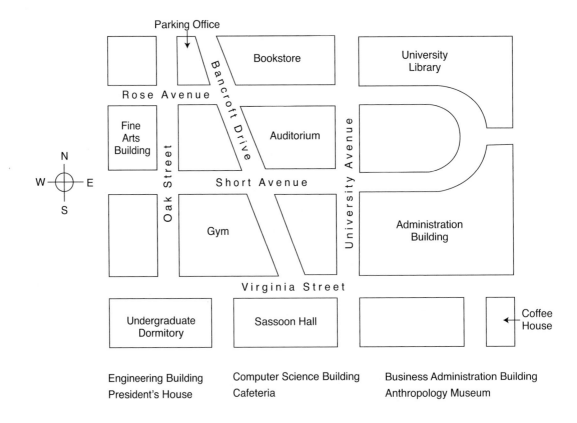

Engineering Building   Computer Science Building   Business Administration Building
President's House   Cafeteria   Anthropology Museum

8 **Role-Play** page 35

Role-play these phone conversations. Take turns playing Student A and Student B. Read the information for your role and be sure to use the expressions for opening and closing a phone conversation.

Student A

Situation 1 You are a student. Your friend told you about a very nice room for rent with an American family. Call the family to get information about the room. Then make an appointment to go see it.

You can ask about the following things (choose three or four):

- who lives in the house
- rent and utilities
- furniture, telephone
- any restrictions (smoking, visitors, pets, etc.)

Situation 2 You are the manager of an apartment building. You have a vacant apartment. It has two bedrooms, one bathroom, air conditioning, and parking for two cars. It is fully furnished in a secure building. The rent is $800 a month. It is 30 minutes away from the local college. You will only rent to someone serious and mature. A smoker is OK, but pets are not. A student calls and asks about the apartment.

1 **Listening for Clues to Relationships Between People** page 45

Pair A

1. You will read the following short conversation with your partner.

Conversation

A: Can I get you anything to drink?

B: Just water, thanks.

Add titles or nicknames to show the following relationships between A and B, and practice the conversation three times.

   a. two male friends

   b. secretary and boss

   c. child and mother

2. With the other pair of students in your group, take turns role-playing your three conversations. Listen for titles and nicknames. Use them to guess the relationships. The other pair will say if you guessed correctly.

2 Role-Play page 46

Role-play situations in an apartment building.

Student A

Situation 1 You are a tenant in a large apartment building. Your refrigerator has broken for the third time in less than six months. Call the manager to express your frustration and to tell him or her you also want the refrigerator replaced.

Situation 2 You are a music major in college. You love to play your CDs while you do your homework at night. The problem is that your downstairs neighbor goes to bed early and does not like your music. This neighbor complained once, and since then you have tried to be quieter at night. However, you refuse to stop listening to music. Now it is 12:30 A.M., and someone is knocking on your door.

3 Requesting and Giving Directions page 48

Look at the map. Ask your partner for directions to the places listed at the bottom of your map. When you find the place, write its name on your map. Then give your partner directions to the places that he or she asks about, from where it says, "Start here each time." At the end of this activity, your two maps should look the same.

Example

Student A: How do I get to the print shop?

Student B: That's easy. Go two blocks north on Pine Street. Turn left and go one block west on 3rd Avenue. The print shop will be on your left, in the middle of the block, next to the hardware store.

Student A: Thanks!

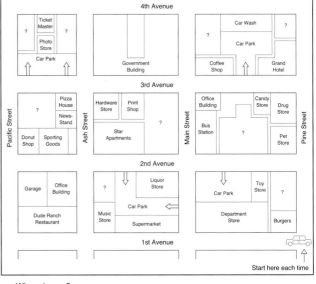

Where is . . . ?

the bakery	the public library	the Laundromat
the post office	the movie theater	Trinity College
the Chinese restaurant	the supermarket	the gas station

7 **Using Vocabulary** page 57

The following list contains statements using the idioms from this section. Read an item from your list. Student B will select the appropriate response from his or her list.

Student A

1. You look worried. What's wrong?

2. I can't make ends meet on $600 a month. I need more income!

3. What's the secret to living on a budget?

4. Why didn't you go to the concert?

4 **Pair Practice with Teens and Tens** page 67

Student A

1. Your partner will read some sentences with numbers to you. Circle the numbers you hear.

   1. 13   30
   2. 115   150
   3. $14.05 $40.05
   4. $16.60 $60.60
   5. 1919   1990
   6. 7040   7014
   7. 1.14   1.40

2. Now read the following sentences to your partner.

   1. I pay $70 a month for parking.
   2. She is 160 centimeters tall.
   3. The president's house has 19 rooms.
   4. She paid $50.50 for a haircut.
   5. Her family has lived here since 1830.
   6. Please deliver the package to 1670 Loyola Street.
   7. That cookie contains only 114 calories.

7 **Reviewing Vocabulary** page 80

The following section contains statements using the new vocabulary from this section. Read an item from your list. Student B will select the appropriate response from his or her list.

Student A

1. How was your trip to New York last December?

2. Did you do anything about the broken elevator in your building?

3. Do you want to go to the beach this afternoon?

4. I heard your mother got a full-time job.

5. What's your brother doing these days?

4 **Asking and Answering Negative Tag Questions** page 93

Use the statements below to make negative tag questions. Decide if the intonation should rise or fall. Then ask your partner the questions.

Student A

1. You're from _____ (name of country, city, or area), aren't you?

2. Last night's homework was _____ (hard, easy, boring, confusing, etc.)...

3. This _____ (book, pen, etc.) is yours...

4. It's _____ (cold, hot, pleasant) today...

5. Our next test is _____ (day or date)...

6. This classroom is _____ (comfortable, too small, etc.)...

7 Using Vocabulary page 106

The list below contains statements using the new vocabulary from this section. Read an item from your list. Student B will select the appropriate response from his or her list.

Student A

1. It's 3 o'clock in the morning! Why aren't you sleeping?

2. Are you leaving?

3. Wake up, Sally. It's 7 A.M.

4. Hello? Is anybody home?

5. Who takes care of your kids while you're working?

6. What's wrong with this light? It's not working properly.

7. How's the baby doing?

8. Why did George quit his job?

8 Asking for a Favor page 107

Read the situations below and ask your partner for help or for a favor. Your partner must give an appropriate response.

Example

It's Thursday. Your library books are due tomorrow. Ask your partner to return the books to the library for you.

A: My library books are due tomorrow. Could you please return them to the library for me?

B: I'm sorry, but I'm not going there today.

Student A

1. Your arms are full of books. Ask your partner to open the door for you.

2. It's raining and you don't have a car. Ask your partner to drive you home after class.

3. You're trying to concentrate. Ask your partner to speak on the phone more quietly.

6 Using Vocabulary page 154

The following list contains statements using the new vocabulary from this section. Read an item from your list. Student B will select the appropriate response from his or her list.

Student A

1. Do you understand tonight's homework assignment? I don't.

2. When do you think you'll be able to speak English fluently?

3. I'm here to see Dr. Brown at 3 P.M.

4. Jerry is a two-faced liar. He told my girlfriend I was seeing another woman!

5. Claudette's friendliness is the reason everyone likes her.

6. I've known my best friend since we were three years old.

7. I've told John six times that I don't want to go out with him, but he keeps asking me.

8. Why is it so hard to make friends with Americans?

2 Using Interjections page 165

Work in pairs to practice using interjections.

Student A

1. Say the following sentences to your partner and wait for a response.

    1. Did you understand last night's homework?

    2. Oops! I forgot my listening book at home.

    3. Ouch! My leg!

    4. The teacher looks really annoyed.

2. Now listen to your partner and choose the proper response from the following list.

    a. Huh? Could you repeat that?

    b. Uh-huh. Let's go home before it starts.

    c. Let's go see if it's still there.

    d. I'll pick it up.

6 **Reviewing Vocabulary** page 178

Student A

1. What is this delicious dish?

2. Sally has a new boyfriend. To be honest, I'm not crazy about him.

3. What do you think of action movies?

4. Did you have a good time in San Diego last weekend?

5. Why did you break up with your girlfriend?

6. I don't care for this new chair you bought. It's not very comfortable.

Chapter 10   **Part 3**

3 **Asking and Answering Affirmative Tag Questions** page 236

Use the statements below to make affirmative tag questions with rising intonation (asking for information). Your partner should answer truthfully.

Example

You read: You're not from France.

You ask: You're not from France, are you?

Your partner answers: Yes, I am (if he or she is from France).

No, I'm not (if he or she is not from France).

Student A

1. You don't smoke…

2. There's no homework tonight…

3. It isn't raining…

4. You don't have children (grandchildren, sisters, brothers)…

5 **Reviewing Vocabulary** page 24

Ask your partner for the locations of the places listed under your map. Ask "Where is _____?" Your partner will use expressions of location. Then ask your partner to repeat the description. Write the name of the place on the map. When you are finished, your two maps should be the same.

Example

Student B: Where is the University Library?

Student A: It's on University Avenue, up the street from the Administration Building.

Student B: Is it north or south of Short Avenue?

Student A: North.

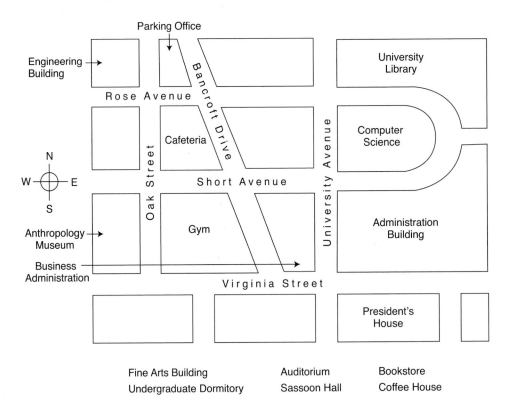

8 Role-Play page 35

Role-play these phone conversations. Take turns playing Student A and Student B. Read the information for your role and be sure to use the expressions for opening and closing a phone conversation.

Student B

Situation 1 You live in a large house with your husband or wife and two children. You have an extra bedroom that you want to rent to a student. The room is furnished. It has a private phone and bath. The rent is only $300, but the student must agree to do ten hours a week of babysitting. Also, you have two large dogs, so the student cannot have any pets. You definitely do not want a smoker. A student calls and asks about the room.

Situation 2 You are a university student looking for a place to live. You saw the following ad in the campus housing office. You can afford to spend $900 a month on rent, and you don't have a car. Therefore, it's important for you to rent an apartment close to the college. Call the owner and get more information about the apartment. Decide if you want to see the place or not. If so, make an appointment with the manager.

> **FOR RENT:**
>
> 2br, 1ba for $800. A/C, furnished, secure bldg.

1 Listening for Clues to Relationships Between People page 45

Pair B

1. You will read the following short conversation with your partner.

   Conversation

   A: Can I get you anything to drink?

   B: Just water, thanks.

   Add titles or nicknames to show the following relationships between A and B, and practice the conversation three times.

   a. grandson and grandfather

   b. boyfriend and girlfriend

   c. waiter and customer

2. With the other pair of students in your group, take turns role-playing your three conversations. Listen for titles and nicknames. Use them to guess the relationships. The other pair will say if you guessed correctly.

2 Role-Play page 46

Role-play situations in an apartment building.

Student B

Situation 1 You are the manager of a large apartment building. You have one tenant who frequently complains about problems in his or her apartment. This takes up a lot of your time. Now the tenant calls you with a new complaint. You feel that this tenant should pay for the repairs because you think the tenant doesn't take good care of the apartment.

Situation 2 The neighbor above you plays loud music late at night. You wrote this neighbor a polite note about it, but the problem has not stopped. Now it is 12:30 A.M. and you cannot sleep because of the music. You are very frustrated. You go upstairs, knock on the neighbor's door, and tell the neighbor you want the problem to stop.

3 Requesting and Giving Directions page 48

Look at the map. Ask your partner for directions to the places listed at the bottom of your map. When you find the place, write its name on your map. Then give your partner directions to the places that he or she asks about, from where it says, "Start here each time." At the end of this activity, your two maps should look the same.

Example

Student A: How do I get to the print shop?

Student B: That's easy. Go two blocks north on Pine Street. Turn left and go one block west on 3rd Avenue. The print shop will be on your left, in the middle of the block, next to the hardware store.

Student A: Thanks!

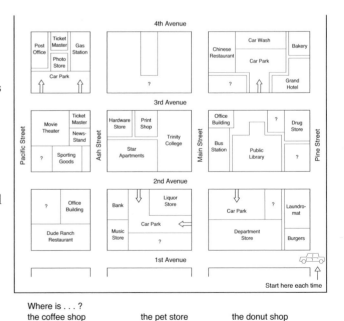

Where is . . . ?

the coffee shop	the pet store	the donut shop
the pizza house	the garage	the toy store
the government building	the supermarket	the candy store

7 **Using Vocabulary** page 57

The following list contains statements using the idioms from this section. Student A will read an item from his or her list. Select the appropriate response from your list.

Student B

a. Don't spend more than you earn.

b. Because the tickets cost an arm and a leg.

c. I'm broke again. I can't pay my rent.

d. Maybe you should get a part-time job.

4 **Pair Practice with Teens and Tens** page 67

Student B

1. Read the following sentences to your partner.

   1. I have only 30 cents in my wallet.

   2. She weighs 115 pounds.

   3. The sweater cost $40.05.

   4. Your change is $60.60.

   5. She was born in 1919.

   6. Our business office is at 7040 Adams Street.

   7. Today one U.S. dollar traded for 1.14 Euros.

2. Your partner will read some sentences with numbers to you. Circle the numbers you hear.

   1. $17 $70

   2. 160   116

   3. 90   19

   4. $15.50 $50.50

   5. 1813   1830

   6. 1617   1670

   7. 140   114

7 **Reviewing Vocabulary** page 80

The following list contains statements using the new vocabulary from this section. Student A will read an item from his or her list. Select the appropriate response from your list.

Student B

a. Yeah. I complained about it to my apartment manager.

b. Yeah. She's supporting me while I finish my B.A.

c. It was the worst. It snowed for five days straight.

d. He spends all his time studying. I almost never see him.

e. No thanks. I'm not in the mood.

4 **Asking and Answering Negative Tag Questions** page 93

Use the statements below to make negative tag questions. Decide if the intonation should rise or fall. Then ask your partner the questions.

Student B

1. You speak _____ (language)... , don't you?

2. _____ (an actor or actress) is from England...

3. The verb tenses in English are difficult to understand...

4. The textbook for this class is (expensive, useful, etc.)...

5. The capital of Canada is Toronto*...

6. The _____ (type of food) at _____ (name of restaurant) is _____ (delicious, terrible, etc.)...

* The capital of Canada is not Toronto; it's Ottawa.

7 **Using Vocabulary** page 106

The following list contains statements using the new vocabulary from this section. Student A will read an item from his or her list. Select the appropriate response from your list.

Student B

a. Yeah, come on in.

b. I have to finish this paper by 10 A.M. Time is running out.

c. I just checked up on her. She's sleeping.

d. I'm tired! I don't want to go to school today!

e. He decided to stay home for a couple of years and bring up his kids.

f. My mother.

g. Yes, it's getting dark. I'd better take off.

h. I know. I told the manager, and he's going to look into it.

8 **Asking for a Favor** page 107

Read the situations on the following list and ask your partner for help or for a favor. Your partner must give an appropriate response.

Example

It's Thursday. Your library books are due tomorrow. Ask your partner to return the books to the library for you.

B: My library books are due tomorrow. Could you please return them to the library for me?

A: I'm sorry, but I'm not going there today.

Student B

1. Your partner speaks English very well. Ask your partner to read your composition and check the grammar.

2. Ask your partner to help you paint your bathroom on Saturday.

3. You need to move a heavy table. Ask your partner to help you.

6 Reviewing Vocabulary page 154

The following list contains statements using the new vocabulary from this section. Student A will read an item from his or her list. Select the appropriate response from your list.

Student B

a. I guess he's a little slow to catch on.

b. Please have a seat. The doctor is with another patient right now.

c. Really? You're lucky to have such a close friendship.

d. No, I'm in the dark too.

e. That's hard to say. In just a few years, I hope.

f. You have to be patient. Friendships don't happen so quickly.

g. He did? I thought he was your best friend!

h. I agree. She always smiles when I see her.

2 Using Interjections page 165

Work in pairs to practice using interjections.

Student B

1. Listen to your partner and choose the proper response from the following list.

   a. Uh-oh, I wonder what's wrong.

   b. What happened? Are you hurt?

   c. Uh-uh. The directions were too confusing.

   d. You can share mine.

2. Now say the following sentences to your partner and wait for a response.

   1. Do you think it's going to rain tonight?

   2. You need the past participle here, not the present.

   3. Uh-oh, I left my wallet in the restroom!

   4. Here's your dictionary... oops!

6 Reviewing Vocabulary page 178

The following list contains statements using the new vocabulary from this section. Student A will read an item from his or her list. Select the appropriate response from your list.

Student B

a. I can't stand them. I prefer comedies.

b. It's hummus. It's from the Middle East. I love it too.

c. No. It rained all day Saturday and Sunday, so we came home early.

d. Really? What's his name?

e. OK. I'll take it back to the store.

f. Because we didn't see eye to eye on anything.

Chapter 10 Part 3

3 Asking and Answering Affirmative Tag Questions page 236

Use the statements on the list below to make affirmative tag questions with rising intonation (asking for information). Your partner should answer truthfully.

Example

You read: You're not from France.

You ask: You're not from France, are you?

Your partner answers: Yes, I am (if he or she is from France).

No, I'm not (if he or she is not from France).

Student B

1. You don't eat meat…

2. There's no test tomorrow…

3. You don't have a computer (cell phone)…

4. Milk isn't good for adults…

Chapter 4 Part 2

11 **What Would You Do?** page 89

Read about your background and qualifications before the interview.

A. *Applicants for Manager*

1A. Education: High school graduate

Experience: Two years as the night manager at another supermarket

Skills: Well-organized; good communication skills with the workers

2A. Education: B.A. in management

Experience: Managed a fast-food restaurant in London for five years; good recommendations

Skills: None specifically related to managing a supermarket, but highly motivated and eager to learn

3A. Education: B.A. in chemistry

Experience: Four years managing another supermarket; had some trouble communicating with the workers there

Skills: Have also worked as a checker, stock clerk, butcher, and truck driver

B. *Applicants for Butcher*

1B. Education: High school graduate and completed trade school for butchers

Experience: None

Skills: Know how to cut and prepare every kind of meat

2B. Education: High school graduate

Experience: Worked in parents' butcher shop during the summers since age 12

Skills: Know how to cut and prepare most kinds of meat

* This is the person who puts groceries in bags after the checker has entered the price in the cash register.

3B. Education: Master's degree in sociology

Experience: Worked as a butcher's helper at another supermarket for four years

Skills: Know how to cut and prepare most kinds of meat; speak three languages

C. *Applicants for Stock Clerk*

1C. Education: High school graduate

Experience: None

Skills: Honest and willing to work hard; need this first job in order to get experience

2C. Education: Tenth grade

Experience: Worked as a stock clerk in another supermarket; work was good but sometimes was late

Skills: Nothing special

3C. Education: High school graduate

Experience: Worked in an office for six months; excellent references

Skills: Can read and follow directions very well

D. *Applicants for Checker*

1D. Education: Eighth grade

Experience: Worked as a checker at another market for 15 years

Skills: Know how to operate cash register; polite and helpful

2D. Education: High school graduate

Experience: None in a supermarket

Skills: Learned how to operate cash register while working in a department store; received Employee of the Month award for outstanding customer service

3D. Education: B.A. in English

Experience: Worked at another market as a stock clerk and bagger* for four years

Skills: Don't know how to use a cash register yet, but learn quickly

Chapter 5 Part 2

9 **What Would You Do?** page 112

"The Tokyo District Court… rejected the husband's demand for damages but did ask the woman to return her wedding rings and a cash gift of $8,000."

Chapter 7 Part 3

3 **Guessing Meanings of Slang Expressions** page 165

1. freaked out—to become extremely upset
2. to shoot some hoops—play basketball
3. cheesy—tacky
4. goofy—silly
5. lose it—to lose control, or lose one's temper
6. pigged out—to overeat
7. chill—relaxed
8. bummed out—discouraged, depressed
9. wiped out—exhausted
10. chickened out—to back out of something because of fear

Sample Abbreviations and Symbols to Use in Taking Notes

Mathematical symbols to use in expressing relationships among ideas:

=	is like, equals, means (in defining a term)
≠	is unlike, not the same as
#	number
<	is smaller than
>	is larger than
+	plus, in addition, and

Other useful symbols:

&	and
%	percent
$	dollars
@	at
?	question, something unclear
~	approximately
↑	increase, go up
↓	decrease, go down
→	causes (as in A → B)
♀	male
♂	female
"	same as above (repeated or used again)
∴	therefore, as a result

Other useful symbols:

A.M.	morning	w/o	without
P.M.	afternoon or evening	yr.	year
e.g.	for example	mo.	month
i.e.	that is, in other words	wk.	week
re:	concerning or regarding	no.	number
etc.	and so on	pd.	paid
vs.	versus	ft.	foot
ch.	chapter	lb.	pound
p., pp.	page, pages	cm	centimeter
w/	with	km	kilometer

Audioscript

CHAPTER 1

Education and Student Life

PART 1 Conversation: On a College Campus

3 **Comprehension Questions** page 5

4 **Listening for Stressed Words** page 6

Nancy: Good morning! Are you here for the English placement test?

Mari: Yes, I am.

Nancy: What's your name?

Mari: Mariko Honda.

Nancy: Could I see some identification?

Mari: Is my passport OK?

Nancy: Yes. All right.... let me find your name on our list... OK Mariko, you can go in. The test will start in about ten minutes.

Mari: Thank you.

Mari: Excuse me, is this seat taken?

Alex: Pardon?

Mari: Is anyone sitting here?

Alex: Ah, no.

Mari: Thanks. I'm glad the test hasn't started yet. I thought I was going to be late.

Alex: Me too. I had to rush here to be on time. I'm Alex, by the way.

Mari: Oh, nice to meet you. My name is Mariko. Or just Mari, for short.

Alex: Nice to meet you, Mari.

Mari: Where are you from?

Alex: Mexico. And you?

Mari: Japan.

Alex: Really? Your English accent is really good.

Mari: Oh, that's because my grandmother is American. We always spoke

English when I was little, so I can speak pretty well, but my reading and writing are really weak.

Alex: I see. So, um, are you planning to go to college here?

Mari: Yes, exactly.

Alex: What's your major?

Mari: Business administration. How about you?

Alex: The same!

Mari: Cool! How long have you been studying here?

Alex: You mean in the English program?

Mari: Yeah.

Alex: This is my second semester.

Mari: Oh, so you know the campus pretty well?

Alex: Oh, yeah.

Mari: Could you tell me how to get to the gym? I want to go work out after the test.

Alex: The gym? Yeah, it's next to the Student Center, across from the grad dorms.

Mari: Sorry... the what?

Alex: The grad dorms. Um, the dormitories for graduate students. Here, I can show you on the campus map...

Mari: That's OK, I know.

Alex: I'm actually planning to go there, too. Want to go together?

Mari: Sounds great.

Announcement:

Good morning everyone. The test is going to start in about five minutes. Please put away your cell phones, iPads, all electronic devices. Start filling out the green information sheet and raise your hand if you have any questions. I or one of the other teachers will be happy to help you.

Alex: The green paper... here it is. Well, good luck on the test.

Mari: Thanks, you too.

6 Listening for Reductions page 8

1.

Student: Hi. I'm here to take the English placement test.

Teacher: OK. What is your name?

Student: Phailin Montri.

Teacher: Could you spell that for me, please?

2.

Paul: I have to leave early tomorrow. This morning I had to rush to catch the bus and I was almost late to work.

Marine: What time are you going to leave?

Paul: Around 7:30.

3.

Lara: Ann, this is my friend Richard.

Richard: Nice to meet you. Where are you from?

Ann: Toronto.

Richard: Oh, you mean you're Canadian?

Ann: Right.

PART 2 Lecture: Academic Honesty

3 Taking Notes on the Introduction page 12

Teacher: Good morning. Welcome to English 4. How's everyone doing? Did everyone get a chance to look at the course syllabus online? No? OK, well since this is our first meeting, I'd like to go over a couple of things quickly. First, if you looked at the syllabus, then you saw that we're going to do a lot of writing in this course—at least four essays and a term paper. And you probably saw that I said something about academic honesty also. Did you get that? Actually, I'd like to spend a little time on that topic right now, just to be sure. I mean, everyone knows that cheating is not okay, but I want to go over the specific types of cheating that students are sometimes confused about—especially international students who come from different cultures, with different customs. So let's talk about types of cheating, how to avoid it and finally, about what can happen if you get caught.

4 Taking Effective Lecture Notes (Part 1) page 13

Teacher: To start, who can give me some examples of cheating?

Student A: Um, copying test answers from another student…

Teacher: Yes, obviously…

Student B: Using notes during an exam.

Teacher: Yeah, what else?

Student C: Copying homework from a classmate?

Teacher: Right. What else?

Student: Texting the answers to someone.

Teacher: Yes. That's why I don't allow students to use phones in my class. Anything else?

Teacher: What about plagiarism? It's right here at the bottom of my syllabus: P-L-A-G-I-A–R-I-S-M. This is especially important in a writing class. Plagiarism means using other people's paragraphs, sentences or unique ideas as your own writing. In other words, it's borrowing other peoples' writing or ideas and not using quotation marks or saying where you found them. So now let me ask you: Are these things considered plagiarism? One: cutting and pasting information from a website.

Class: Yes.

Teacher: Right. OK, two: copying information from a book, magazine, newspaper or any other published source.

Class: Yes/No.

Teacher: The answer is yes. I'll explain why in a minute. OK, next: buying an essay or term paper online, you know, from places like easyessays.com and services like that.

Class: Yes.

Teacher: Good. In addition, asking your friend or cousin to write your essay or term paper is also plagiarism. And this includes asking them to write several sentences or paragraphs for you, even if it's not the whole paper.

Now, I want to mention that people in different cultures think of cheating, of plagiarism, in different ways. In some traditional cultures in Asia and the Middle East, teachers expect students to use words and ideas of famous, well-respected people. And they're not expected to change those words or even mention the source. That's because the teachers already should know where the words came from. But in Western cultures, we believe that words and original ideas belong to their owners. You know, like this computer on my desk here belongs to me. The same with my ideas. If you repeat my ideas, you need to give me credit. You need to mention my name, that you got it from me. And that's what I want to talk about next. How to give credit, how to mention the source so that you can avoid plagiarism.

6. Taking Effective Lecture Notes (Part 2) page 14

Teacher: OK, so let's talk about how to avoid plagiarism.

To show clearly that sentences or ideas are not yours, there are two things you can do. One, you can quote them. Quote means repeating a speaker's exact words. If you do this, you have to put quotation marks at the beginning and at the end of the text you're quoting. Like these.

The second thing you can do is paraphrase or summarize the original text. Basically this means presenting the original information but in your own way, using your own words. So you can change the original vocabulary, the original grammar, but you can't change the original meaning. And you can't add your opinion to it. For example, if I say "We're going to have a test two weeks from today," the paraphrase would be "The teacher is going to give an exam the week after next." See how I changed the sentence but not the meaning? This was a simple example, but paraphrasing

and summarizing are not easy to do. I'll teach you some specific ways later this semester.

And finally—and this is really important—whether you use an exact quote or paraphrase or summarize, always remember to cite sources. By cite, I mean give information about who said the original words and where you found them. If the information came from a website, give the web address and the date you visited the website. If it's from a newspaper article, of course you'll need to cite the name of the newspaper, the name of the writer, the date, the page, etcetera. Don't worry; later in this course, I'll teach you exactly how to do this as well, you know, how to cite sources in the right way.

OK, I think you all got my point. I want you to produce original work in my class. I don't expect perfect writing, just honest, original work. If you don't, if you cheat, I'll have to follow university rules. And I'm sorry to say, the rules, the penalties, are very strict. Let's talk about those next.

PART 3 Strategies for Better Listening and Speaking

Focus on Testing: Using Context Clues page 17

Conversation 1

A: Are they posted yet?

B: No, they're coming out on Friday.

A: I think I'm gonna get a C.

B: Oh, come on, you always say that.

Question 1:
What are the women talking about?

B: Don't worry. I'm sure you'll get a good grade. You always do.

Conversation 2

Man: … I hate economics.

Woman: You've been saying that all semester. Why don't you switch?

Man: It's too late! I'm already in my third year. I'm supposed to graduate next year.

Woman: Why did you choose it if you hate it so much?

Man: I didn't. My parents wanted me to study it, and I didn't want to disappoint them.

Question 2: *Why is the man unhappy?*

Man: Economics is the wrong major for me, but now I have to finish it.

Conversation 3

A: Do you have time to go get some coffee?

B: No, I have an appointment with Dr. Brown in the academic affairs office.

A: About what?

B: About studying abroad next year. I'm spending next semester in Brazil, remember? Dr. Brown is gonna help me select my classes.

A: Well, good luck. I've heard he's really helpful.

Question 3: *Who is Dr. Brown?*

B: Yeah, I'm lucky to have him as my advisor.

Conversation 4

Student: Professor Cates?

Professor: Oh, hello Darla, come in.

Student: You said you wanted to talk to me about my essay?

Professor: Yes. Well, I checked the originality of your paper on the Internet. According to the website I used, only 25 percent of your essay is original.

Student: Uh... really? Only 25 percent? But I was really careful to use my own words.

Question 4:
What is the professor probably thinking?

Professor: You need to be more careful about plagiarism, Darla. I'm going to let you rewrite your paper this time, but if it happens again, you will receive an F.

① Listening for Intonation Clues page 18

Conversation 1A

Sarah: Hello?

Mark: Hi Sarah. How's it going?

Sarah: Pretty good, thanks. How are you?

Mark: Good. Listen, I finished work early and I was wondering if you'd like to go to a movie with me.

Sarah: When—tonight?

Mark: Yeah.

Sarah: Oh Mark, I would really love to go with you, but I can't. I have to take care of some things here at my apartment.

Mark: Oh yeah? What's going on?

Sarah: You remember my roommate, Janna?

Mark: Yeah, sure. You're always talking about her. What about her?

Sarah: Well, she's moving out.

Question 1A: *How does the woman sound?*

Mark: That's great! Maybe now you can find a nice new roommate.

Conversation 1B

Sarah: Hello?

Mark: Hi Sarah. How's it going?

Sarah: Pretty good, thanks. How are you?

Mark: Good. Listen, I finished work early and I was wondering if you'd like to go to a movie with me.

Sarah: When—tonight?

Mark: Yeah.

Sarah: Oh Mark, thanks for asking, but I can't. I have to take care of some things here at my apartment.

Mark: Oh yeah? What's going on?

Sarah: You remember my roommate, Janna?

Mark: Yeah, sure. You're always talking about her. What about her?

Sarah: Well, she's moving out.

Question 1B: *How does the woman sound?*

Mark: That's too bad. I know how much you enjoyed living with her.

Conversation 2A

Robby: Hi Mom.

Mom: Hi honey.

Robby: What's up?

Mom: I'm just calling to remind you it's grandma's birthday…

Robby: I know…

Mom: … so you don't forget to call her this time.

Robby: I won't forget, Mom.

Mom: Because last year you forgot, and she was upset.

Robby: I know Mom. It won't happen again.

Mom: Yeah, well, that's what you said about Dad's birthday, and you forgot that, too.

Robby: I know. I had a big test that day.

Mom: So call Grandma, OK?

Robby: OK, I will!

Question 2A: *How does Robby sound?*

Robby: You know, Mom, it's really annoying when you keep telling me the same thing over and over again.

Conversation 2B

Robby: Hi Mom.

Mom: Hi honey.

Robby: What's up?

Mom: I'm just calling to remind you it's grandma's birthday…

Robby: I know…

Mom: … so you don't forget to call her this time.

Robby: I won't forget, Mom.

Mom: Because last year you forgot, and she was upset.

Robby: I know Mom. It won't happen again.

Mom: Yeah, well, that's what you said about Dad's birthday, and you forgot that, too.

Robby: I know. I had a big test that day.

Mom: So call Grandma, OK?

Robby: OK, I will.

Question 2B: *How does Robby sound?*

Robby: Tell you what, I'll do it right now so that I don't forget.

3 **Expressions of Location in Context** page 23

1. The library is across the quad from the Language Arts building.

2. There's a student parking lot at the intersection of Lass Avenue and Dale Ave.

3. The Information Technology building is between the stadium and the gymnasium.

4. The Fine Arts building is next to the sculpture garden.

5. There are parking lots on both sides of Dale Ave.

6. The bookstore is opposite the student center.

7. The Computer Science building is beside the Fine Arts building.

8. The Language Arts building is beside the Cafeteria.

CHAPTER 2 **City Life**

PART 1 Conversation: Finding a Place to Live

3 **Comprehension Questions** page 29

4 **Listening for Stressed Words** page 30

Nancy: Hello?

Mari: May I speak to Nancy, please?

Nancy: Speaking.

Mari: Uh hi, uh, my name is Mari, and I'm calling about the room for rent. I saw your ad at the campus housing office.

Nancy: Oh, right. OK, uh, are you a student?

Mari: Well, right now I'm just studying English, but I'm planning to start college full-time in March.

Nancy: I see. Where are you living now?

Mari: I've been living in a house with some other students, but I don't like it there.

Nancy: Why? What's the problem?

Mari: Well, first of all, it's really noisy, and it's not very clean. The other people in the house are real slobs. I mean they never lift a finger to clean up after themselves. It really bugs me! I need a place that's cleaner and more private.

Nancy: Well, it's really quiet here. We're not home very much.

Mari: What do you do?

Nancy: I teach English at the college.

Mari: Wait a minute! Didn't we meet yesterday at the placement exam?

Nancy: Oh... you're the girl from Japan! What was your name again?

Mari: Mari...

Nancy: Right. What a small world!

Mari: It really is. By the way, who else lives in the house? The ad said there are three people.

Nancy: Well besides me there's my husband, Andrew, and my cousin, Jeff. He's a musician and a part-time student. Uh, are you OK with having male roommates?

Mari: Sure, as long as they're clean and not too noisy.

Nancy: Don't worry. They're both easy to live with.

Mari: OK. Um, is the neighborhood safe?

Nancy: Oh sure. We haven't had any problems, and you can walk to school from here.

Mari: Well, it sounds really nice. When can I come by and see it?

Nancy: Can you make it this evening around five? Then you can meet the guys too.

Mari: Yeah, five o'clock is good. What's the address?

Nancy: It's 3475 Hayworth Avenue. Do you know where that is?

Mari: No, I don't.

Nancy: OK. From University Village you go seven blocks east on Olympic Avenue. At the intersection of Olympic and Alfred, there's a stoplight. Turn left and go up one and a half blocks. Our house is in the middle of the block on the left.

Mari: That sounds easy.

Nancy: Yeah, you can't miss it. Listen, I've got to go. Someone's at the door. See you this evening.

Mari: OK, see you later. Bye.

Nancy: Bye-bye.

 6 **Listening for Reductions** page 33

Conversation 1

Mari: Hey Jeff, where are you going?

Jeff: I want to get a present for Nancy. It's her birthday, you know.

Mari: Yeah, I know. What do you think I should get her?

Jeff: Well, she likes music. How about a CD?

Conversation 2

Nancy: How do you like my new haircut, Mari?

Mari: It's great! Who's your hairstylist?

Nancy: His name's Jose.

Mari: Can you give me his phone number?

Nancy: Sure, but he's always very busy. You can try calling him, but he might not be able to see you until next month.

Conversation 3

Andrew: What do you want to do tonight, Nancy?

Nancy: Nothing special. I've got to stay home and correct my students' compositions.

PART 2 Lecture: Neighborhood Watch Meeting

4 Taking Notes on Statistics page 38

1. A year ago there were 48 burglaries in your area; this year it's gone up to 60 so far.

2. The number of car thefts has almost doubled.

3. Did you know that in half of all burglaries, 50 percent, the burglars enter through unlocked doors or windows?

5 Listening for Transitions page 39

6 Taking Notes page 40

Part 1

Police Officer: Good evening. My name is Officer Jenkins. Thanks for inviting me tonight. OK, so, as you know, there have been a number of break-ins recently in your neighborhood, and even though it's true that there's been very little *violent* crime, um, especially compared to other parts of the city, burglary and car theft are both up in this area. Let me give you some statistics. OK, a year ago there were... 48 burglaries in your area; this year it's gone up to 60 so far, and the number of car thefts has almost doubled, too. Now, I'm not here to try to scare you. What I want to do tonight is to give you some simple suggestions that will make your homes and automobiles safer. OK?

So first of all, let's talk about lights outside the house. If you live in a house, you need to have lights both in the front of your house and in the back, and be sure to turn on those lights at night. In my opinion this is the most important thing you can do to prevent burglaries.

Next, let's talk about lights inside the house. It's...

Woman in Audience: Excuse me, what about apartments? I mean, I live in an apartment building...

Police Officer: Yeah, good question. If you live in an apartment building, you want to have good, bright lighting in the garage, the hallways, and by the door to your apartment. If a light is broken, don't ignore it. Report it to your manager immediately. And whether you live in a house or an apartment, it's a good idea to put automatic timers on your lights. You know what a timer is, right? It's like a clock that turns on your lights automatically, so it looks like someone is home even if you're out. Are you with me on that?

All right, then... the next topic I want to discuss is locks. First of all, forget cheap locks 'cause they're not safe. Every door in your place should have a deadbolt... um, a deadbolt at least one inch thick. Also, there are special locks you can buy for your windows. By the way, did you know that in half of all burglaries, 50 percent, the burglars enter through unlocked doors or windows? I'm telling you, even in a peaceful neighborhood like this, where you know all your neighbors, you have to get into the habit of keeping your windows and doors locked.

Part 2

Police Officer: OK, now let's move on and talk about how you can prevent car theft. First, if you have a garage, use it for your car, not for your Ping-Pong table! But seriously, the most important thing is—and I hope this is obvious—if you've got valuables in the car, hide them in the trunk. Don't leave them out on the seat, not even for five minutes! Last week we got a report from a guy who left his laptop on the car seat while he ran in to buy a cup of coffee. When he came back it was gone. The thief just broke the car window and reached in and took it. And also...

Man in Audience: What about a car alarm?

Police Officer: Well, most research shows that noisy alarms don't do anything to prevent car theft. It's better to have the kind of device thieves can see, like a lock on your steering wheel. But the best thing of all is just to lock your car and keep valuables out of sight.

All right. Now my last point is what you,

as neighbors, can do to help each other. The main thing is that when you go on vacation, ask someone to watch your house for you, to collect your mail, take in your newspaper, stuff like that. Also, if you see something unusual, like a strange van or truck in your neighbor's driveway, or people carrying furniture out, *don't* go out there and try to stop it. Just call the police! And one more thing. Each of you should put this Neighborhood Watch decal—this picture right here of the man in a coat looking over his shoulder—in your front window. This tells criminals that this area has a Neighborhood Watch and that someone might be watching them. OK, are there any questions?

Man in Audience: Yeah, there's something I want to know… Do you think it's a good idea to keep a gun in the house?

Police Officer: Well now, that is a very complicated question. I think that it's a bad idea to have a gun in your house, especially if you have kids. Thousands of people die in gun accidents each year in this country. So, in my opinion, it's just not safe to have a gun in your house. But of course it *is* legal to have a gun, if that's what you want. Just make sure you get the proper license and that you take a course in gun safety, OK? All right. Anything else?

PART 3 Strategies for Better Listening and Speaking

Focus on Testing:
Using Context Clues page 44

Conversation 1

Manager: Yes? Who is it?

Tenant: It's Donna from 206. I've got a check for you.

Manager: Oh, it's you. Do you know it's the fifth of the month?

Tenant: Yes, Mr. Bradley. I'm sorry. I know it was due on the first, but my grandma got sick, and I had to go out of town suddenly.

Question 1: *Who is the man?*

Manager: Look, my job as manager here

is to collect the rent on the first. If you're late again next month you'll have to look for another place to live.

Conversation 2

Tenant: OK, Mr. Bradley. But look, while I'm here, I need to talk to you about a couple of things.

Manager: Yeah?

Tenant: First, about the cockroaches. They're all over the kitchen again. I'm sick of them!

Manager: Have you used the spray I gave you?

Tenant: It's no good. I need something stronger to kill those horrible bugs once and for all.

Question 2:
Who will the manager probably need to call?

Manager: OK, I'll call the exterminator next week.

Conversation 3

Tenant: Next week?! Last week you said you'd fix the hole in the ceiling, and you still haven't done that! I'm fed up with waiting for you to fix things around here!

Question 3: *What can you guess about Donna's apartment?*

Tenant: Why should I pay so much rent for a place in such bad condition?

Manager: Well, you're not the only tenant in this building. If you don't like it, why don't you move out?

Conversation 4

John: Hi, Donna. What do you need this time?

Donna: Hello, John. A couple of eggs. Do you mind?

John: No, come on in.

Question 4:
How does John feel about Donna's request?

Donna: Thanks so much, John!

John: You're welcome!

Conversation 5

John: Hi, Donna. What do you need this time?

Donna: Hello, John. A couple of eggs. Do you mind?

John: No, come on in.

Question 5:
How does John feel about Donna's request?

Donna: Thanks, John.

John: OK, but next time go ask somebody else, all right?

PART 4 Real-World Task: Following Directions

2 **Following Directions** page 48

1. You are at the X. Go two blocks west on 2nd Avenue. Turn left and go down one block. What is on your left?

2. You are at the intersection of Main Street and Third Avenue. Go one block south on Main. Turn left. Go straight for half a block. What is on your left?

3. You have just eaten dinner at the French restaurant on the corner of 4th and Pine. Go south on Pine Street to 2nd Avenue. Turn right. Go one block west on 2nd. Turn left. Go down Main Street for half a block. What is on your right?

4. You work in the office building at the intersection of 3rd and Main. After work you decide to go shopping. Go one block east on 3rd. Turn left and go one block up Pine Street. Turn right. Go one block east until you reach Oak Street. What is on your right?

CHAPTER 3 Business and Money

PART 1 Conversation: Borrowing Money

3 **Comprehension Questions** page 53

4 **Listening for Stressed Words** page 54

Dad: Hello?

Jeff: Hi, Dad.

Dad: Jeff! How are you?

Jeff: I'm fine, Dad. How's Mom? Did she get over her cold?

Dad: Yes, she's fine now. She went back to work yesterday.

Jeff: That's good. Um, Dad, I need to ask you something.

Dad: Sure, son, what is it?

Jeff: Well, uh, the truth is, I'm broke again. Could you lend me $200 just till the end of the month?

Dad: Broke again? Jeff, when you moved in with Nancy and Andrew, you said you could make ends meet. But this is the third time you've asked me for help!

Jeff: I know, I know, I'm sorry. But, see, my old guitar broke, and I had to buy a new one. I can't play on a broken guitar, right?

Dad: Look Jeff, if you want to play in a band, that's OK with me, but you can't keep asking me to pay for it!

Jeff: OK, OK, you're right. But what do you think I ought to do? Everything costs an arm and a leg around here.

Dad: Well, first of all, I think you'd better go on a budget. Make a list of all your income and all your expenses. And then it's simple. Don't spend more than you earn.

Jeff: But that's exactly the problem! My expenses are always larger than my income. That's why I need to borrow money from you.

Dad: Then maybe you should work more hours at the computer store.

Jeff: Dad! I already work 15 hours a week! How can I study and work and find time to play with my band?

Dad: Come on, Jeff, when I was your age…

Jeff: I know, I know. When you were my age you were already married and working and going to school.

Dad: That's right. And if I could do it, why can't you?

Jeff: Because I'm not you, Dad, that's why!

Dad: All right, Jeff, calm down. I don't expect you to be like me. But I can't lend you any more money. Your mother and I are on a budget too, you know.

Jeff: Maybe I should just drop out of school, work full-time, and play in the band in the evenings. I can go back to school later.

Dad: I wouldn't do that if I were you.

Jeff: Yeah, but you're not me, remember? It's my life!

Dad: All right, Jeff. Let's not argue. Why don't you think about this very carefully and call me back in a few days. In the meantime, you'd better find a way to pay for that new guitar.

Jeff: Yes, Dad.

Dad: All right. Good-bye, son.

Jeff: Bye.

6 Listening for Reductions page 56

Customer: Hi, my name is Chang Lee.

Teller: How can I help you?

Customer: I want to check my balance.

Teller: OK. Can I have your account number, please?

Customer: 381335.

Teller: Your balance is $201.

Customer: OK. And I asked my father to wire me some money. I'd like to know if it's arrived.

Teller: I'm sorry, your account doesn't show any deposits.

Customer: Oh, no. I need to pay my rent tomorrow. What do you think I ought to do?

Teller: Well, we're having some computer problems today. So, why don't you call us later to check again. Or you can come back. We're open till five.

Customer: OK, thanks.

Teller: You're welcome.

9 Distinguishing Between *Can* and *Can't* page 58

1. Sue can pay her bills by herself.
2. Jeff can't work and study at the same time.
3. I can't find my wallet.
4. You can pay with a credit card here.
5. You can't open an account without identification.
6. Anna can't work in the United States.
7. I can lend you five dollars.
8. We can't make ends meet.
9. You can apply for a loan at the bank across the street.
10. Jeff can play the guitar very well.

PART 2 Lecture: Entrepreneurs

3 Taking Notes page 61

4 Outlining the Lecture page 63

Lecturer: How many of you know the name Jeff Bezos? OK, how about Amazon.com? Have you heard of that? Well, Amazon is the world's first and largest Internet bookstore. And Jeff Bezos is the man who started Amazon back in 1995. Five years later, Amazon was serving millions of customers in 120 different countries. Amazing, right? And this is the reason why, in 1999, Jeff Bezos was selected as *Time* magazine's Person of the Year, a very great honor.

Now, Jeff Bezos is actually not the topic of my lecture today, but he is a perfect example of my topic, which is entrepreneurs. That's *entrepreneurs*, spelled E-N-T-R-E-P-R-E-N-E-U-R-S. *Entrepreneur* is a French word meaning a person who starts a completely new business or industry; um, someone who does something no one else has done before; or who does it in a completely new way, like Jeff Bezos. Entrepreneurs like Jeff Bezos are very highly respected in American society and, I think, in many other countries too. So, in today's lecture I want to talk about three things. First, the characteristics of entrepreneurs—I mean, what kind of people they are. Second, the kind of background they come from. And third, the entrepreneurial process, that is, the steps entrepreneurs follow when they create a new business.

OK, let's begin by looking at the characteristics or, um, the qualities, of entrepreneurs. There are two qualities that I think all entrepreneurs have in common. First, entrepreneurs have vision. I mean that they have the ability to see opportunities that other people simply do not see. Let's look again at the example of Jeff Bezos. One day in 1994, he was surfing the Internet when suddenly he had a brilliant idea: why not use the Internet to sell products? Remember, at that time, no one was using the Internet in that way. After doing some research, Bezos decided that the product he wanted to sell was books. That's how Amazon got its start.

The other quality that I think all entrepreneurs have is that they're not afraid to take risks. I mean they're not afraid to fail. As an example, let me tell you about Frederick Smith. He founded FedEx, the company that delivers packages overnight. Smith first suggested the idea for his company in a college term paper. Do you know what grade he got on it? A *C*! Clearly, his professor didn't like the idea, but this didn't stop him. Today FedEx is worth more than 20 billion dollars and employs more than 130,000 people.

OK, we've just seen that all entrepreneurs have at least two important qualities in common. But now let's take a look at some differences. We'll see that their backgrounds can be very different. First of all, some entrepreneurs are well educated, like Jeff Bezos, who graduated from Princeton University. But others, like Bill Gates, the founder of Microsoft, never even finished college. Next, some entrepreneurs come from rich families, like Frederick Smith, the founder of FedEx. In contrast, other entrepreneurs come from poor families, and many are immigrants or the children of immigrants. A great example is Jerry Yang, one of the men who started Yahoo dot com. He was born in Taiwan and came to America as a young boy in the 1970s.

OK, another difference is that although many entrepreneurs start their businesses at a young age, lots of others don't start until age 40 or later. And finally, I think it's important to remind you that entrepreneurs are not always men. A famous woman entrepreneur, for example, is Anita Roddick. She founded The Body Shop. You can find her natural cosmetics shops all over the world. So, to conclude this section, you can see that entrepreneurs come from many different backgrounds.

5 **Taking Notes on a Process** page 64

Lecturer: I want to move on now and take a look at the entrepreneurial process. There are six basic steps that most entrepreneurs follow when they start their businesses. In the first step, they identify a problem; in other words, they see a need or a problem that no one else sees. Then, in the second step, they think of a solution, what needs to be done to solve the problem or meet the need. I think we've already seen several examples today of people who saw a need or an opportunity and then came up with a creative solution.

Step three is to prepare a business plan. This means looking at things like equipment, location, financing, marketing, and so on. There are thousands of details to think about when you start a new business; as a result, this stage can take months or even years.

The next step, the fourth step, is putting together a team—in other words, hiring the right people to work with the entrepreneur in the new business. After that, the fifth step is something called test marketing. That's test marketing. This involves making and selling a small amount of the product or service just to try it out and see if customers like it. And if they do, then, finally, entrepreneurs go to the sixth step, which is raising capital. Capital is another word for money. The entrepreneur has to raise a lot of money, you know, from the bank, or friends, or family, in order to produce and sell the product or service in large quantities.

I want to say, in conclusion, that entrepreneurs like Jeff Bezos are among the most respected people in the United States. They are cultural heroes, like movie stars or sports heroes. Why? Because, starting with a dream and working very hard, these people created companies that solved serious, important problems. They provided jobs for millions of people, and in general their companies made life easier and more pleasant for all of us. If you ever order a book from Amazon, or use natural make-up from the Body Shop, say thanks to the remarkable people who created these companies.

PART 3 Strategies for Better Listening and Speaking

Focus on Testing:
Using Context Clues page 66

Advertisement 1

Every person has valuable possessions that are difficult or impossible to replace; for example, family photographs, jewelry, a passport, old coins, or insurance policies. You should protect these priceless valuables by putting them in a safe place. Lock up your treasures in International Bank, and you'll never have to worry about losing your valuables again.

Question 1: *The speaker is talking about...*

The International Bank Safe-Deposit Box—safety and protection the easy way!

Advertisement 2

Right now International Bank can lend you money for dozens of projects. For instance, remodeling a kitchen or a bathroom can change an old house into an exciting new one. Thinking about solar heating? Need a new roof? International Bank can help you finance them.

Question 2: *The speaker is talking about...*

For any home improvement loan, talk to International Bank first.

Advertisement 3

With an Insta-Teller Card from International Bank, you're close to your money night or day. The Insta-Tellers operate 24 hours a day, seven days a week, 365 days a year. It's an easy way to get cash, pay your bills, make a deposit, or check your balance even when your bank is closed.

Question 3: *The speaker is talking about...*

Insta-Teller automated teller machines—any transaction, any time.

Advertisement 4

How would you like to earn 4.5 percent interest and still be able to take out money any time you need it? You can do both! Just deposit $5,000 and keep a minimum average balance of $500. Come in and ask about our investor's plan.

Question 4: *The speaker is talking about...*

International Bank Investor's Plan—a savings account and more!

3 Distinguishing Between Teens and Tens page 67

1. He paid forty dollars and ten cents for the bottle of wine.

2. **Woman:** How much does this dictionary cost?

   Man: Sixteen ninety-nine.

3. Most credit card companies charge 18 percent interest per month on your outstanding balance.

4. We drove at a speed of ninety miles per hour.

5. I bought my coat in Paris for two hundred and thirty euros.

6. The plane from Buenos Aires carried two hundred and sixty passengers.

7. My dog weighs fourteen and a half kilos.

8. The rent on this apartment is two thousand, two hundred fifteen dollars a month.

9. My aunt lives at seventeen sixty four Wilson Avenue.

10. International Bank is located at eighteen ninety West Second Street.

PART 4 Real-World Task: Balancing a Checkbook

3 Balancing a Checkbook page 70

George: Let's see here. Check number 200. October 25th. Did you write this check?

Martha: Hmm. Thirty dollars and twenty-one cents. Oh, yes. That was last Thursday. ABC Market.

George: OK, so that leaves a balance of four hundred ninety dollars and thirty-one cents. Next: number two-oh-one. Electric bill. Fifty-seven eighty-two. So now we have four hundred thirty-two dollars and forty-nine cents. Next: October 27th. *Time* magazine. I forgot to enter the amount.

Martha: I remember that. It was $35.

George: OK. So that leaves three ninety-seven forty-nine. Now what's this $70?

Martha: That was for your sister's birthday present.

George: Oh, yes. OK.... And here's check two-oh-five. When did we pay the dentist?

Martha: The same day I deposited my paycheck. November first.

George: Fine. So after the deposit, the balance was one thousand three hundred ninety-seven dollars and eighteen cents. And then I made the house payment, check number two-oh-six. That's four hundred twelve dollars, and the credit card payment—that's a hundred fifty-five, so now our balance is eight hundred thirty dollars and eighteen cents.

Martha: You know, George, we should really pay off our credit card balance. The interest is 18 percent a year.

George: You're right. But we can't afford it right now. Look at this car insurance bill! Three hundred five dollars to Auto Insurance of America. And that's just for four months. And what's this... another traffic ticket?

Martha: Last month it was you, this month it was me.

George: Oh, man... How much was it this time?

Martha: Sixty-eight dollars. OK, so what's the balance now?

George: Four hundred fifty-seven dollars and eighteen cents. I guess we're OK for the rest of the month as long as we don't get any more traffic tickets.

CHAPTER **4** Jobs and Professions

PART 1 Conversation: Finding a Job

3 Comprehension Questions page 77

4 Listening for Stressed Words page 78

Mari: Hey, Jeff, what's going on?

Jeff: Oh, I'm looking at the classified ads. It looks like I have to get a job.

Mari: I thought you had a job, at a computer store or something.

Jeff: Yeah, but that's part-time. I need something full-time.

Mari: Really? But what about school? What about your band? How can you work full-time?

Jeff: Well, to tell you the truth, I'm probably going to drop out of school for a while. I'm just not in the mood for studying these days. I'd rather spend my time playing with my band. But my father won't support me if I'm not in school.

Mari: I see... Well, what kind of job do you want to get?

Jeff: Well ideally, something involving music, like in a record store. But if that's not possible... I don't know, but whatever I do, it'll be better than my first job.

Mari: Oh yeah? What was that?

Jeff: Believe it or not, the summer after I finished high school I worked at Burger Ranch.

Mari: You? In a fast-food place? What did you do there?

Jeff: I was a burger flipper. You know, I made hamburgers all day long.

Mari: That sounds like a pretty boring job!

Jeff: It was the worst. And I haven't gone inside a Burger Ranch since I quit that job.

Nancy: Hi, what's so funny?

Jeff: Do you remember my job at the Burger Ranch?

Nancy: Oh yeah. That was pretty awful. But actually, it doesn't sound so bad to me right now.

Mari: Why, Nancy? What's wrong?

Nancy: Oh, I'm just really, really tired. I'm teaching four different classes this term and two of them are really large. Sometimes I think I've been teaching too long.

Mari: How long have you been teaching?

Nancy: Twelve years. Maybe it's time to try something else.

Mari: Like what?

Nancy: Well, I've always wanted to be a writer. I could work at home…

Jeff: Oh, don't listen to her, Mari. She always talks this way when she's had a bad day at school. At least *you* have a good *job*, Nancy. Look at me: I'm broke, and Dad won't lend me any more money…

Nancy: Oh, stop complaining. If you're so poor, why don't you go back to the Burger Ranch?

Mari: Listen you two, stop arguing. Look at me! I can't work at all because I'm an international student.

Jeff: OK, OK. I'm sorry, Nancy. Tell you what. Let's go out to dinner. I'll pay.

Nancy: But you're broke!

Jeff: All right, *you* pay!

6 Listening for Reductions page 80

Manager: I'm going to ask you some questions, OK? What kind of jobs have you had?

Applicant: Mostly factory jobs. The last five years I worked in a plastics factory.

Manager: What did you do there?

Applicant: I used to cut sheets of plastic.

Manager: What do you want to do here?

Applicant: I don't know… I'll do anything. I'm good with my hands, and I'm a hard worker.

Manager: Why don't you fill out an application in the office. It looks like we're going to have an opening next week. I'll call you.

Applicant: Thanks.

PART 2 Lecture: Changes in the U.S. Job Market

5 Listening and Taking Notes on Causes and Effects page 85

1. Because of technology, we're able to manufacture goods by using machines instead of human workers.

2. As a result, thousands of manufacturing jobs don't exist anymore.

3. We're going to need more medical services because people are living longer and longer.

4. Also, because of developments in medical technology, people with serious illnesses are able to live much longer than they could in the past.

5. The main reason for the huge growth in this category is that most married women now work outside the home.

6 Taking Notes on Statistics page 85

1. According to the United States government, approximately 2.5 million manufacturing jobs have disappeared just since the year 2001.

2. At the same time that the number of manufacturing jobs is decreasing, the number of service jobs is probably going to grow by more than 20 million just in the next ten years!

3. Almost half of the jobs on the list are in the field of health care.

4. According to the United States Department of Labor, the number of healthcare jobs will increase by almost 3 million in the next ten years.

5. The number of jobs in the computer industry is expected to grow by almost 30 percent in the next ten years.

7 Taking Notes page 86

8 Outlining the Lecture page 86

Part 1

Lecturer: If you'll be graduating from high school or college in the next year or two, then I'm sure you're very concerned about finding a job. There are two questions that young people like you always ask me. First, what are the best jobs going to be? And second, how can I prepare myself to get one of those good jobs? Well in the next few minutes, I want to try to answer these questions for you, and I hope this information will help you make the right choices about your future career.

Let's start with a little history. In the last 100 years, there's been a big change in the U.S. job market, from a manufacturing economy to a service economy. What does that mean? Well, in a manufacturing economy people *make* things, like cars or furniture or clothes. In a service economy, people *do* things. Uh, they cut your hair, they fix your shoes, they sell you a computer. Uh, airline pilots, doctors, restaurant workers—all of these are examples of service workers. OK? So again, my point is that the number of manufacturing jobs has been going down for quite a long time. Now why do you think that is? What's the cause?

Student 1: I think automation, you know, robots, computers…

Lecturer: That's one reason, yes. Because of technology, we're able to manufacture goods by using machines instead of human workers. As a result, thousands of manufacturing jobs don't exist anymore. OK, can you think of another reason?

Student 2: Foreign competition. I mean… most manufacturing is done outside of the U.S. now, in countries where the labor costs are cheaper.

Lecturer: Yes, that's right. According to the U.S. government, approximately 2.5 million manufacturing jobs have disappeared just since 2001. And that trend is definitely going to continue as we move further into the 21st century.

But now let's talk about service jobs. Here the trend is exactly the opposite. At the same time that the number of manufacturing jobs is decreasing, the number of service jobs is probably going to grow by more than 20 million just in the next ten years! Now, would everybody please look at the handout I gave you, which shows a list of the occupations that will grow the fastest between the years 2002 and 2012. If you study the list carefully, you'll see that most of the jobs on the list are in three categories: health care, computers, and personal care and services. Let me say a few words about each of these categories.

Part 2

Lecturer: First, health care. Almost half of the jobs on the list are in the field of health care. Uh, medical assistants, physician assistants, physical therapy aides, dental hygienists— these are just a few examples. According to the U.S. Department of Labor, the number of healthcare jobs will increase by almost 3 million in the next ten years. And why is that? Simple. We're going to need more medical services because people are living longer and longer. Also, because of developments in medical technology, people with serious illnesses are able to live much longer than they could in the past. And many of them need a lot of special care and medical help.

All right, now, getting back to the list, you can see that there will be many new jobs related to computers. We're going to need people who can design and build computers, like engineers, but in addition, there will be lots of jobs for people who manage and operate computers, like database administrators. As you know, computers are used in everything these days from rockets to coffee machines, so it's no surprise that the number of jobs in the computer industry is expected to grow by almost 30 percent in the next ten years.

Now let me explain the third category, personal care services. Some examples of jobs in this group are caterers, home health workers, and daycare providers. One reason for the huge growth in this category is that most women now work outside the home. So a lot of the work that women used to do in the home, like cooking and taking care of small children, is now done by service workers.

OK, now, while we're looking at the list, there's one more thing I'd like you to notice. Look at all the jobs that have a salary rank of 1. OK? And what do you notice about the educational requirements for those jobs? That's right. They all require at least a bachelor of arts degree.

So in conclusion, let me go back to the two questions I mentioned at the beginning of this talk. First, where will the good jobs be? We've seen today that the areas of greatest growth will be in the fields of computers, health care, and personal services. If you still haven't decided which career you want to follow, you should think about getting a job in one of these fields. However, it's important to remember that many service jobs don't pay very well. The best jobs all require a college education. So the answer to the second question—how you can prepare yourself to get a good job—the answer is simple. Go to college and get a degree. That's the bottom line.

PART 3 Strategies for Better Listening and Speaking

Focus on Testing: Using Context Clues page 91

Conversation 1

Woman: May I see your driver's license, please?

Man: What did I do?

Woman: You ran a red light.

Man: But I'm sure it was yellow.

Question 1: *What's the woman's job?*

Woman: Are you trying to argue with a police officer?

Conversation 2

Woman: Is this your first visit?

Man: No, I come in every six months for a check-up.

Woman: Oh, I see. Did you bring your insurance form with you?

Man: Here it is.

Woman: OK. Take a seat, and the dentist will be with you shortly.

Question 2: *What is the woman's job?*

Man: You're new here, aren't you? What happened to the other receptionist?

Conversation 3

Man: Do you have a reservation?

Woman: Yes, Jackson, party of four.

Man: Inside or out on the patio?

Woman: Outside. And could you bring us some coffee?

Question 3: *What's the man's job?*

Man: I'm the host. I'll ask the waiter to bring you some coffee right away.

Conversation 4

A: Hi Jim. It's Carl. It looks like I'm going to need your professional services this year.

B: I thought you always did your taxes by yourself.

A: Yeah, but this year things are too complicated. I lost money in the stock market, and then I inherited my uncle's house, remember?

B: Hmm. You need professional help, for sure.

Question 4: *What is Jim's job?*

B: But you know, it's not a good idea to use your best friend as your accountant. I think you should find someone else.

Conversation 5

Man: May I help you?

Woman: The sleeves on this jacket are too short. How much will it cost for you to make them longer?

Man: Let me look at it… I can do it for 30 dollars.

Woman: That much?

Question 5: *What's the man's job?*

Man: Well, that's what any tailor would charge.

3 Recognizing the Intonation of Tag Questions page 92

1. We're having a staff meeting tomorrow, aren't we?

2. You're the programmer from Turkey, aren't you?

3. This exercise is easy, isn't it?

4. The supervisor is married, isn't she?

5. Smoking is forbidden here, isn't it?

6. That test was really hard, wasn't it?

7. The secretary speaks Arabic, doesn't he?

8. That training video was really boring, wasn't it?

9. The marketing director speaks beautiful Japanese, doesn't she?

10. We need to sign our names on these reports, don't we?

PART 4 Real-World Task: A Homemaker's Typical Day

4 Sequencing Events page 95

Do you want to know what I do on a typical day? Well, I'll tell you what I did yesterday as an example. I woke up before my wife and son, and the first thing I did was to come into the kitchen and make the coffee. Then I made my son's lunch, you know, to take to school, and after that I started cooking breakfast. I made eggs, oatmeal, and toast because I always want my family to start the day with a full stomach. Then my wife and son came into the kitchen and sat down to eat. While they were eating, I threw a basket of laundry into the washing machine and then I also sat down to eat.

After breakfast I walked my son to the bus stop, and I waited with him until the bus came. I kissed him good-bye and walked home. As soon as I entered the house, the phone rang. It was my mother-in-law. She wanted to know if my wife was still there, but I told her she had just left. So I talked with her for a few more minutes, about the weather and her garden, and then I got off the phone. After

that, uh, let's see, I spent three hours cleaning the house, and after lunch I went shopping for groceries. By then it was three o'clock, and it was already time to pick up my son at the bus stop. I helped him with his homework, and then my wife came home. Normally she gets home at about 6 P.M., but yesterday she was a few minutes early. I was so busy all day that I hadn't had time to water the garden, so I did it while my wife made dinner. Finally, after dinner I washed the dishes while my wife put our son to bed. And then both of us just collapsed in front of the TV.

And that was my day. Nothing glamorous— just really busy!

CHAPTER 5 Lifestyles Around the World

PART 1 Conversation: A Single Mother

3 Comprehension Questions page 103

4 Listening for Stressed Words (Part I) page 104

1. Come on in.

2. They want me to look into a computer problem right away.

3. If he wakes up, just give him a bottle.

4. Listen, I've got to take off.

5. Thanks so much, Jeff, for helping me out.

6. I take care of him from time to time when Sharon's busy.

7. I worried that time was running out.

8. I could never bring up a baby by myself.

9. I'd better check up on Joey.

5 Listening for Stressed Words (Part II) page 104

Jeff: Who's there?

Sharon: It's Sharon and Joey!

Jeff: Hi! Come on in. What's happening?

Sharon: Jeff, can you do me a big favor? I

just got a call from the office. They want me to look into a computer problem right away. Would you mind watching Joey until I get back?

Jeff: Sure, no problem. Is he asleep?

Sharon: Yeah, he just fell asleep ten minutes ago. He usually sleeps for a couple of hours at this time of day. But if he wakes up, just give him a bottle.

Mari: Ooh, what a cute baby! He's so little!

Jeff: Mari, this is our neighbor, Sharon, and her son, Joey. Sharon, this is our new roommate, Mari.

Mari: Nice to meet you.

Sharon: You too. Listen, I've got to take off. Thanks so much, Jeff, for helping me out.

Jeff/Mari: Bye!

Mari: Hey, Jeff, I didn't know you liked babies.

Jeff: Well, Joey is special. I take care of him from time to time when Sharon's busy. And then she does favors for me in return. Like last week she lent me her car.

Mari: And her husband? Is he…

Jeff: She's not married. I don't think she ever was, actually.

Mari: Never?

Jeff: Nope, never. I think she's happy being a single mother.

Mari: Oh. Is that pretty common in America?

Jeff: Well, it's certainly becoming more and more common. Even Nancy used to talk about it. You know, before she got married.

Nancy: Hi, guys.

Jeff/Mari: Hi.

Nancy: Uh, what were you saying about me?

Jeff: That you used to talk about having a baby by yourself before you met Andrew.

Nancy: Oh yeah, I worried that time was running out. You know, like, what if I never got married…

Mari: Maybe I'm old-fashioned, but I could never bring up a baby by myself. I think it would be so difficult…

Nancy: Yeah, raising a child is tough. I'm really lucky I met Andrew.

Mari: And, if you have a baby, you'll have Jeff here to help you with babysitting.

Jeff: We'll see. Speaking of babysitting, I'd better check up on Joey.

PART 2 Lecture: Changes in the American Family

③ Taking Notes on Examples page 109

1. Women today are working in professions that were not as open to them 30 or 40 years ago. To give just one example, today more than half the students in American medical schools are women.

2. Most American homes don't have a full-time homemaker anymore. And that creates new problems for families; problems like who takes care of babies and old people; who shops, cooks, and cleans; who volunteers at the children's school; and so on.

3. In some countries, companies are required by law to give new parents a paid vacation when they have a new baby. Canada, for instance, has a law like that, but the United States does not.

④ Taking Notes (Part I) page 110

⑤ Outlining the Lecture page 110

Lecturer: Have you ever seen the old television show *Father Knows Best*? You probably haven't because it was a popular comedy show in the 1950s—way before you were born. It was about a family: a father, who went to work every day; a mother, who stayed home and took care of the house; and the children—two or three, I can't remember. Anyway, in those days that was considered to be a typical American family.

But today, the American family is very different. First, families are smaller today than before. I mean, people are having fewer children. Second, more and more children are growing up in single-parent families—families with only a mother or only a father. I'm not going to go into the reasons for that here because I want to focus on the third and biggest change in the American family: the role of married mothers and the effects of this new role. Consider these statistics: In the 1950s, only 11 percent of married mothers worked outside the home. In 2002, about 70 percent of mothers were employed.

Why is that? Well, there are two important reasons. The first one, very simply, is that they need the money. These days the cost of living is so high that most families need two salaries in order to make ends meet.

The other reason why married mothers are working in larger and larger numbers is that they have more opportunities than they did 30 or 40 years ago. There are laws in the United States that give women the same opportunity as men to go to college and get jobs. As a result, women today are working in professions that were not as open to them 30 or 40 years ago. To give just one example, today more than half of the students in American medical schools are women.

So, to summarize so far, we've seen that the American family has changed dramatically since the days of those old television shows. In the typical two-parent family today, both the father and the mother have jobs. This means that most American homes don't have a full-time homemaker anymore. And that creates new problems for families: problems like who takes care of babies and grandparents; who shops, cooks, and cleans; who volunteers at the children's school; and so on.

6 Taking Notes (Part II) page 111

Lecturer: To help families with working parents deal with these new problems, some American businesses have introduced new programs and policies to make it easier to work and raise children at the same time. Let me give you five examples of these policies and programs.

The first policy is paid maternity leave. What we're talking about is a woman taking time off from work when she has a baby. American law requires companies to give a woman up to 12 weeks of leave when she has a baby. But the problem is that the companies aren't required to pay for those 12 weeks. As a result, many women are forced to go back to work much sooner than they want to. Recently some companies, at least the big ones, have started to offer paid maternity leave. But it's still kind of rare. By the way, a small percentage of companies now also offer *paternity* leave—that means that fathers can take time off for a new baby. I would like to see a law that requires all companies to give paid leave to both mothers and fathers for a new baby. Canada, for instance, already has a law like that.

OK, moving along. Here's another example of a policy that helps working families. As you know, big companies like IBM or General Motors often transfer their employees to other cities, right? Well, if a company transfers the husband, for instance, this might create a problem for the wife because now she has to find a new job too. So now there are companies that will help the husband or wife of the transferred worker find a new job.

A third policy that many companies now offer is called "flextime." Here's what that means. In the United States, a normal workday is from 9 A.M. until 5 P.M.—eight hours. With flextime, workers can choose the hour that they start work in the morning and can go home after eight hours. So, for instance, a worker who comes in at 7 can leave at 3. Or a worker can come in at 10 and leave at 6. You can imagine how useful this flexibility is for people who have children.

The fourth change I want to describe is telecommuting. Or sometimes we say "teleworking." With telecommuting, people work at home and use the computer or phone to communicate with their workplace. It's estimated that about 15 percent of the U.S. workforce telecommutes now. But the percentage is growing all the time because it saves people time and money. And if parents are allowed to work at home, their children might not have to spend as much time in child care.

And speaking of child care, the fifth program offered by many of the best companies is day care; that is, some companies have daycare centers at the office where trained people take care of the employees' children. This means workers come to work with their young children, leave them at the center, and can visit them during lunch or whatever. Then the parents and kids drive home together at the end of the day. With day care at work, parents don't need to worry about their kids because they're right there.

OK, let me review what I've been talking about. I've given you five examples of company policies and programs that make life a little easier for working mothers and fathers. But it's important for me to tell you that only some large companies can afford these kinds of programs. For most people, trying to work and take care of a family at the same time is still very, very difficult. In my opinion, our government and our society need to do a lot more to help working parents and their children.

conclusion

PART 3 Strategies for Better Listening and Speaking

Focus on Testing: Using Context Clues page 115

Conversation 1

Senior Citizen Man: Well, I tell you, things get pretty tough by the end of the month. I don't have any pension—just Social Security—and that's only $800 a month. Sometimes the check is late, and the rent is due on the first of the month. Do you think the landlord cares?

Question 1: *The speaker is...* *retirement, pensioner*

Senior Citizen Man: Sometimes I think no one cares about retired people in this country.

Conversation 2

17-year-old girl: Sometimes I feel like I'm in a prison. "Come home by ten." "Don't go there." "Don't do that." "Turn down the music." They treat me like a baby. They have no respect for my privacy.

Question 2: *The speaker is talking about...* *herselves parents*

Girl: My parents forget that I'm 17 years old. I'm not a child anymore.

Conversation 3

Man: My ex-wife and I agreed that the kids would live with me. At first it was hard with all the work and no help. But it's exciting to watch my kids grow up.

Question 3: *This man...* *is divorced*

Man: And fortunately, there are organizations to help divorced fathers like me.

Conversation 4

Young man: I lived with my parents until I was 18, then I left home to go to college and lived with roommates in an apartment near the campus. When I graduated, I got a job with an engineering firm and got my own place. But last year I lost my job and ran out of money. So what could I do? I came back home.

Question 4: *This person probably lives...* *with parents*

Young man: Boy, it's not easy living with your parents again after all these years.

Conversation 5

Senior Citizen Woman: After I broke my hip, it was too hard to go on living by myself. So I tried living with my son and his family for a while, but their house is small and noisy, and I want my privacy, too. So I came here. And it really isn't bad. I have my own doctor, good food, and plenty of friends my own age.

Question 5: *This woman is living in...* *with her son*

Senior Citizen Woman: This retirement home is really the best place for me.

PART 4 Real-World Task: Using Numbers, Percentages, and Graphs

② **Completing Line Graphs** page 118

Graph number 1

Graph 1 gives statistics on American women in the U.S. labor force. In 1960, 37.8 percent of American women had jobs. By 1980, it had jumped to 51.1 percent. In 1990, it was 57.5 percent. And in 2003, 61 percent of American women were working.

Graph number 2

Graph 2 shows the divorce rate in the United States. In 1960, the divorce rate was just 2.2 per 1,000 people. In 1970, it rose to 3.5, and in 1980 it jumped to 5.2. However, it declined in 1990 to 4.7, and in 2003 declined even more, to 3.8 per 1,000 people.

Graph number 3

Graph 3 presents information on people over age 65 who lived alone from 1970 to 2000. You need to make two sets of points here. Use an O for men and an X for women.

In 1970, 35.9 percent of elderly women lived alone, compared to 10.8 percent of elderly men. In 1980, the percentage was 31.9 for women and 8.1 for men. In 1990, 51.8 percent of women lived alone, compared to 21.5 percent for men. And finally, in 2000, 40 percent of women and 17 percent of men were living by themselves.

CHAPTER 6 Global Connections

PART 1 Conversation: Taking Classes Online

3 Comprehension Questions page 127

4 Listening for Stressed Words page 127

Jeff: [saying some words in Chinese]

Mari: Oh, sorry, am I interrupting?

Jeff: No, that's okay. I'm just catching up on my Chinese homework.

Mari: Oh, I didn't know you were taking Chinese.

Jeff: Yeah, I'm taking it online.

Mari: Online? Doesn't the college offer Chinese classes?

Jeff: They do, but the regular face-to-face classes were full. I like this class better anyway.

Mari: Really? How come?

Jeff: Well, for one thing, it's so convenient. I mean, I don't need to worry about fitting it into my schedule. I can just go online whenever I want and do my work.

Mari: Whenever? Don't you have deadlines?

Jeff: Yeah, we have to post the homework and participate in group discussions by a certain date. But I don't feel pressured, you know, the way I do in a regular class.

Mari: I see what you mean. I'm not always ready to participate in class.

Jeff: Uh-huh. And another thing I like: the people in the class. My classmates are from all over the States and even from abroad. There's someone from Canada and people from Germany and Brazil.

Mari: Wow. That's a lot of different time zones! Seems like the whole world wants to learn Chinese these days.

Jeff: Yup. And get this: the instructor is in Beijing.

Mari: That's so cool. But how does he correct your pronunciation? Don't you need the face-to-face contact?

Jeff: No, he listens to our voice recordings and gives us feedback. And once a week we talk on Skype.

Mari: So you know what everyone looks like?

Jeff: Sure. We've all become friends and chat on Facebook all the time, too. And we've all agreed to stay in touch after the course ends and meet next year in China!

Mari: Oh, so you'll get some face-to-face contact after all!

Jeff: Of course. You can't really get to know a culture without traveling there.

Mari: True. That's exactly why I came here. Not just to learn English but also to get to know the lifestyle and customs.

Jeff: Right. But anyway, you should really try an online class some time. Almost all American colleges and universities offer them, you know.

Mari: I probably will. You certainly got me interested.

6 Identifying Intonation Patterns page 130

1. Don't you need face-to-face contact?
2. How much does the online class cost?
3. What countries are your classmates from?
4. May I interrupt?

5. Can you give me feedback?

6. Do you want to meet in Beijing next year?

7. Which hotel should we stay at?

8. Why do you want to study abroad?

PART 2 Lecture: Body Language Around the World

3 Taking Notes on Similarities and Differences page 135

1. In the U.S. there is kind of a general rule, which is that people stand about one arm's length or about 70 centimeters apart when they are talking. In contrast, Latin Americans usually stand much closer to each other.

2. In Arab cultures, for instance, you will also notice that men sit and stand very close to each other. On the other hand, in East Asia, people usually stand farther apart than Americans do.

3. Next let's talk about eye contact, which is the way people look at each other, or don't look at each other, when they're talking. In the U.S. the rules are simple. You should look at a person's eyes when you speak with them. To Americans this is a sign of respect and attention. If I'm talking to you in class and you're looking away from me, I might think you're not listening to me. But the exact opposite is true in many cultures. In some parts of Africa and the Caribbean, for example, children are taught to look down when they're talking to a person with greater authority, such as a parent or a teacher.

4. Similarly, in Japan an employee would not make direct eye contact with an employer. It would be disrespectful.

5. The rules for touching are very different from one culture to another. Some cultures are more affectionate than others. So, in Latin cultures such as Mexico and Italy, it's normal for strangers to hug each other on happy occasions. And it's similar in France, where, maybe you know, everybody, even total strangers, kiss each other as a form of greeting. But in Japan and many other countries it is not proper for strangers to touch each other, and even married people may avoid touching in public.

4 Taking Notes (Part I) page 135

5 Outlining the Lecture page 135

Professor: Good afternoon, class. As I announced last time, we're starting a new unit today, and the topic is nonverbal communication or body language as it's often called. As you know, we humans convey a lot of information without using any words, by using our heads, our hands, our eyes, and so on. The thing is, body language, like spoken language, differs from culture to culture; and there is a lot of potential for misunderstandings if people aren't aware of these differences. So today I'm going to give you an overview, an introduction, to four categories of nonverbal communication. Those categories are movement, distance, eye contact, and touching. I'll define each of the categories and give examples. And I'll be asking you for examples as well.

OK, the first category I mentioned is movement, and this includes gestures, um, movements of the hands and arms, and also movement of the head and even the feet. There's a famous photo of Bill Clinton, who was president from 1993 to 2001, making the American gesture for OK: you make a circle with your first two fingers, and you hold up the other three fingers, like this. And this photo caused some confusion in other countries, like Russia, where this gesture means "zero." And in Brazil, where it's a really offensive gesture. This is just one example of how the same gesture can mean different things in different places. Can someone give me another example? Yes, Adi?

Adi: When I first came here I saw American people pointing with the second finger, and I was really shocked because in my country, Indonesia, this is very rude. If you want to point at someone you use your thumb or your open hand.

Professor: Thank you, that's interesting. Does anyone have another example? Maybe something that involves another part of the body? OK, Moussa?

Moussa: In Arab cultures you never, never, show the bottom of your shoe or even point to someone's feet. It's really terrible. I was so surprised the first time I saw a teacher sitting with one foot on his knee, and I could see the bottom of his shoe. I thought he was so disrespectful.

Professor: Another great example. Thank you, Moussa. All right, I think we need to move on to the second category I mentioned, and that's distance. I mean how close or far people are comfortable sitting or standing from each other. In every culture people have what we call their personal space, which is like an invisible bubble around them. And if a stranger steps inside their personal space, they feel uncomfortable. In the U.S. there is kind of a general rule, which is that people stand about one arm's length or about 70 centimeters apart when they are talking. This is also true for Northern European countries like Sweden. In contrast, in Latin cultures, people usually stand much closer to each other. So imagine a party where, let's say, a person from Sweden is talking to a person from Italy. The Italian stands close to the Swede because that's normal in his culture, but the Swede keeps moving backwards because to him the Italian is standing too close for comfort. The conversation may have started in the middle of the room but soon the Italian has unintentionally pushed the Swede against a wall. The poor Swede looks really uncomfortable and the poor Italian is confused because he doesn't understand what he's doing wrong!

Other cultures also differ from Americans in their use of personal space. In Arab cultures, for instance, you will also notice that men sit and stand very close to each other. On the other hand, in East Asia, people usually stand farther apart than Americans do.

 6 Taking Notes (Part II) page 136

Professor: Next let's talk about eye contact, which is the way people look at each other, or don't look at each other, when they're talking. In the U.S. the rules are simple. You should look at a person's eyes when you speak with them. To Americans this is a sign of respect and attention. If I'm talking to you in class and you're looking away from me, I might think you're not listening to me. But the exact opposite is true in many cultures. In some parts of Africa and the Caribbean,

for example, children are taught to look down when they're talking to a person with greater authority, such as a parent or a teacher. Similarly, in Japan an employee would not make direct eye contact with an employer. It would be disrespectful. Yes, Angie? You want to say something?

Angie: I read about a case where a woman didn't get a job because the employer said she didn't look at him during the interview, so he felt like she was hiding something, like she was dishonest.

Professor: Exactly. That is how most Americans would react, I think.

All right, finally I want to introduce the topic of touching. First let me tell you a little story. A young woman from Mexico, let's call her Inez, is invited to the wedding of her Japanese classmate, Yuki. After the wedding ceremony everyone stands in line to greet the bride and groom and their families. When Inez is introduced to Yuki's mother, she leans in and tries to hug her. Yuki's mother looks horrified and immediately steps away from Inez. Inez looks hurt. Can someone explain what happened here?

Female: I think Inez was trying to offer congratulations to Yuki's mother, but maybe the mother wasn't comfortable touching someone she didn't know.

Professor: That's correct. The rules for touching are very different from one culture to another. Some cultures are more affectionate than others. So in Latin cultures, like Mexico and Italy, it's normal for strangers to hug each other on happy occasions. And it's similar in France, where, maybe you know, everybody, even total strangers, kiss each other as a form of greeting. But in Japan and many other countries it is not proper for strangers to touch each other, and even married people may avoid touching in public. You can see why Yuki's mother was uncomfortable and Inez was offended in the example I gave you.

All right, let's review what we've discussed so far. I've introduced four categories of nonverbal communication—uh, movement, distance, eye contact, and touching. Next time we'll look at each of these categories in greater detail. For now, what I hope you've gotten is the general message that body language differs from culture to culture in the same way that spoken language does, and because of these differences there is always the potential of people misunderstanding one another. In today's globalized world, where we are interacting with one another in business, in the classroom, and in the workplace, it's important to know something about nonverbal communication in other cultures so that we can work together harmoniously and avoid misunderstandings.

PART 3　Strategies for Better Listening and Speaking

Focus on Testing: Using Context Clues page 139

Conversation 1

A: I want to go overseas next summer but I can't afford it.

B: You can—if you stay at a hostel.

A: How is that different from a hotel?

B: A hostel, especially a youth hostel, is more like a dormitory. You share a room with a bunch of other travelers, often from all over the world.

A: Wow, it sounds like a great way to meet new people.

B: Yeah. And it's a lot cheaper than a hotel.

Question 1: *A hostel is probably...*

Conversation 2

A: How was your vacation?

B: Fantastic! We stayed at a great apartment in the center of Paris, totally free.

A: A free apartment in Paris? Wow. How did you do that?

B: We exchanged apartments with a French family.

A: Oh, so your friends stayed at your place in New York while your family stayed at theirs?

B: Well, yeah, but they're not our friends. Actually, we met them online through a company called homeexchange.com.

A: That sounds great. Can I find an apartment in Bangkok that way? I'm planning to visit Thailand next summer.

B: Definitely. Just sign up online and pay a small fee.

Question 2: *What is probably true about home exchanges?*

Conversation 3

A: After I graduate, I want to see and learn about other parts of the world.

B: Me too. But I don't want to be just a tourist. Have you heard about something called volunteer travel?

A: I think so. You go abroad and do volunteer work, like at a hospital, a school, an orphanage, places like that. Right?

B: Yeah. There are all sorts of organizations you can join, depending on where you want to go and what kind of work you want to do.

A: Are they all free?

B: I don't think so. When my cousin volunteered at a hospital in Mexico, he had to pay for his travel expenses. But the housing and food were free.

A: How long was he there?

B: A year, I think. But you can volunteer for short periods, too. Let's look into it.

Question 3: *Volunteer travel is probably a good experience for...*

Conversation 4

A: Wow. Look at this advertisement: "Discover nature, protect the environment and help improve the lives of local people."

B: Sounds like a travel ad.

A: Yes, it's an ad for a trip to Brazil. Not to famous cities like Rio, though, but to natural areas. Like the rainforest.

B: Hmm. Isn't the rainforest disappearing very quickly? How does it help the environment to have more and more tourists visiting there?

A: Well, the purpose of this trip is to teach visitors about nature, how to protect it and not to damage it. And some of the money from the tourists will go directly to the local people.

B: Oh, I get it. I think this kind of travel is called "ecotourism."

Question 4:
What are "eco-tourists" interested in?

Conversation 5

A: Where are you going to stay when you go to Tokyo?

B: I'm going to try couch surfing.

A: Couch what?

B: Couch surfing. It's a kind of international club. Members volunteer to host you in their homes, give you a tour of their city, or just give you advice. And you host people in your home, too.

A: It sounds wonderful. But aren't these people total strangers?

B: Yup. But it's really safe. I've stayed with people in Europe and Asia. And I've hosted people from Sweden, Russia and Japan.

A: Hm. I'll check out their website and see if this is for me.

Question 5:
Couch surfing is an organization for...

PART 4 Real-World Task: Participating in a Survey

2 Listening to a Phone Survey page 144

A: Hello?

B: Yes, I'd like to speak to Ms. Julie Salsedo.

A: Speaking.

B: Oh. Ms. Salsedo, my name is Ken. I'm calling from the International Gallop Poll organization. I wonder if you have a few minutes to participate in a survey.

A: Um, a survey? What kind of survey?

B: A survey about charity and volunteering. It's very short, just five questions.

A: OK, I guess I can do that. Go ahead.

B: Terrific. OK, my first question is: In the past month, have you donated money to an organization?

A: What kind of organization? Like a charity, or...?

B: It can be any organization—a charity, or a school, or even a political organization.

A: No, I haven't. Not since the economy has gone down, you know, it's been hard...

B: I see. That's OK. You can just give yes/no answers. So, here is my second question. During the past month, have you volunteered time to an organization?

C: Yes, I have. I volunteered at my daughter's school.

B: OK. Next, in the past month, have you helped a stranger? Or someone you didn't know who needed help?

A: Hmm. Let's see. I think so.

B: So your answer is "Yes"?

A: Yes. Some tourists asked me for directions, and I helped them out. I actually took them to the place they were looking for.

B: Great. OK, next: Which country do you think has the most generous people?

A: Oh, that's a tough one. I think you can find generous people and selfish people everywhere.

B: Right. But which country do you think has the most generous people?

A: Hmm. I suppose the richest countries because they have the most money and time to give. So I'm going to pick, um, Switzerland.

B: OK, thank you. Next, can you tell me how you feel about your life? How satisfied are you with your life on a scale of 1 to 10? One means very unhappy, and 10 means very happy, very satisfied.

A: Hmm. I guess I'm pretty happy. I'd say 8.

B: OK, Ms. Salsedo. That's all the questions I have. I just need some personal information. What is your age range? Are you between 20 and 30? Between 30 and 40? Between 40 and 50?

A: The last one. Between 40 and 50.

B: And your income level? Is your yearly income between 20,000 and 40,000…

A: I'm sorry, I'm really not comfortable answering that.

B: Oh, that's OK. No problem. Thank you very much for your time, Ms. Salsedo.

A: You're welcome.

B: Bye-bye.

<table>
<tr><td>CHAPTER 7</td><td><h2>Language and Communication</h2></td></tr>
</table>

PART 1 Conversation: What Do People Really Mean?

3 **Comprehension Questions** page 152

4 **Listening for Stressed Words**
page 152

Mari: Yolanda! Hi!

Yolanda: Hi, Mari, how are you?

Mari: Fine, thanks. Um, is anyone sitting here?

Yolanda: No, have a seat.

Mari: Thanks. So how have you been?

Yolanda: Oh, you know, busy. I've got school, and work, and I'm getting ready for my brother's wedding next month.

Mari: Oh, yeah.

Yolanda: Anyway, it's going to be a huge wedding and…

Mari: Oh, excuse me, uh… Nancy! Over here!

Nancy: Hi!

Mari: Nancy, this is Yolanda. She works in the library. Yolanda, this is my housemate, Nancy. She teaches English here.

Nancy: Nice to meet you, Yolanda.

Yolanda: You too. Well, listen, actually, I've got to go. I have to be at work in ten minutes. I'll see you soon, Mari. We'll go to a movie or something.

Mari: Sure. How about Thursday night?

Yolanda: Uh, I have to check my calendar. I'll call you, OK?

Mari: OK, see you.

Mari: I don't understand Americans.

Nancy: Huh?

Mari: Did you hear what she said? "I'll call you, we'll go to a movie." But every time I try to pick a specific day or time, she says she's busy, she has to check her calendar. And then she doesn't call.

Nancy: Mm hmm…

Mari: Why do Americans say things they don't mean? They act so nice, like they always say, "How are you," but then they keep on walking and don't even wait for your answer. They're so… how do you say it… two-faced?

Nancy: I know it seems that way sometimes, Mari. But it's not true. It's just that for Americans, friendliness and friendship aren't always the same thing.

Mari: What do you mean?

Nancy: Well, as you know, Americans can be very open and friendly. Like, they invite you to sit down, they ask you questions, they tell you all about their families. So naturally you think they're trying to make friends with you. But actually, friendship, real friendship, doesn't happen so quickly.

Mari: So, when people say, "How are you," they're just being polite? They don't really care?

Nancy: Not exactly. The thing you have to understand is that "How are you" isn't a real question. It's more like a greeting, a way of saying hello.

Mari: Aha, I get it! And "Have a nice day" is just a friendly way to say good-bye?

Nancy: Exactly. Now you're catching on.

Mari: But I'm still in the dark about Yolanda. Does she want to be my friend or not?

Nancy: It's hard to say. Maybe she's just too busy these days. I guess you'll just have to be patient.

Mari: Hmm. That's good advice, I guess. Thanks.

5 Understanding Statements with Rising Intonation page 154

1. You're going?

2. You remember my friend Yolanda?

3. He hasn't done his homework yet?

4. It's at the intersection of First and Main?

5. Jack is Rose's brother?

PART 2 Lecture: Differences Between British and American English

homework

3 Classifying Lecture Organization
page 158

Lecture 1

Personal computers have revolutionized the way people work and communicate. I could talk for hours about the wide use of personal computers, but today we only have time to introduce three major uses of computers: at home, in business, and in education.

Lecture 2

In today's lecture I will provide the most recent information concerning the growth and characteristics of the U.S. population.

Lecture 3

You may have guessed by now that my topic for today's lecture is differences between American and British English. In particular, I want to examine three categories of difference. First, and most obvious, is pronunciation; second, vocabulary; and third, grammar.

4 Taking Notes (Part I) page 159

5 Outlining the Lecture page 159

Lecturer: Good afternoon. To introduce my topic today, I'd like you to listen to two speech samples and tell me where the speakers are from. Ready? OK, here's the first one.

Speaker 1: "Today's weather forecast calls for partly cloudy skies in the morning, clearing by mid-afternoon with winds up to 15 miles an hour out of the west. The high temperature will be 80 degrees Fahrenheit, and the low will be 64."

Lecturer: OK. Now, where do you think that speaker was from?

Audience: America… the United States… Canada.

Lecturer: Yes, most of you got it. That was what we call a *standard* American accent. Which means the accent that is spoken by the majority of people who live in the United States and Canada.

Now, listen to a different speaker reading the same text.

Speaker 2: "Today's weather forecast calls for partly cloudy skies in the morning, clearing by mid-afternoon with winds up to 15 miles an hour out of the west. The high temperature will be 80 degrees Fahrenheit, and the low will be 64."

Lecturer: And where is that speaker from?

Audience: England… the United Kingdom… Great Britain.

Lecturer: Yes, of course. That was British English. So you may have guessed by now that my topic for today's lecture is differences between standard American and British English. In particular, I want to examine three categories of difference. First, and most obvious, is pronunciation; second, vocabulary; and third, grammar.

So to begin, let's go back to the subject of accent, or pronunciation. You had no trouble identifying the North American and British accents because each of them has a unique sound. What is it? Well, one obvious difference is in the pronunciation of the letter *a*. For example, most Americans say /kænt/, but the British say /kant/. Or Americans say /bæth/ and the British say /bath/. The /æ/ sound is very common in American English, but not very common in British English.

Another noticeable difference between American and British pronunciation is the /r/ sound. In British English, the /r/ sound is very often dropped; it disappears. To give some examples, Americans say /kar/ but the British say /ka/. Americans say /fʏrst/ but British say /fʌst/. A big American city is "New /yɔrk/ " for Americans, but "New /yok/" to the British. In the two speech samples you heard at the beginning of this lecture, the American speaker said /forekæst/, but the British said /fohcast/. In that single word you can hear the difference both in the *a* vowel and in the pronunciation of /r/. Listen again: /forkæst/, /fohkast/.

A third difference is the pronunciation of the /t/ sound in the middle of words. In British English it is normally pronounced, but in American English it changes to a /d/ or disappears. For example: a British person will say "little," but an American says "liddle." You can hear this difference particularly with numbers: Brits say "twenty-one, twenty-two," and so on, but Americans drop the /t/ and say "twenny-one, twenny-two," and so on.

So there you have just three of the differences that give American and British pronunciation their unique sounds. There are many more. But now let's go on to talk about vocabulary.

6 Taking Notes (Part II) page 160

Lecturer: Some people believe that American English vocabulary and British English vocabulary are very different, but actually they are not. The English language has more than one million words. Yet there are only a few hundred words and expressions that are different in American and British English. You can see a few of them in the chart right here. So for instance, Americans say, "truck," but the Brits say "lorry." Another well-known example is "elevator," which is used in the United States and "lift," which is the British term. Now, although the number of vocabulary differences is small, funny misunderstandings can sometimes occur. For instance, if an American says, "I'm going to wash up," he would go into the bathroom and wash his hands and face. But a British person may be quite surprised to see him go to the bathroom because in England, to "wash up" means to

wash the dishes.

Vocabulary differences can also create some confusing situations in restaurants. If an Englishman traveling in the United States enters a restaurant and orders "bangers and mash," the American waiter would be totally confused. He wouldn't know that the man wanted sausage and mashed potatoes.

Finally, let's talk a bit about grammar. I've left this category for last because in the area of grammar, standard American and British English are nearly identical. One common difference, however, involves the past participle of the verb *get*. For example, an American might ask, "Have you gotten your grade yet?" whereas a Brit would ask, "Have you got your grade yet?" Another difference is in the use of the verb *have*, especially in questions. Americans say, "Do you have any ideas?" but the British say, "Have you any ideas?" There are also differences in prepositions. So for instance in the United States, it's correct to say that John is different *from* Mary, but the British will say that John is different *than* Mary. But these differences are very small and few in number.

And this brings me to my conclusion, which is this: Standard British and standard American English are so similar that most speakers of these two types will have no trouble understanding one another. American and British English are not two different languages. Rather, they are two dialects, two varieties, of the same language, English.

PART 3   Strategies for Better Listening and Speaking

Focus on Testing: Using Context Clues page 163

Conversation 1

A: Have you ever heard of Esperanto?

B: Huh?

A: Esperanto. It's a language.

B: Really? I've never heard of it. Where is it spoken?

A: Lots of places. According to this article,

it's actually an artificial language; it was invented in 1887 by a man from Poland.

B: That's interesting. So who speaks this language now?

A: Well, it says here that there may be as many as 15 million people who speak Esperanto as a second language.

B: What does Esperanto mean, anyway? It doesn't sound like Polish.

A: It's not. The vocabulary of Esperanto comes from lots of different languages. Esperanto means "hope" in Latin.

B: Well, I hope I never have to learn it. It's hard enough trying to learn English.

Question 1: *What is Esperanto?*

Question 2: *Where did the woman get her information about Esperanto?*

Question 3: *Which of the following is probably true about Esperanto?*

Conversation 2

A: Look, there's a beehive under the roof.

B: I guess we'd better call an exterminator.

A: Yeah, you're right… But I really don't want to kill them. Did you know bees can communicate with one another?

B: Really? How?

A: They use body language to show where food is, how far away it is, and how much food is available.

B: No kidding…

A: Yeah, see that one there? See how she's going around and around in circles, like she's dancing? That means food is nearby. If the food is farther away, the bee points to it with her body. And the faster she dances, the more food is available.

B: How do you know so much about bees?

A: I took an entomology class in college. I was a biology major, and I thought it would be interesting to learn something about bugs.

Question 4: *Why does the man want to call an exterminator?*

Question 5: *Which information about food is not conveyed by the bee's body language?*

Question 6: *What is entomology?*

Conversation 3

Man: Why are you talking to your computer?

Woman: I'm not talking to it. I'm giving a dictation.

Man: What do you mean?

Woman: It's this great software program. It understands what I'm saying and writes down the words.

Man: Wow. So you don't have to type at all?

Woman: No, that's the point. I'm a slow typist, so this program is a lifesaver.

Man: Can I try it?

Woman: Well, first you have to train the computer to recognize your voice.

Man: Oh. Why?

Woman: Because everybody's pronunciation is different. If it doesn't know your voice, it makes mistakes.

Man: I see. I should get one of these for my computer. I have three term papers due this month.

Question 7: *Why does the woman use this software program?*

Question 8: *What will the man probably do next?*

Question 9: *What is probably true about this computer program?*

Understanding Interjections page 165

Conversation 1

Student: Can we use a dictionary on the test?

Teacher: Uh-huh.

Conversation 2

Mother: Here, let me brush your hair.

Child: Ouch! Not so hard!

Conversation 3

Father: Could you please carry this bag of groceries into the house? Be careful; it's heavy.

Son: Sure… oops! Sorry.

Conversation 4

A: The computer is down because of a virus that crashed the hard drive.

B: Huh?

Conversation 5

A: I'm expecting an important letter. Has the mail arrived yet?

B: Uh-uh.

Conversation 6

A: Did you remember to buy stamps when you went to the post office?

B: Uh-oh.

PART 4   Real-World Task: Spelling Bee

2   Identifying Spellings   page 168

Teacher: Our contestants in today's spelling bee are Jack, Marisa, Yolanda, Evan, and Tony. As you know, I will say the word and then say it in a sentence. Are you ready to begin?

All: Ready. Yes.

Teacher: All right. The first word is for Tony. The word is *tries*. "He always tries to do a good job."

Tony: Tries. OK, T-R-I-E-S.

Teacher: Correct. All right. The next word is for Jack. Your word is *choose*. "Which flavor ice cream will you choose?"

Jack: Choose. C-H-O-S-E.

Teacher: I'm sorry, but that is wrong. The correct spelling of *choose* is C-H-O-O-S-E. Good try, Jack. OK, the next word goes to Marisa. Your word is *effect*. "Jogging has a good effect on our health."

Marisa: Effect. E-F-F-E-C-T.

Teacher: Right! Marisa, you stay in the game. The next word is for Evan. Your word is *quizzes*. "We had two grammar quizzes last week."

Evan: OK, quizzes. Uh, Q-U-I-Z-Z-E-S.

Teacher: Yes, that's right. Now, for Yolanda, your word is *succeed*. "You must study hard if you want to succeed."

Yolanda: Hmm. Succeed. S-U-C-C-E-D-E.

Teacher: I'm sorry, Yolanda, that's wrong. It's S-U-C-C-E-E-D. Good try. OK, let's see who's still in the game: Marisa, Evan, and Tony. Are you ready for the second round?

All: Yes, yeah, let's go.

Teacher: OK, Tony. Your word is *ninety*. "The shoes cost ninety dollars."

Tony: N-I-N-E-T-Y. Ninety.

Teacher: You're right! Well done. The next word is for Marisa. *Analyze*. "After a test, you should analyze your mistakes."

Marisa: Wow, that's hard. OK: A-N-A-L-I-Z-E. Analyze.

Teacher: Sorry, Marisa. It's A-N-A-L-Y-Z-E. Please sit down. Evan, you're next. Your word is *possibility*. "There is a possibility of snow tonight."

Evan: Possibility. OK. P-O-S-S-I-B-I-L-I-T-Y.

Teacher: Great! OK, it's down to Tony and Evan. First Tony. Your word is *mysterious*. "During the night we heard mysterious noises."

Tony: Um, M-I-S-T-E-R-I-O-U-S. I think.

Teacher: Oh no, that's not correct. It's M-Y-S-T-E-R-I-O-U-S. You almost got it. Well, that leaves Evan. If you spell this word correctly, you'll be the winner today. The last word is *lightning*. "We were scared by the thunder and lightning."

Evan: L-I-G-H-T-N-I-N-G. Lightning.

Teacher: Right! Congratulations, Evan! You're our winner today.

CHAPTER 8	Tastes and Preferences

PART 1 Conversation: What Do You Like to Do for Fun?

3 Comprehension Questions page 175

4 Listening for Stressed Words page 176

Jeff: Come in!

Dan: Hi.

Jeff: Hey, Dan, how ya doin'?

Dan: Great, thanks. Hey, I burned you some new CDs.

Jeff: Cool.

Dan: Hi. You were at our show last night, right?

Mari: Yeah, I was.

Jeff: Sorry, Mari, this is Dan. Dan, this is Mari.

Mari: It's nice to meet you.

Dan: Nice to meet you, too.

Jeff: Oh, let me get that. I'll be right back.

Dan: OK. So, Mari, did you have a good time at the club last night?

Mari: Yeah, it was pretty wild.

Dan: What did you think of our band?

Mari: Well, your music is great for dancing, but to tell you the truth, it was kind of loud. I guess I really prefer jazz.

Dan: Do you go to concerts much?

Mari: No, not very often. I can't afford them. They're so expensive!

Dan: Yeah, I know what you mean. Well, what do you like to do for fun?

Mari: I love to eat! I love going to different ethnic restaurants and trying new dishes.

Dan: What's your favorite kind of food?

Mari: Well, Japanese, of course. What about you?

Dan: Well... I'm not crazy about sushi or sashimi. But I really like Mexican food.

Mari: Ooh, I can't stand beans, and I don't like cheese. Uh... What about Indian food?

Dan: I don't care for it. Too spicy. Um... Do you like American food? You know, hamburgers, hot dogs, French fries...

Mari: Yuck! All that fat and salt and sugar... We don't see eye to eye on anything, do we?

Dan: Well, let's see. What's your opinion of modern art? There's a wonderful show at the county museum right now.

Mari: To be honest, I don't get the modern stuff. I prefer 19th century art, you know, Monet, van Gogh, Renoir.

Dan: Hmm. How do you feel about sports? Are you interested in football?

Mari: American football? I hate it!

Dan: Basketball?

Mari: It's OK.

Dan: How about tall musicians with brown hair?

Mari: It depends.

Dan: OK, I got it. How about tall musicians with brown hair who invite you to a movie?

Mari: Science fiction?

Dan: Sounds great!

Mari: Finally we agree on something!

5 Listening for Reductions page 177

1. A: Do you like Chinese food?

   B: Not really.

   A: Japanese?

2. A: Phew! What a day!

   B: Tired?

3. A: Anybody home?

   B: I'm here. I'm in the kitchen.

4. A: I guess it's time to go.

B: Leaving already?

5. A: Does he have a wife?

B: Yes.

A: Kids?

PART 2 Radio Interview:
Generation Y

5 Taking Notes (Part I) page 182

6 Rewriting Your Notes page 182

Host: Dr. Harris, thank you for joining us today.

Dr. Harris: My pleasure.

Host: To begin, could you tell us the meaning of the term "Generation Y"?

Dr. Harris: Sure. Generation Y refers to young Americans who were born between the late 1970s and the early 1990s, uh, that is between 1977 or 1978 and 1993 or 1994. In other words, the youngest ones are still teenagers, and the oldest ones are young adults. And there are more than 70 million of them.

Host: Is that number significant?

Dr. Harris: It is extremely significant. Generation Y is the second-largest generation in U.S. history, and by the year 2020 it will be the largest. So this generation is the future market for almost all consumer brands. Marketers know they have to stay in touch with this generation if they want their products to succeed.

Host: What are some of the most important characteristics of this generation?

Dr. Harris: Well, first let me give you some statistics, OK? One-fourth, that is one in four people in this generation, grew up in single-parent homes. Three-fourths, I mean 75 percent, have mothers who work. And one-third are not Caucasian. To put it another way, this is the most diverse generation in U.S. history.

Host: Would you say they are tolerant?

Dr. Harris: Very tolerant. Also optimistic, confident, independent, and... rich!

Host: Rich? Explain that.

Dr. Harris: OK. Here are some more statistics: According to a study by the Harris company, members of Generation Y have total incomes of $211 billion a year. These kids spend an average of $30 on every trip to the mall. And if you have teenagers, you know that this generation practically lives at the mall.

7 Taking Notes (Part II) page 184

Host: Two hundred and eleven billion. That's an incredible amount of money. What do they spend it on?

Dr. Harris: Fashion, fast food, movies, CDs, electronics, concert tickets. Generation Y-ers like to have fun.

Host: Are there special brands that this generation prefers?

Dr. Harris: No, not in the way that their parents preferred Levi's jeans or SUVs. Generation Y-ers like anything that's hip or hot at the moment, but that can change very fast.

Host: So what do marketers need to know if they want to sell to this group?

Dr. Harris: I think the main thing to remember is that this is the Internet generation, the generation of instant messaging. They have grown up with the media, so they are very smart shoppers. They don't like traditional advertising techniques. And as I said, they are not loyal to specific brands. And they love fads, like right now graphic T-shirts and flip-flops are totally in.

Host: Is Generation Y found only in the U.S. or is it in other countries as well?

Dr. Harris: Generation Y is actually an international phenomenon, although it has different characteristics in different countries. In Eastern Europe, for example, it's the first generation to grow up without communism. And in other countries like, oh, Korea and Greece, this is the first generation to grow up with a high standard of living. These young people want to be modern. I mean they are not interested in the traditional way of life. Also, they identify more closely with the West, and that can cause conflict between them and the generations that came before them.

Host: Dr. Harris, before we conclude, may I ask you a personal question?

Dr. Harris: Go ahead.

Host: What generation are you?

Dr. Harris: I'm a baby boomer, born in 1960. But my daughter, who was born in 1984, is Generation Y. And believe it or not, she loves listening to my old Beatles records.

Host: No kidding. Dr. Harris, this has been very interesting. Thank you for being with us today.

Dr. Harris: You're welcome.

PART 3 Strategies for Better Listening and Speaking

2 Distinguishing Among *Do, Does,* and *Did* page 188

1. Do you have time to eat lunch?
2. Does he play the piano?
3. Did they need help?
4. Do I look like my sister?
5. Did she understand the instructions?
6. Do we sound good?

7. Did they own a house?
8. Do we need to rewrite the composition?

3 *Do, Does,* and *Did* in Questions page 188

1. Did he decide to take the job?
2. When do we eat?
3. Do I have to rewrite this composition?
4. Where did we park the car?
5. Do they know what to do?
6. Did she miss the bus again?
7. Do you usually walk to school?
8. Did you remember to turn off the light?

Focus on Testing: Using Context Clues page 189

Conversation 1

Woman: Look at that! Isn't it interesting? I love the colors and shapes.

Man: What's it supposed to be?

Woman: It's not supposed to "be" anything. It's modern. Don't try to analyze it.

Man: Well, how much does it cost?

Woman: Let's see. Five thousand dollars. What do you think?

Question 1: *What are the speakers talking about?*

Man: Five thousand dollars? For *that* painting? I don't think so.

Conversation 2

Woman: Don't wear the brown one.

Man: Why not? What's wrong with it?

Woman: Well, it doesn't go with your suit. Brown and black don't look good together.

Man: Well, what if I wear it with my other suit?

Question 2:
What are the man and woman talking about?

Woman: No, you should just wear a different tie. I don't really like brown anyway.

Conversation 3

A: Do you want to try it? It's really fun!

B: No thanks. It's too cold and windy. And honestly, I'm not crazy about the idea of flying down a mountain on one thin piece of wood.

A: But that's the fun part!

Question 3:
What sport are the people talking about?

B: I'm sorry, snowboarding isn't for me. I'd rather stay inside by the fire.

Conversation 4

Teen girl: You colored your hair.

Teen boy: Yeah, I finally did it. Do you like it?

Girl: Uh, you look so... different!

Boy: What do you mean "different"?

Question 4:
How does the girl feel about the boy's hair?

Girl: Uh, I'm not crazy about it. Sorry.

Conversation 5

Teen girl: You colored your hair!

Teen boy: Yeah, I finally did it. Do you like it?

Girl: You look so different!

Boy: What do you mean "different"?

Question 5:
How does the girl feel about the boy's hair?

Girl: I love it! It's so cool!

PART 4 Real-World Task: Choosing Someone to Date

2 Comparing People's Qualities
page 192

David: I don't know what to do. Katherine and Jean are both wonderful women. So how am I supposed to choose between them? Take Katherine. We went to the same high school and college, and my parents are crazy about her. Also, Katherine is very intelligent, and she's interesting to talk with; we spend hours discussing art and politics and books.

Now Jean is also very smart, but she's much quieter than Katherine. It's not as easy to talk to her. But even though she's quiet, she's crazy about sports, just like me, and she has a great sense of humor; I mean, she tells the funniest jokes, and I love the way she laughs. On the other hand, Katherine is sometimes too sensitive; what I mean is she doesn't understand that I'm just joking, so she gets offended.

And another thing I don't like about Katherine is that she's not good at managing money. She has a very good job and a good salary, but somehow she never seems to have any money! That's not very responsible, is it? But Jean is great with money. She even insists on sharing the cost of our dates.

On the other hand, I want to have children, but Jean says she's not sure. That could be a problem later on. Katherine loves kids, but sometimes she has a bad temper; she gets angry whenever I'm five minutes late!

I'm really confused. Katherine and Jean— they're so different and I really like them both. But you know, I don't know if either one is serious about me anyway. What do you think I should do?

CHAPTER 9 New Frontiers

PART 1 Conversation: Living in a "Smart" House

3 Comprehension Questions page 200

4 Listening for Stressed Words
page 200

Andrew: Nancy!

Nancy: Yeah?

Andrew: Look at this utility bill. We're spending way too much on electricity.

Nancy: Ugh, I know. It's because *some* people in this house never remember to turn off lights.

Mari: Um, *I* turn off lights all the

time. In Japan, we're very careful about saving energy.

Andrew: Well, if we had a smart house, we wouldn't have to worry about this so much.

Mari: A smart house?

Nancy: Yeah, we've been talking about that for ages. Go ahead, Andrew, explain what it is.

Andrew: Well, a smart house is a house that has automatic systems for controlling the lights, temperature, windows and doors…

Mari: You mean the lights turn off by themselves?

Andrew: Yes, they can turn on or off at a specific time that you decide.

Nancy: Or the system can tell if someone is in the room or not. If the room is empty, the lights go off.

Andrew: And the heating and air conditioning work the same way.

Mari: That's very cool.

Andrew: And you can program other appliances to do stuff, too.

Mari: Like which ones? How?

Andrew: Like your security system recognizes you and opens your door, your music turns on when you enter a room, your refrigerator tells you when you run out of food…

Mari: So it's all computerized, right?

Nancy: Right. And get this, you control everything remotely from your phone or tablet.

Andrew: So let's say you're on vacation or at work, but don't remember if you turned off your stove, it's all very convenient.

Nancy: And efficient!

Mari: You just need an app on your phone and that's it?

Andrew: Well, yes, an app, but you also have to install a control system,

you know, the hardware, then some software…

Nancy: Yeah, it can get a little complicated. And expensive!

Andrew: But we will definitely turn this house into a smart one eventually…

Nancy: OK, but in the meantime, let's all be smart about saving energy. Um, who left the TV on in the bedroom?

Andrew: Oops.

PART 2 Lecture: Facial Recognition Software

3 **Listening for Persuasive Language** page 206

1. According to a study published in the *New York Times* newspaper, the average American teenager now spends more than 11 hours each day using some kind of electronic device to get information, communicate with friends, listen to music, or watch videos. You might think that sounds totally normal. But in reality, this amount of media use, day in and day out, can have very serious consequences.

2. Unless the people in town start conserving water right away, we are going to face serious water shortages as early as next summer. We all need to take action to avoid running out of water. Here are three things you need to do starting today. First…

3. **A:** That's a pretty bad sunburn.

   B: Yeah. I went to the beach yesterday.

   A: You really need to start using sunscreen.

   B: I don't like the way it feels.

   A: You'll get used to it. Believe me, with your light skin and blue eyes, it's crucial to use sunscreen every day, unless you want to get skin cancer.

4. If you're concerned about protecting your privacy on the Internet, it's essential to write your government representatives and say you want them to pass laws that protect people's privacy. Do it today!

5. The police have estimated that approximately

72 miles of city property such as walls, fences, freeway overpasses, park benches, and so on, are covered in graffiti. Now I know some people say that graffiti is a kind of street art, that people have a right to freedom of expression. But it's a fact that graffiti attracts crime and lowers property values.

4 Taking Notes and Outlining (Part I)
page 207

Part 1

I want you to imagine this situation. Let's say you're in a shopping mall, and you walk by one of those digital advertising displays, and you decide to stop and look. Suddenly an ad appears for running shoes, followed by an ad for men's deodorant. And then one for an energy drink. It's like the sign "knows" that you're a 20-year-old guy who loves sports. Well, guess what: It *does* know! That's because, um, when you looked at the sign, a computer scanned your face and selected ads that matched your age, sex, and body. The technology that does this is called facial recognition software.

In my speech today I'm gonna explain what facial recognition technology is and some of the positive ways that we can use it. But then, in the second part of my speech, I'm gonna tell you about some negative aspects of this technology. Especially the negative impact on privacy. And I'm gonna argue that this technology is something that we and the government need to control very carefully.

OK. To begin, what is facial recognition software? Well, actually, there are two kinds of facial recognition technology. One kind recognizes human faces, but it can't identify who the person is. This is the kind of software that I told you about in my introduction. It's already being used in advertising, for example, in subway stations in Tokyo. Another interesting use of this software is in bars in the city of Chicago. It's used to identify the number of men and women in a bar at one time. So then the bars send out this information, for example on Twitter, and then customers can decide if they want to go there or not. Cool, huh?

OK. Now the second kind of software *does* have the ability to recognize who you are. It

works by measuring the distance between your eyes, the shape of your nose, the width of your mouth, etc., and it's really useful for catching criminals and potential terrorists. In London, for example, in England, you know, there are cameras in most public places. In the fall of 2011, police used facial recognition software to analyze photos of people who were involved in riots.

Now, I can imagine what you are thinking. Facial recognition software is great! It can help businesses sell products, and it can help police fight crime! What's wrong with that? Well, I agree that those are excellent uses of facial recognition software.

5 Taking Notes and Outlining (Part II) page 208

Part 2

The problem is that facial recognition software also has the potential to take away your privacy.

I mean, everybody here has a Facebook account, right? I read that each month, 2.5 *billion* photos get posted to Facebook. So probably there is a photo of you, either on Facebook or somewhere else on the Internet, and that photo probably has your name and other information attached to it. So, let's say you're walking down the street and a camera takes a picture of you. Someone could use face recognition software to match that photo to your photo on the Internet. And in that way they can get your name, your age, your city, your likes and dislikes, and all kinds of other private information.

Maybe you think that this is not a big deal, but to me, well, I think it's dangerous. Imagine a world where a picture of your face will allow anybody to know your name, your age, your political beliefs, your employment history, your shoe size… And remember those digital billboards in malls that I talked about at the beginning? Imagine if those billboards could match your face with your medical history and display an ad for an antidepressant or heart medication right there for anybody to see. I think that would be incredibly embarrassing, don't you?

All right, so if you are concerned about protecting your privacy, what can you do about it? Well, there are two things you need to do right away. First, try to limit the number of photos online that are connected with your name. Like, don't let people tag your photos on Facebook.

In the second place, it's essential to support laws that protect people's privacy. In Germany, private companies have to get your permission before they're allowed to store your photo or information about you in their databases. But we don't have a law like that in the U.S., and I think we should.

In conclusion, facial recognition software already exists, and there is no way to go back in time and make it disappear. But if you care about your privacy and want to keep your freedom to walk down the street without people knowing all your secrets, then you and the government should take steps to control it before it's too late.

PART 3 Strategies for Better Listening and Speaking

Focus on Testing: Using Context Clues page 210

Passage 1

Someday soon, your car may be able to drive itself. In 2010, Google introduced a fully automated, driverless car that went 140,000 miles without an accident. According to the World Health Organization, more than 1.2 million people die every year in traffic accidents. Nearly all these accidents are caused by human error; therefore, driverless cars, which are controlled by computers, could prevent thousands of deaths each year. Driverless cars could also give greater freedom to disabled people and reduce the need for parking spaces, since the cars could drive themselves home after dropping off passengers.

Question 1:
What can we conclude from this information?

Passage 2

Each year Americans use more than 330 billion gallons of water to wash their clothes.

Now a British company called Xeros has developed a machine that uses 90 percent less water than normal washing machines. It cleans clothes with reusable nylon beads that remove stains and dirt. This is good news both for the environment and for your monthly water bill. The nearly waterless machine became available in 2011.

Question 2: *The passage implies that the new washing machine...*

Passage 3

"Geo-engineering" is the process of changing things in our environment in order to reduce global warming. A simple example of geo-engineering is the practice of painting buildings, roofs, and streets white. In hot countries like Greece, people have been doing this for generations. Professor Steven Chu, who won the Nobel Prize for Physics in 1997, explains that white surfaces are cooler because they reflect sunlight back into space. Painting both houses and cars white would reduce the need for air conditioning and save a lot of energy. In the U.S. it would be like taking all cars off the roads for a period of 11 years.

Question 3:
What can we infer from the passage?

Passage 4

Would you eat a hamburger that was grown in a laboratory? Maybe not today. However, by the year 2050, the world will have 9 billion people, and finding ways to feed them will be a major challenge. One answer may be artificial food. In fact, scientists in Holland and Britain have already succeeded in developing artificial meat in laboratories, and the first artificial hamburger could be developed soon. But don't expect it to taste like McDonald's!

Question 4:
What can we conclude from the passage?

Passage 5

Imagine a car that flies. Or is it an airplane that you can drive? Both, according to the builders of the Transition—the world's first vehicle that can travel both in the air and on land. The Transition gets 30 miles per gallon, almost 13 km per liter on land, and it can fly two passengers about 500 miles, 805 km, at a speed of 105 miles, about 170 km per hour. It can fly in and out of any airport. Once it lands, the wings fold up and the pilot can drive it home and park it in the garage. The vehicle, which has both airbags and a parachute, costs $200,000.

Question 5: *We can infer that the greatest advantage of the Transition is...*

3 **Distinguishing Among –ed Endings** page 214

1. smoked
2. rubbed
3. lifted
4. mopped
5. changed
6. directed
7. wished
8. removed
9. added
10. surfaced
11. solved
12. selected
13. erased
14. telephoned
15. numbered

PART 4 Real-World Task: Tracking a Journey on a Map

3 **Following a Journey on a Map** page 217

One. Zac started his voyage across the Pacific Ocean from a place called Marina del Rey, in California. He crossed the Pacific Ocean to his first stop, Hawaii.

Two. Next, he sailed to the Marshall Islands, where he met the president of that country.

Three. Next, he traveled to Papua New Guinea, a country in Australia.

Four. After leaving Australia, he ran into some pirates in the Indian Ocean. Luckily, he escaped without any problems and continued to his next destination, the island nation of Mauritius. At this point, he was halfway through his journey.

Five. Near the eastern coast of Africa, strong storms damaged Zac's boat. However, he was able to repair the damage and sail on to Durban, South Africa.

Six. In South Africa, he also stopped at Cape Town, where he met the oldest person to sail around the world: Minoru Saito, age 75, from Japan.

Seven. After leaving South Africa, Zac sailed across the Atlantic Ocean and landed in Panama.

Eight. He crossed the Panama Canal to the Pacific Ocean, and after a couple of stops in Mexico, he sailed up the coast back to California, completing his journey in 13 months and two days.

CHAPTER 10 **Ceremonies**

PART 1 Conversation: A Baby Shower

3 **Comprehension Questions** page 223

4 **Listening for Stressed Words** page 224

Mari: Hi, Jeff. Hi, Sharon. Look what I got in the mail.

Jeff: Hey.

Sharon: Hi, Mari.

Jeff: "Join us for a baby shower honoring Nancy Anderson, April 5th, 11 A.M.... hosted by Sharon Smith and Carolyn Freeman..."

Sharon: Oh good, you got the invitation. So can you make it?

Mari: I think so, but, well, what is a baby shower exactly?

Jeff: You know, it's a party for a woman who's going to have a baby. Um, it's like a welcoming ceremony for the new baby.

Mari: It's a party? Then why do you call it a "shower"?

Jeff: Because the custom is to *shower* the woman with gifts for the baby. Get it?

Mari: I see. Are you invited too, Jeff?

Jeff: No way! No men allowed!

Mari: Really?

Sharon: Well, not exactly. Lots of baby showers include men these days, but traditionally showers are hosted by a woman's girlfriends or female relatives, and they're only for women.

Mari: Hmm. But isn't Nancy and Andrew's baby due at the end of May? And this invitation says April 5th.

Sharon: Well, yes. The custom is to have a shower before the baby is born, when the woman is seven or eight months pregnant.

Mari: Very interesting. And everybody brings a gift?

Sharon: Right. Something for the baby: You know, toys or clothes or something for the baby's room.

Mari: OK. The invitation says it's for lunch, so…

Sharon: Yeah, we'll have lunch, and afterwards we'll play games.

Mari: Games? What kind of games?

Jeff: Girl games.

Sharon: Silly games like bingo, or guessing games, or baby trivia games. And the winners get small prizes.

Mari: It sounds like fun.

Sharon: It is. And then, at the end of the party, there's usually a cake with baby decorations, and then the mother-to-be opens her presents.

Mari: While the guests are still there?

Sharon: Sure. That's my favorite part! Everybody gets to see the gifts.

Jeff: And go "oooh, aaah…"

Sharon: And see how happy the woman is.

Mari: Wow. That's so different from our custom. In Japan we usually don't open a gift in front of guests.

Sharon: Really? That *is* different.

Mari: Well, what kind of gift do you think I should get for her?

Sharon: She's registered online, so you can see what she's already gotten and what she still needs. Would you like me to write down the Internet address for you?

Mari: Sure. That would be great. Uh, is there anything I can do to help with the party? Maybe do the flower arrangements or something?

Sharon: Oh, thanks, but it's not necessary. Everything is all taken care of. Just come and have fun.

PART 2 Lecture: Water in Traditional Ceremonies

3 Recognizing Digressions page 231

So I thought I'd focus on that today: the role of water in celebrations around the world.

Let's take Thailand as an example. I'll never forget my first time there. It was April, the hottest part of the year. And by the way, Thailand doesn't have four seasons like we do here. Um, depending on which part of the country you're in, there are three seasons, the dry season from November to February, the hot season from March to June, and the rainy season from about July to October. Um, so anyway, back to our topic. I was walking down the street in the small village where I lived and suddenly, two teenagers walked past me and as they did, they threw water on me! I was kind of shocked but didn't really mind because it was so hot. Then I realized that it was the 13th, which is Songkran, the Water Festival in Thailand. On that day, people throw water on each other, and also wash the hands of their elders with scented water. It's a custom based on the belief that water will wash away bad luck.

4 Taking Notes page 231

5 Outlining the Lecture page 231

Host: And now I'd like to introduce our speaker, Josh Harrison. Josh has just returned from his latest overseas assignment as a Peace Corps volunteer. He's served in at least three different countries and has traveled to many more than that; that's why I thought he'd be the perfect speaker for today's topic: ceremonies and celebrations around the world. Welcome, Josh.

Speaker: Thank you, Diane. And thanks for inviting me. Well, I've thought about the topic and I thought, gosh, how am I going to narrow this down? I mean, I have seen and participated in so many fascinating celebrations in many different cultures. Then I remembered something I noticed just recently: Even though the cultures I experienced were completely different, many of their ceremonies had something interesting in common: the use of water. Yeah, water. Some ceremonies involve drinking the water, some involve pouring it, and some involve dunking or going under water. To me, that was a very interesting discovery. So I thought I'd focus on that today: the role of water in celebrations around the world.

Let's take Thailand as an example. I'll never forget my first time there. It was April, the hottest part of the year. And by the way, Thailand doesn't have four seasons like we do here. Um, depending on which part of the country you're in, there are three seasons, the dry season from November to February, the hot season from March to June, and the rainy season from about July to October. Um, so anyway, back to our topic. I was walking down the street in the small village where I lived and suddenly, two teenagers walked past me and as they did, they threw water on me! I was kind of shocked but didn't really mind because it was so hot. Then I realized that it was the 13th, which is Songkran, the Water Festival in Thailand. On that day, people throw water on each other, and also wash the hands of their elders with scented water. It's a custom based on the belief that water will wash away bad luck.

Now, this idea of washing away bad things, of cleansing or purifying, is also found in Islamic cultures. For example, when I lived in Saudi Arabia, I learned that traditional Muslims pray five times a day, and before they do, they always wash their faces, hands, and feet with water. And the water has to be very clean and pure. This ritual washing symbolizes the removal of sin and disease; in other words, the cleansing of both body and soul, before speaking to God.

All right, now, another religion where water plays an important role is Christianity. And one particular ritual that comes to mind is baptism. Baptism is a ceremony that welcomes a new baby into the Christian religion and the community. Now, since there are many branches of Christianity, there are also many different ways that baptism can be performed. When I lived in Latin America, I attended several Catholic baptisms. And what they do is they bring the baby to the church, where a priest pours or sprinkles some water on the baby's head. This water symbolizes the washing away of sin—somewhat similar to the meaning in Islam. And then, while pouring the water, the priest says a prayer and tells the parents to raise the baby as a good Christian.

So as you can see, water has different symbolic meanings in different cultures. In some cultures it's believed to keep away bad luck, as in Thailand. In Islamic and Christian cultures it's used to purify and wash away sin. Water has rich symbolism in nearly all cultures. So now I'd like to know what you think and see if you can share some of your own traditions. How does water play a part in celebrations in *your* culture?

PART 3 Strategies for Better Listening and Speaking

Focus on Testing: Using Context Clues page 234

Conversation 1

Man 1: And now, on behalf of our entire staff, I'd like to present this gold watch to Mr. Harry Kim and express our appreciation for 35 years of dedicated service to our company. Congratulations, Mr. Kim!

Man 2: Thank you, Mr. President. All I can say is, it's been a pleasure working with you all these years. This company has been like a second family to me.

Man 1: What are you going to do with your time from now on?

Man 2: I'm going to play a lot of golf, work in my garden, and visit my grandchildren.

Conversation 2

Woman: Well, that was a very moving service. And I've never seen so many flowers. She sure had a lot of friends.

Man: Yep. And the minister spoke beautifully, didn't he? I'm sure it was a comfort to the family.

Woman: I am really going to miss Myra. She was a good neighbor and a good friend.

Man: I can't imagine what Ralph is going to do without her. They were married, what, 40 years?

Woman: Something like that, yes. Poor Ralph.

Conversation 3

Girl: Here they come! Look Mommy, there's Shawna!

Mother: Where?

Girl: She's walking in behind that really tall guy, see?

Mother: Oh yes, yes, I see her. Doesn't she look elegant in her cap and gown, honey? So grown up…

Girl: What's gonna happen now?

Father: After everyone sits down there'll be speeches, and then they'll give out the diplomas.

Mother: I can't believe that three months from now our little girl is going to be starting college.

Father: I know. Where did the time go?

Conversation 4

Daughter: And now I'd like to propose a toast. To my parents, Lena and Richard: May your next thirty years together be as happy and prosperous as the first thirty have been. Thanks for being an inspiration to us all. Cheers!

All: Cheers! Congratulations!

Father: Thank you, Betsy, and thank you all for coming out to celebrate with us on this happy occasion. You're the best group of friends anyone ever had and we're very grateful. And now *I'd* like to propose a toast: To my wife Lena, who's as beautiful today as she was on our first date more than 30 years ago. To you, darling!

All: Cheers!

Conversation 5

Mother: How are the plans coming?

Daughter: I met with the caterer yesterday and tomorrow we'll order the flowers. We have the rings, and oh, my dress will be ready next Wednesday.

Mother: What about the band for the reception?

Daughter: We hired them months ago. And we ordered the cake too.

Mother: Speaking of cake… you and Robert aren't going to shove cake in each other's faces, are you?

Daughter: No, Mom, don't worry.

2 **Recognizing the Meaning of Affirmative Tag Questions** page 235

1. Alia didn't forget to buy flowers again, did she?
2. That wasn't a very long ceremony, was it?
3. We don't need to bring a present, do we?
4. You're not going to wear that shirt to the party, are you?
5. There aren't many people here, are there?
6. You're not bringing your dog, are you?
7. The wedding hasn't started yet, has it?
8. You didn't like the party, did you?

Real-Word Task: Making Wedding Plans

② **Taking Notes on Wedding Preferences** page 240

Katsu

Consultant: OK, Katsu, to get started, why don't you look at this list for the wedding ceremony, and let me just ask you first of all if there are any items that you have really strong feelings about, like you absolutely must do this or you absolutely refuse to do that.

Katsu: Hmm… Well, I really don't want a religious service. I think a big, traditional American service would be very strange for my parents. So I'd prefer to get married outdoors, in a garden or something, and have a justice of the peace perform the service.

Consultant: OK. Have you and Sandra discussed a date?

Katsu: Not an exact date but we agree that we'd like to do it in April or May.

Consultant: Got it. What else?

Katsu: I'd like it small, just our families and close friends. And informal. I don't want to wear a tuxedo, and I don't want bridesmaids and all those extra people. I think it would be nice if each of us walked in with our parents and that's it. I really want to honor my parents at my wedding.

Consultant: OK, Katsu, obviously you know that Sandra's family is Christian and they've been in America for generations. So let me ask you, is there anything from that tradition that you really like and would want to include in your ceremony?

Katsu: Let's see… Well, I'm sure Sandra will want to wear a white dress and that's fine. And, um, well, I don't like organ music, but maybe we could have a flute and a violin, something soft like that.

Consultant: And what about Japanese culture? Is there something you'd like to include from that?

Katsu: Wow. That's a hard question. I've never been to a traditional Japanese wedding.

But I know that in Japan purple is, like, the color of love, so maybe Sandra could carry purple flowers.

Sandra

Consultant: OK, Sandra, to start off I'm going to ask you the same question I asked Katsu. Look at this list of items in a typical wedding ceremony and tell me if there's anything you feel very strongly about.

Sandra: Well, I've always dreamed of having a big traditional wedding, you know, in a church, with an organ playing, and bridesmaids and groomsmen, and a beautiful white dress. But that was before I met Katsu. His family isn't Christian, you know, and my family's not *super* religious either, so maybe we could have a garden wedding instead of a church wedding. But I'd like my family's minister to perform the service, and I definitely want my father to walk me down the aisle, and I want my little cousin to be our flower girl. I guess the most important thing is to be able to include everybody. My family is huge, and I want to invite them all.

Consultant: So you want to wear a white dress?

Sandra: Of course.

Consultant: And what about Katsu?

Sandra: He hates anything formal. It's fine if he wears a suit.

Consultant: OK, Sandra. Tell me, do you like the color purple?

Sandra: Purple? At a wedding?

Consultant: Katsu suggested you could carry purple flowers. He says that in Japanese culture purple is the color of love.

Sandra: Hmm… purple. That could work. I love irises, and maybe the bridesmaids' dresses could be violet.

Consultant: That sounds like a wonderful idea. What about music?

Sandra: Well, if we're outdoors then we can't have an organ, can we; so, hmm, how about something soft like classical guitar or flute?

Vocabulary Index

Chapter 7

catch on
category
dialect
friendliness
friendship
Have a seat.
identical
in the dark
It's hard to say.
majority
make friends
noticeable
sample
standard
two-faced
unique
whereas
while

Chapter 8

brand — *trend*
can't stand —
Caucasian
confident
conflict
consumer
developed country
dish
diverse
don't/doesn't care for
have a good time
hip (informal)
I'm crazy about it!
identify with
income
loyal
optimistic
phenomenon
see eye to eye
significant
standard of living
tolerant

Chapter 9

antidepressant
appliances —
aspect
billboard
convenient —
display
efficient —
essential —
facial —
for ages!
impact —
install
in the meantime
leave on
match — *game*
potential
privacy
remotely
riot —
scan
turned into
utility bill
width →

Chapter 10

allowed
cleanse
due
fascinating
focus on
go "ooh and ah"
host
involve
mother-to-be
narrow (something) down
play a part in
pour
pray
prayer
pregnant
priest
pure
purify
register
ritual
shower
silly
sin
sprinkle
symbol
symbolism
symbolize

imply —
infer —

if verb ends with p, t, ch, k = /t/
with b, d, j, g = /d/

Skills Index